The Cross

and

Its Shadow

BY

STEPHEN N. HASKELL

Author of "The Story of Daniel the Prophet" and
"The Story of the Seer of Patmos"

"A glorious high throne from the beginning is the place
of our sanctuary." Jer. 17:12

THE BIBLE TRAINING SCHOOL,
SOUTH LANCASTER, MASS.
1914.

Facsimile Reproduction

Printed by

REVIEW AND HERALD® PUBLISHING ASSOCIATION
Washington, DC 20039-0555
Hagerstown, MD 21740

PRESS OF
SOUTH LANCASTER PRINTING CO.,
SOUTH LANCASTER, MASS.

AUTHOR'S PREFACE

ETERNITY can never fathom the depth of love revealed in the cross of Calvary. It was there that the infinite love of Christ and the unbounded selfishness of Satan stood face to face. The entire system of Judaism, with its types and symbols, was a shadow of the cross, extending from Calvary back to the gate of Eden, and contained a compacted prophecy of the gospel.

At the present day the person who comes to the study of the New Testament through the interpreting lights of the types and symbols of the Levitical services, finds a depth and richness in the study that are found in no other way. It is impossible to have exalted views of Christ's atoning work if the New Testament is studied without a previous knowledge of the deep, blood-stained foundations in the Old Testament gospels of Moses and the prophets.

" In every sacrifice, Christ's death was shown. In every cloud of incense His righteousness ascended. By every jubilee trumpet His name was sounded. In the awful mystery of the holy of holies His glory dwelt."

AUTHOR'S PREFACE

In the light shining from the sanctuary, the books of Moses, with their detail of offerings and sacrifices, their rites and ceremonies, usually considered so meaningless and void of interest, become radiant with consistency and beauty. There is no other subject which so fully unites all parts of the inspired Word into one harmonious whole, as the subject of the sanctuary. Every gospel truth centers in the sanctuary service, and radiates from it like the rays from the sun.

Every type used in the entire sacrificial system was designed by God to bear resemblance to some spiritual truth. The value of these types consisted in the fact that they were chosen by God Himself to shadow forth the different phases of the complete plan of redemption, made possible by the death of Christ. The likeness between type and antitype is never accidental, but is simply a fulfilment of the great plan of God.

In " The Cross and Its Shadow," the type and the antitype are placed side by side, with the hope that the reader may thus become better acquainted with the Saviour. It is not the intention of the author of this work to attack any error that may have been taught in regard to the service of the sanctuary, or to arouse any controversy, but simply to present the truth in its clearness.

The book is the result of many years of prayerful study of the types and symbols of the sanctuary service, and is sent forth with a prayer that the reading of it may arrest the attention of the thoughtless, give the Christian new views of Christ's character, and lead many into the sunlight of God's love.

INTRODUCTION

IN THE government of God, law is the basis upon which everything is made to rest. Law is the foundation of God's throne, the stability of His government and character, and the expression of His love and wisdom. Disobedience of this law caused the fall of Satan and his host. Disobedience to God's commands by Adam and Eve opened the flood gates of woe upon the world, and plunged the whole human family into impenetrable darkness. But divine love had conceived a plan whereby man might be redeemed. This plan was revealed in the promise, " I will put enmity between thee and the woman, and between thy seed and her seed; it shall bruise thy head, and thou shalt bruise His heel."

Since the divine law is as sacred as God Himself, only one equal with God could make atonement for its transgression. Hence, the seed of the woman could refer to none other than the Lord Jesus Christ. In this promise to our first parents a gleam of hope penetrated the gloom that enveloped the minds of the sinful pair, and when a system of sacrifices was made known to them that demanded the life of an innocent victim, they could see more clearly the import of the promise,— that it involved the death of God's dear Son to atone for their sin and meet the claims of the broken law. Through this system of sacrifices, the shadow of the Cross reached back to the beginning, and became a star of hope, illuminating the dark and terrible future, and relieving it of its utter desolation.

It was the reflection from the Cross that reached back to the antediluvian age, and kept alive the hope of the faithful few in those years of weary waiting. It was the faith in the Cross that sustained Noah and his family during that terrible experience when God was punishing the world for its transgression of His holy law. It was a knowledge of the Cross and its significance that caused Abraham to forsake his country, his kindred, and his father's house, and sojourn with his sons in a land of strangers. It is written of him, " He believed in the Lord, and he accounted it to him f o r righteousness."   In prophetic vision, Moses was permitted to see the Cross of Christ, and understand more fully the significance of the brazen serpent he had lifted up in the wilderness for the healing of the people. It was this view that took away the sting of punishment for his own sin, and reconciled him to the decree that, " he must die in the mount, and be gathered to his people."

The simple system of sacrifices instituted by the Lord in the beginning to symbolize, or prefigure, Christ, was almost totally lost sight of during the bondage of the children of Israel in Egypt. Upon their return to Canaan, Moses, by divine direction, gave them a more elaborate system, designated in the Scriptures as the " sanctuary and its services." This earthly sanctuary, with every minutia of its construction, equipment, and service, was to be built and operated in harmony with the pattern of the heavenly shown to him in Mount Sinai. Every form, ceremony, and detail of this service had a significance, and was designed to give the worshiper a more complete understanding of the great remedial system.

In the sanctuary, the Cross of Christ is the great center of the whole scheme of human redemption. Around it clusters every truth of the Bible. From it radiates light from the beginning to the end of both dispensations. Nor does it stop here. It penetrates the great beyond, and gives the child of faith a glimpse of the glories of the future eternal state. Yea, more than this, is accomplished by the Cross. The love of God is manifest to the universe. The prince of this world is cast out. The accusations which Satan has brought against God are refuted, and the reproach which he has cast upon heaven is forever removed. The justice and immutability of God's law are sustained, and angels, as well as men, are drawn to the Redeemer. The Cross of Christ becomes the science and song of the universe.

It can be truthfully said of the author of " The Cross and Its Shadow," as it was of one of old, that he is " mighty in the Scriptures." In this book he is giving to the world, in condensed form, the results of the study of years upon this great theme. Through the figures and symbols used in the ministration in the earthly sanctuary, the author has made the closing work of Christ in the heavenly Sanctuary very clear. The similarity and connection between type and antitype have been made so plain that no one can fail to comprehend the great central truths of the plan of salvation as unfolded in the service and ministration of the earthly sanctuary.

In these days of superficial study, and the consequent man-made theory of the plan of salvation, it is refreshing to find a book like " The Cross and Its Shadow," which lifts up Jesus, and presents Him to the world as revealed in types, as shadowed in symbols, as prefigured in the revelations of the prophets, as

INTRODUCTION

unveiled in the lessons given to His disciples, and as manifested in the wonderful miracles wrought for the sons of men.

As the Word is honored by the author, may the Holy Spirit, the great Teacher of righteousness, honor the author by making his book the means of saving many souls in God's eternal kingdom.

G. A. IRWIN,

Loma Linda, California.

CONTENTS

xi

SECTION V. VARIOUS OFFERINGS

SECTION VI. SERVICES OF THE SANCTUARY

SECTION VII. THE AUTUMNAL ANNUAL FEASTS

SECTION VIII. LEVITICAL LAWS AND CEREMONIES

SECTION IX. THE TRIBES OF ISRAEL

SECTION I

The Sanctuary

The Heavenly Sanctuary

THERE is a house in heaven built,
 The temple of the living God,
The tabernacle true, where guilt
 Is washed away by precious blood,

Long since, our High Priest entered there,
 Who knows the frailties of our frame,
Who loves to hear his people's prayer,
 And offer to our God the same.

The daily ministry he bore,
 Till ended the prophetic days;
He opened then the inner door,
 To justify the sacred place.

Before the ark of ten commands,
 On which the mercy-seat is placed,
Presenting his own blood, he stands,
 Till Israel's sins are all erased.
                    —*R. F. Cottrell.*

CHAPTER I

LIGHT IN THE DARKNESS

TO every voyager on the storm-tossed sea of life, the Lord has given a compass which, if rightly used, will safely guide him into the eternal haven of rest. It was given to our first parents at the gate of Eden, after they had admitted sin into this beautiful earth as well as into their own lives. The compass consists of the following words, which were spoken by the Lord to Satan: " I will put enmity between thee and the woman, and between thy seed and her seed," [1] In every heart God has planted an enmity to sin, which, if heeded, will lead to righteousness and eternal life. Any man, whatever his station or rank in life, who will abso-

[1] Gen. 3 : 15.

lutely follow the divine compass placed in his heart, will accept Christ as his Saviour and be led out into the sunlight of God's love and approval.[1]

As the result of our first parents' eating of the forbidden fruit, over all the earth hung the gloom of the divine decree, " In the day that thou eatest thereof dying thou shalt die." [2] The marks of death and decay were soon seen in the falling leaves and withered flowers. There was no escaping the decree, " The wages of sin is death." [3] But a ray of light pierced the darkness when God spoke the following words to Satan: " It (the seed of the woman) shall bruise thy head, and thou shalt bruise His heel." [4] These words revealed the fact that for those who would cherish the enmity against sin which God had placed in the heart, there was a way of escape from death. They would live, and Satan would die; but before his death he would bruise the heel of the seed of the woman. This was necessary in order that the death of Satan might be made sure, and that mankind might escape eternal death. [5]

Before man was placed on trial, the love of the Father and the Son for him was so great that Christ pledged His own life as a ransom if man should be overcome by the temptations of Satan. Christ was " the Lamb slain from the foundation of the world." [6] This wonderful truth was made known to our first parents in the words spoken by the Lord to Satan, " It (the seed of the woman) shall bruise thy head, and thou shalt bruise His heel."

In order that man might realize the enormity of sin, which would take the life of the sinless Son of God, he was required to bring an innocent lamb, confess his sins over its head, then with his own hands take its life, a type of Christ's life. This

[1] John 1:9. [2] Gen. 2:17, margin. [3] Rom. 6:23.
[4] Gen. 3:15. [5] Heb. 2:14. [6] Rev. 13:8.

sin-offering was burned, typifying that through the death of Christ all sin would finally be destroyed in the fires of the last day. [1]

It was difficult for man, surrounded by the darkness of sin, to comprehend these wonderful heavenly truths. The rays of light which shone from the heavenly sanctuary upon the simple sacrifices, were so obscured by doubt and sin, that God, in His great love and mercy, had an earthly sanctuary built after the divine pattern, and priests were appointed, who "served unto the example and shadow of heavenly things." [2] This was done that man's faith might lay hold of the fact that in heaven there is a sanctuary whose services are for the redemption of mankind.

Rays of light from the heavenly sanctuary shone upon the simple sacrifice.

The prophet Jeremiah grasped this great truth, and exclaimed, "A glorious high throne from the beginning is the place of our sanctuary." [3] David knew of God's dwelling-place in heaven, and when writing for the generations to come, he said, "He (God) hath looked down from the height of His sanctuary; from heaven did the Lord behold the earth." [4] The

[1] Mal. 4: 1-3. [2] Heb. 8: 5. [3] Jer. 17: 12.
[4] Ps. 102: 19.

faithful ones have always understood that when they sought God with all the heart, "their prayer came up to His holy dwelling-place, even unto heaven." [1]

All the worship in the earthly sanctuary was to teach the truth in regard to the heavenly sanctuary. While the earthly tabernacle was standing, the way into the heavenly tabernacle was not made manifest; [2] but when Christ entered heaven to present His own blood in man's behalf, God revealed through His prophets much light in regard to the sanctuary in heaven.

To John, the beloved disciple, were given many views of that glorious temple. He beheld the golden altar, on which, mingled with fragrant incense, the prayers of earthly saints are offered up before God. In vision he saw the candle-stick with its seven lamps of fire burning before the throne of God. The veil into the most holy was lifted, and he writes, "The temple of God was opened in heaven, and there was seen in His temple the ark of His testament." [3]

It is in this "true tabernacle, which the Lord pitched, and not man," that Christ pleads His blood before the Father in behalf of sinful men. [4] There is the throne of God, surrounded by myriads of the angelic hosts, all waiting to obey His commands; [5] and from there they are sent to answer the prayers of God's children here on earth. [6]

The heavenly sanctuary is the great power-house of Jehovah, whence all the help necessary to overcome *every* temptation of Satan is sent to each one who is connected with it by faith.

The heavily laden electric car, with its slender arm reaching up to the wire above, through which it receives strength

[1] 2 Chron. 30 : 27.   [2] Heb. 9 : 8.   [3] Rev. 11 : 19.
[4] Heb. 8 : 2.   [5] Ps.   103 : 19, 20,   [6] Dan. 9 : 21-23,

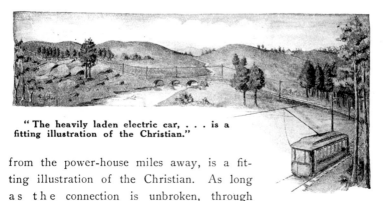

" The heavily laden electric car, . . . is a fitting illustration of the Christian."

from the power-house miles away, is a fitting illustration of the Christian. As long as t h e connection is unbroken, through the darkest night, the car runs smoothly up and down hill alike, not only shedding light on the immediate track ahead, but casting its bright rays of light into the darkness far and near. But the instant the connection is broken, how great is the change! The car remains in darkness, unable to go forward.

So it is that Christ, our great High Priest in the heavenly sanctuary, reaches His hand down over the battlements of heaven to clasp the hand of every one who will reach up by faith and take hold of the proffered help. The one whose faith lays hold of that help, can pass securely over the steepest hills of difficulty, his own soul filled with light while diffusing light and blessing to others. As long as he by faith keeps a firm hold of God, he has light and power from the sanctuary above; but if he allows doubt and unbelief to break the connection, he is in darkness, not only unable to go forward himself, but a stumbling-block in the way of others.

The one who allows nothing to break his connection with heaven becomes an earthly dwelling-place for the Most High;

"for thus saith the high and lofty One that inhabiteth eternity, whose name is Holy; I dwell in the high and holy place, with him also that is of a contrite and humble spirit." [1]   He who separates from sin and puts it far from him, becomes a temple of the Holy Ghost. [2]   God loves to dwell in the hearts of His people, [3] but sin cherished in the heart prevents His Spirit from abiding there. [4]   Christ knocks at the door of every heart, inviting all to exchange sin for righteousness, that He may come in and abide with them. [5]

There are three temples brought to view in the Bible,— the heavenly temple, the dwelling-place of the Most High, where Christ intercedes in our behalf; the temple of the human body, where God's Spirit rules and reigns; and the earthly temple, with its typical services, designed to teach mankind how to receive divine help from the great storehouse above, so that God can honor them by abiding with them continually.

The earthly sanctuary with its types and symbols is like the powerful lenses of the telescope, which make it possible to view heavenly bodies that otherwise would be invisible. To the eye of the ignorant those wonderful lenses appear like ordinary glass; but the astronomer, who longs to know of the wonders of the heavens, is filled with rapture as he gazes through them.

"The astronomer . . . is filled with rapture as he gazes."

In like manner the Christian who will study the typical service of the earthly sanctuary, not as a collection of dry, lifeless relics of ancient worship, but as a wonderful art gallery, where, by the hand of a master-artist, the different parts

[1] Isa. 57: 15.   [2] 1 Cor. 6: 19, 20.   [3] Eph. 3: 17-20.
[4] 1 John 3: 15.   [5] Rev. 3: 20.

of the marvelous plan of redemption are portrayed, will be astonished at the beauty revealed. The figures fairly speak to him, as it were, from the canvas. They tell the beautiful story of the Saviour's love until his very soul is filled with rapture as he gazes upon them. He sees the vivid picture of the priest in snow-white robe leading the red heifer out to the rough uncultivated valley, there to offer it a sacrifice for sin. He sees him sprinkle its blood on the rough stones of the val- ley, to teach that Christ died for the most worth- less, for the veriest out- cast. Who can gaze on that picture without having his heart filled with love for such a compassionate Re- deemer?

Again he views a picture of the destitute sinner, longing to be free from sin; and be- holding his wealthy brethren pass with their lambs for sin-offerings, the poor ones with their

"Only a handful of flour will answer."

pigeons and doves, he sinks back into despondency, for he has no living thing to offer. Then the light of hope springs into his face as one tells him, "Only a handful of flour will answer." And as the sinner watches the priest offer the crushed wheat as an emblem of the blessed body to be broken for him, and hears him say, "Thy sin is forgiven," his heart leaps for joy, as did the heart of the poor man by the pool of

Bethesda, who had no one to help him, when the blessed Master told him to take up his bed and walk. [1]

If the one who longs to know more of Christ and His infinite love, will study the types and symbols of the earthly sanctuary, connecting each with its glorious antitype, his soul will be filled with rapture. Like the lenses of the telescope, they reveal wondrous beauties in the character of our blessed Redeemer, beauties that are revealed in no other way.

There is a separate and distinct heavenly lesson taught by each of the different types and symbols of the earthly sanctuary service; and when they are all viewed together, they form a wonderful Mosaic painting of the divine character of Christ as none but a heavenly artist could portray it.

Names given the heavenly sanctuary
by different Bible writers.

" Thy dwelling-place,"	Solomon,	2 Chron. 6 : 39.
" A palace,"	David,	Psalm 48 : 3.
" His holy temple,"	David,	Psalm 11 : 4.
" Temple of God,"	John,	Rev. 11 : 19.
" Habitation of Thy holiness,"	Isaiah,	Isa. 63 : 15.
" True tabernacle which the Lord pitched,"	Paul,	Heb. 8 : 2.
" My Father's house,"	Jesus,	John 14 : 2.
" Place of His habitation,"	David,	Psalm 33 : 14.
" His holy habitation,"	Jeremiah,	Jer. 25 : 30.
" The sanctuary,"	Paul,	Heb. 8 : 2.
" Holiest of all,"	Paul,	Heb. 9 : 8.

[1] John 5 : 2-9.

Names given the earthly sanctuary.

" A worldly sanctuary,"	Heb. 9: 1.
" The first tabernacle,"	Heb. 9: 8.
" A figure for the time then present,"	Heb. 9: 9.
" Patterns of things in the heavens,"	Heb. 9: 23.
" Not the very image of the things,"	Heb. 10: 1.
" Holy places made with hands,"	Heb. 9: 24.
" Figures of the true,"	Heb. 9: 24.
" The temple,"	1 Cor. 9: 13.

XXXXXXXX

The body of the Christian is called the temple.

" Jesus answered and said unto them, Destroy this temple, and in three days I will raise it up. . . He spake of the temple of His body." John 2: 19, 21.

" Know ye not that your body is the temple of the Holy Ghost?" 1 Cor. 6: 19.

" If any man defile the temple of God, him shall God destroy; for the temple of God is holy, which temple ye are." 1 Cor. 3: 17.

CHAPTER II

THE TABERNACLE

HE tabernacle as pitched in the wilderness was a beautiful structure. Around it was a court enclosed with linen curtains, which were suspended by silver hooks from pillars of brass trimmed with silver. Viewed from any side, the tabernacle was beautiful. The north, south, and west sides were formed of upright boards, ten cubits high, covered with gold within and without, and kept in position by silver sockets underneath, and by bars overlaid with gold, which passed through golden rings, and extended around the building. [1] The front, or east end, was enclosed by a curtain " of blue, and purple, and scarlet, and fine twined linen, the work of an embroiderer." [2] It was hung upon five pillars of acacia wood overlaid with gold, and added much to the beauty of the entrance. The rich rainbow tints of the curtain, inwrought with

[1] Ex. 26:15-30.   [2] Ex. 36:37, margin.

cherubim, which formed the door of the building where God promised to dwell, was a beautiful "shadow" of the entrance to the heavenly sanctuary. Here, with a rainbow of glory encircling His throne, the Father sits, while ten thousand times ten thousand angels pass to and fro at His command. [1]

The roof, or covering, of the tabernacle consisted of four curtains of cloth and skins. The inside curtain, like that at the entrance of the tabernacle, was of blue, purple, scarlet, and fine twined linen, with golden cherubim wrought in it by a cunning embroiderer. [2] This formed the ceiling, which was a faint representation of the canopy of glory above the throne of God, with the myriads of angels ready to fulfil His commands. [3] Over this was a curtain of goats' hair, above that a covering of rams' skins dyed red, and over all a covering of badgers' skins, all forming a perfect protection from the weather. [4] The different colors in the coverings, blending with the golden wall and the gorgeous entrance curtain, or veil, as it was called, combined to make a structure of surpassing glory.

Over the tabernacle rested the pillar of cloud by day and the pillar of fire by night, which guided the Israelites in all their wanderings. [5] In the midst of the desert heat there was a cool, refreshing shelter beneath the shade of the cloudy pillar for those who served in the tabernacle or worshiped in its court, while without was the scorching heat of the desert. [6] What a beautiful type of the covering God spreads over His people in the midst of this wicked world, so that it is possible to dwell in the secret place of the Most High and abide under the shadow of the Almighty One [7] while in the midst of the turmoil and strife of this wicked world.

At night, when the intense heat abated and darkness covered the desert, then above the holy tabernacle hung the cloud,

[1] Rev. 4 : 2-4; 5 : 11. [2] Ex. 26 : 1, margin. [3] Eze. 1 : 28.
[4] Ex. 26 : 1-14. [5] Ex. 40 : 38. [6] Isa. 32 : 2. [7] Ps. 91 : 1.

"God's immediate, visible presence lighted up the entire encampment."

now a great pillar of fire, " in the sight of all the house of Israel, throughout all their journeys." [1]   God's immediate, visible presence lighted up the entire encampment, so that all could walk safely through the darkness.   What an expressive type was thus given of the Christian's walk!   There may be no visible light; but when the light of God's presence surrounds him, his pathway is light.   David knew this when he wrote, " Blessed is the people that know the joyful sound: they shall walk, O Lord, in the light of Thy countenance." [2]   The weakest trusting child of God can have the blessed privilege of being guided by the light of God's countenance, safe from the pitfalls of Satan, if he will surrender his heart to God.

Within the golden walls of the tabernacle, priests of divine appointment performed a work representing in types and symbols the plan of redemption.

The work of Christ has two distinct phases, one performed in the first apartment of the heavenly sanctuary, the other in the second apartment.   He offers salvation free to every one. Many accept and start out on the Christian pathway.   Christ reaches down His infinite arm to encircle and support every one who calls upon His name, and no power of earth or Satan

[1] Ex.   40:38.   [2] Ps.   89:15.

can force a child of God out of His protecting care. [1] The only way any can be lost is by letting go their hold upon that infinite hand. Like Peter, if they take their gaze from Christ and fix it upon the sea of life, they sink, unless, like him, they cry out, "Lord, save me," and are rescued by the Saviour. [2]

The work of Christ is illustrated by the parable of the marriage of the king's son. All the guests, both bad and good,

"The King comes in to examine the guests."

are gathered at the marriage; but when the king comes in to examine the guests, all are ejected except those who are clothed with the wedding garment of Christ's righteousness. "Many are called, but few are chosen." [3]

There were two apartments in the sanctuary, or tabernacle. In the first apartment a service was performed daily through-

[1] John 10: 28, 29.   [2] Matt. 14: 28-31.   [3] Matt. 22: 1-14.

out the year which typified the work of inviting the guests and gathering them to the marriage. On one day at the end of the year a service was performed in the second apartment which typified the work of choosing out from among the many that have accepted the call, those who are worthy of eternal life, as illustrated in the parable by the king examining the guests.

Type   Antitype

Heb. 8: 1-5. The earthly sanc-   Rev. 11 : 19. There is a tem-
tuary was a shadow of the   ple in heaven.
heavenly sanctuary.

Heb. 9: 1-3. The worldly sanc-   Heb. 9: 24. The heavenly sanctuary had two apartments.   tuary also has two apartments.

CHAPTER III

HISTORY OF THE SANCTUARY

THE history of the typical service, of which the earthly tabernacle was a visible representation, began at the gate of the garden of Eden, where our first parents brought their offerings and presented them before the Lord. Abel showed his faith in the promised Saviour by bringing an animal. He not only presented the shed blood of the sacrifice, but he also presented the fat to the Lord, showing faith in the Saviour and a willingness to put away his sin. [1]

Before the people of God went into Egypt, their worship was simple. The patriarchs lived near the Lord, and did not need many forms or ceremonies to teach them the one grand truth that sin could be atoned for only by the death of One who was sinless. They needed only a rough altar and an innocent lamb to connect their faith with the infinite Sin-bearer.

[1] Gen. 4:4; Heb. 11:4.

(33)

As the patriarchs journeyed from place to place, they set up their altars and offered their sacrifices, and God drew near to them, often showing His acceptance of their offerings by sending fire from heaven to consume the sacrifices.

Of all the sacrifices recorded in the book of Genesis, none comes so near the great antitypical offering as the one required of Abraham when God called him to offer his only son. The test of faith was not simply in the fact that Isaac was his only legitimate son, but Abraham understood that through Isaac's posterity the long-promised Messiah was to come; and in offering Isaac, Abraham was cutting off his only hope of salvation, as well as that of the world. But his faith wavered not. He believed that the same God who had performed a miracle in giving him a son, could bring that son from the dead to fulfil the promise that He had made. [1]

The Lord chose the exact spot for the offering of Isaac. He said to Abraham, " Get thee into the land of Moriah; and offer him there for a burnt-offering upon one of the mountains which I will tell thee of." [2] As Abraham and Isaac went on that memorable journey, they were directed by the Lord to Mount Moriah; and when they came to the place, Abraham built an altar and bound Isaac upon it, ready to sacrifice him; but the Lord stayed his hand.

The spot where such loyalty to God was shown was ever afterward honored by the Lord. But the devil as well as the Lord watched over this place. He knew it was sacred to Jehovah, because there God had tested the faith of the man He honored by calling him His friend. [3]

For more than four hundred years after the children of Israel entered the promised land, Satan held this place. It was a stronghold of the enemy in the midst of Israel. But

[1] Heb. 11 : 17-19.   [2] Gen. 22 : 2.   [3] James 2 : 23.

it was finally captured by David, who made it the capital of his kingdom; afterward Jerusalem was called the "City of David." [1]

The threshing-floor of Ornan the Jebusite, where the angel of the Lord appeared to David, was on this same spot. The prophet told David to erect an altar on the threshing-floor, and there David made a special consecration to the Lord. A few years later the temple, which was erected without sound of hammer, occupied this same plot of land. [2] God had conquered, and He designed the place should ever be hallowed by His presence. But His people were unfaithful, and when the Lord of light came to His own temple, He was despised and crucified, and the holy city and the site of the sacred temple passed into the hands of the Gentiles.

David erected an altar on the threshing-floor.

Satan is guarding this spot vigilantly at the present time, intending never again to relinquish his hold upon it. But the time is coming when, in spite of Satan and all his host, the same Saviour who was rejected in His own temple shall place His feet upon the Mount of Olives, [3] and the entire site of old Jerusalem will be purified; then the New Jerusalem will come

[1] 2 Sam. 5 : 6-9.   [2] 2 Chron. 3 : 1.   [3] Zech. 14 : 4-11.

down from heaven and rest upon that spot made sacred by the consecration of God's chosen people. God's glorious heavenly temple will be upon Mount Zion [Moriah], never-more to fall into the hands of the enemy. God says, " I. . . will set My sanctuary in the midst of them for evermore."

Having briefly outlined the subject from Eden lost to Eden restored, we will go back to the time Israel came out of Egypt.

Subjected to a life of incessant toil and surrounded by heathen darkness, the children of Israel lost sight of the significance of their simple sacrifices. On account of their servitude, they were deprived of the privileges enjoyed by the ancient patriarchs, of spending much time communing with God, and they drifted very near to Egyptian idolatry. When God brought them out of Egypt, He proclaimed His law from Sinai, and then gave them the same system of worship the patriarchs had followed. But He had to deal with them as with children. Because they could not grasp the truths without the simple illustrations, God gave them the system of worship that Abraham, Isaac, and Jacob had followed, but in kindergarten form, just as we would use the kindergarten methods to teach children lessons which adults can easily comprehend.

They had drifted so far away that they could not comprehend how God could live with them, being invisible, so God said, " Let them make Me a sanctuary; that I may dwell among them." [1] The pillar of cloud above the tabernacle and God's visible presence manifested within, helped the Israelites more easily to comprehend the real abiding presence of the Lord with them.

This sanctuary was a shadow, or model, of the heavenly sanctuary; and the service was so planned by the Lord that all the work was a type, or representation, of the work the Son of

[1] Ex. 25:8.

God would do on earth and in heaven for the redemption of
the lost race. It was the most wonderful object-lesson ever
given to mankind.

The sanctuary was completed, while the Israelites were encamped at Sinai, and during their forty years' wanderings in
the wilderness they carried it with them. When they reached
the promised land, it was set up in Gilgal for a few years, [1] and
then removed to Shiloh, [2] where it remained for many years.
When David was fleeing from Saul, the tabernacle was in Nob, [3]
for there the priests set the show-bread before the Lord each

Sabbath day. It
was next set up in
the high place at
Gibeon. [4] The taber-
nacle remained in
Gibeon u n t i l re-
moved by Solomon
to Jerusalem. Jo-
sephus tells us that
Solomon had " the
tabernacle w h i c h

Moses had pitched, and all the vessels that were f o r
ministration to the sacrifices of God," removed to the temple.

David desired to build a house for the Lord; but on account of his many wars the Lord directed that his son should
build the house. When Solomon was established on his throne,
he erected a magnificent structure, and dedicated it to the Lord.
God showed His acceptance by His glory filling the temple.
Solomon did not plan the temple himself; God revealed the plan
to David, as He had that of the tabernacle to Moses. David

[1] Joshua 5 : 10, 11.   [2] Joshua 18 : 1; 19 : 51.   [3] 1 Sam. 21 : 1-6.
[4] 1 Chron. 16 : 39; 21 : 29.

was not to see it built, but when he delivered the plan for the building to Solomon, he said, "The Lord made me understand in writing by His hand upon me, even all the works of this pattern." [1]

The history of Solomon's t e m p l e is really a history of the religious experience of the children of I s r a e l. When they departed from the Lord, the temple was neglected, and sometimes even suffered violence. It was p i l l a g e d by Shishak, king of Egypt. [2] At the instigation of Jehoiada it was repaired by Jehoash, [3] who himself afterward robbed it of its treasures to p r o p i t i a t e the Syrians. [4] Ahaz a little later n o t only spoiled it of its treasures, but

"The Lord made me understand in writing by His hand upon me, even all the works of this pattern."

[1] I Chron. 28 : 11-19.   [2] I Kings 14 : 25, 26.   [3] 2 Kings 12 : 4-14.
[4] 2 Kings 12 : 17, 18.

also defiled its holy precincts. [1]   Under the reign of the good king Hezekiah the temple was purified and its worship restored; [2] but even Hezekiah stripped it of its treasures to procure a treaty with the Assyrians. [3] Again it was polluted by the idolatrous worship of Manasseh. [4] The " good king Josiah," when but a youth of eighteen repaired and purified the temple, and again restored its worship. [5] Finally, on account of the unfaithfulness of the chosen people of God, the holy temple was burned to the ground, and its treasures carried to Babylon. [6]

It was nearly seventy years before the rebuilding of the temple by Zerubbabel was completed and the house dedicated with great rejoicing. [7]   Herod spent forty-six years in repairing Zerubbabel's temple, until in the days of Christ it was a magnificent structure. [8]

God's presence abode with His people in the dwelling-places they prepared for Him, from the time the tabernacle was erected in the wilderness, all the way down through the history of their spiritual wanderings until that memorable day when the types celebrated for four thousand years met their Antitype on the cross of Calvary. Then with a great noise the glorious veil of Herod's magnificent building was rent from the top to the bottom, as the Lord departed forever from His temple. [9] Previous to this, the services were directed of God; henceforth they were but a hollow mockery, for God had left the sanctuary. [10] The temple remained standing until 70 A. D., when it was destroyed by the Romans. To-day the sacred spot is covered by a Mohammedan mosque.

The Epistle to the Hebrews shows that the leading apostle clearly taught the antitypical fulfilment of the types and shadows celebrated for so many years. It should not be forgotten that

[1] 2 Kings 16 : 14, 18.   [2] 2 Chron. 29 : 3-35.   [3] 2 Kings 18 : 13-16.
[4] 2 Kings 21 : 4-7.   [5] 2 Kings 22 : 3-7.   [6] 2 Kings 25 : 9, 13-17.   [7] Ezra 6 : 16-22.
[8] John 2 : 20.   [9] Matt. 27 : 50, 51.   [10] Matt. 23 : 37, 38.

the gift of the Spirit of prophecy and the Sabbath of the Lord were always connected with the sanctuary service. We have no reason to doubt that during the early history of the Christian church, the subject of the sanctuary and the antitypical work of Christ in heaven was clearly understood by the Christians; but when the Bible was taken from them, when the Sabbath of the Lord was hidden, and the voice of the Spirit of prophecy was no longer heard directing the church, then they lost sight of the beautiful antitypical work represented by the ancient sanctuary service.

The Mosque of Omar which occupies the site of the ancient temple.

But the time arrived for the opening of the great judgment in heaven, when the Father and the Son, with their retinue of holy angels, passed in state into the most holy place of the heavenly sanctuary. No earthly pageant could ever compare with that majestic cortege. God designed that it should be recognized on earth, and He caused a message to be proclaimed to the inhabitants of earth, directing their attention to the movements of the Son of God. This is known as the first angel's message of Rev. 14: 6, 7. A large company accepted the message and their attention was centered on the Saviour; but they did not understand the antitypical work of the sanctuary, and hence they expected the Saviour to come to the earth. Instead of coming to the earth, however, He went into the second apartment of the heavenly sanctuary, to take up the work of the judgment.

This company, who had been gathered out by the message of the first angel, loved their Lord; and in their longing desire to find why He had not come to the earth, they drew so near to Him that He, in answer to their earnest prayers, directed their attention to the heavenly sanctuary. There they saw the ark of God's testament containing His holy law, and they acknowledged its claims upon them, and began to keep holy the Sabbath of the Lord. The sanctuary service, the Sabbath, and the Spirit of prophecy were ever united in olden times; and when light from the antitypical sanctuary service came to the people of God, He gave them the Spirit of prophecy again, to reveal to them the solemn truths in regard to Christ's ministry in heaven, which otherwise they would not have comprehended.

SUMMARY

THE TABERNACLE

    Built by Moses in the wilderness,   Ex. 40: 1-38.

    Stored in Solomon's temple,   1 Kings 8: 4;

                               1 Chron. 22: 19.

THE TEMPLE

    Built by Solomon,   2 Chron. chap. 2-5.

    Destroyed by the Babylonians,   2 Chron. 36: 17-19.

Rebuilt by Zerubbabel,   Ezra 6: 13-15.
Repaired by Herod,   John 2 : 20.
Forsaken by the Lord,   Matt. 23 : 37, 39.
Destroyed by the Romans,   Matt. 24 : 2, fulfilled 70 A. D.

SECTION II

The Furniture of the Sanctuary

The Cross and the Crown

NO blood, no altar now,
 The sacrifice is o'er;
No flame, no smoke, ascends on high;
 The Lamb is slain no more!
But richer blood has flow'd from nobler
 veins,
To purge the soul from guilt, and cleanse
 the reddest stains.

We thank Thee for the blood,
 The blood of Christ, Thy Son;
The blood by which our peace is made,
 Our victory is won:
Great victory o'er hell, and sin, and woe,
That needs no second fight, and leaves no
 second foe.

     —H. Bonar.

CHAPTER IV

THE ARK

HE ark was the central figure of the entire sanctuary. The broken law contained in the ark was the only reason for all the sacrificial services, both typical and antitypical. When the Lord gave directions for making the sanctuary, His first instruction was, " They shall make an ark of shittim (acacia) wood: two cubits and a half shall be the length thereof, and a cubit and a half the breadth thereof, and a cubit and a half the height thereof." [1] It was overlaid within and without with pure gold, with a crown of gold around the top.

The cover of the ark was called the mercy-seat, and was of pure gold. On either end of the mercy-seat were cherubim of beaten gold, with their wings stretched forth covering the ark, and their faces looking reverently toward the law of God contained therein.

[1] Ex. 25 : 10.

There is great consolation in the fact that the Lord Himself covered the broken law with a mercy-seat; and then He, the merciful God, took His position upon that seat, so that every sinner who comes confessing his sins, may receive mercy and pardon. That mercy-seat, with the cloud of glory, the visible representation of God's presence, and its covering cherubim, is a figure, or "shadow," of the throne of the great God, who proclaims His name as "merciful and gracious, longsuffering, and abundant in goodness and truth." [1]

Within the ark was the Lord's own copy of that holy law given to mankind in the beginning. "Where no law is, there is no transgression." [2] "Sin is not imputed when there is no law;" [3] therefore the Lord could never have driven our first parents from the garden of Eden [4] on account of their sin, if they had been ignorant of His holy law. How God proclaimed His law to our first parents He never revealed in His Holy Book; but when it was necessary again to make His law known to His people, after their long servitude in Egypt, He had the account of that awe-inspiring event recorded, so that the generations to come might know that God came from heaven and spoke the ten commandments with an audible voice in the hearing of all Israel. [5]

After God had declared the ten commandments from the top of Mount Sinai, He wrote them upon two tables of stone, and gave them to Moses, with the instruction, "Thou shalt put them in the ark." [6] The ark was placed in the most holy apartment of the sanctuary, where no mortal eye, except that of the high priest, could gaze upon it, and he on only one day in the year, when he went in to sprinkle the blood of the Lord's goat before and upon the mercy-seat to atone for the broken law within the ark.

[1] Ex. 34:5-7.   [2] Rom. 4:15.   [3] Rom. 5:13.   [4] Gen. 3:22-24.
[5] Deut. 4:10-13.   [6] Ex. 31:18.

" The wages of sin is death," [1] and the broken law demands the death of every sinner. In the typical service the blood was sprinkled above the law [2] to show faith in the blood of Christ, which would free the righteous from the demands, or curse, of the law. [3]

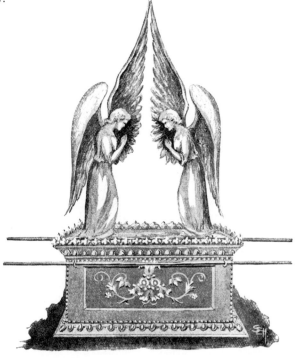

God communed with His people from the cloud of glory which rested above the mercy-seat, between the cherubim. [4] These golden cherubim with outstretched wings were a representation of the covering cherubim that surround the throne of God in heaven. [5]

[1] Rom. 6:23.　　　　[2] Lev. 16:15.　　　　[3] Gal. 3:13.
　　[4] Ex. 25:21, 22.　　　　[5] Eze. 28:14, 16.

There can be no government without law. The very suggestion of a kingdom is always connected with law. There could be no judgment without a law as a standard of judgment. God declares that "as many as have sinned in the law shall be judged by the law." [1] All God's commandments are righteousness. [2] The establishment, or foundation, of His throne is righteousness and judgment. [3]

"There was nothing in the ark save the two tables of stone," [4] is the divine record. The pot of manna was laid up "before the Lord," [5] and Aaron's rod that budded was laid up "before the testimony." [6] Paul, enumerating all the contents of the most holy place in the order that he has, leads some to suppose that at some time the pot of manna and Aaron's rod were placed in the ark; but the ark was made for the one purpose of containing God's holy law. [7]

No profane hands were allowed to touch the ark. Uzzah was smitten for reaching forth his hand to steady it when the oxen which were drawing it stumbled; [8] and thousands of "the men of Bethshemesh" were smitten for looking into it. [9] None but the Levites were allowed to carry the sacred chest. [10]

On the occasion of a battle with the Philistines, the wicked sons of Eli, the high priest, carried the ark on to the battle-field, and it was captured by the Philistines; but God impressed their hearts to return it to Israel with a golden trespass-offering. [11] When Solomon's temple was built, the ark was placed in the holy of holies, where it remained until taken by the prophet Jeremiah and hid in a cave in the mountains before the Babylonian captivity, lest it should fall into the hands of the Gentiles. [12]

The writer of the Apocrypha states that the ark will again

[1] Rom. 2:12.   [2] Ps. 119:172.   [3] Ps. 97:2, margin.   [4] 1 Kings 8:9.
[5] Ex. 16:33, 34.   [6] Num. 17:10.   [7] Deut. 10:1, 2.   [8] 2 Sam. 6:6, 7.
[9] 1 Sam. 6:19.   [10] Deut. 10:8.   [11] 1 Sam. 4:3-11.   [12] 2 Maccabees 2:1-8.

be brought forth in the last times.   Whether that copy of the
law which God gave at Sinai will be brought out again or not,
there will be a copy of that same law, traced as with a pen of
fire in the heavens, before the wondering gaze of the inhabitants of earth, in connection with the second coming of
Christ to the earth. [1]

That holy law is the standard by which all will be judged.
That law will condemn the guilty; for "sin is the transgression of the law." [2]   The same law that condemns the sinner will
witness to the righteousness of those who, through faith in
Christ, have tried to walk in harmony with its holy precepts,
humbly seeking forgiveness for every transgression. [3]

TYPE   ANTITYPE

Ex. 26: 33. The ark was placed   Rev. 11: 19. The ark was seen
in the most holy place.   in the heavenly sanctuary.

Ex. 25: 21, 22. God's visible   Ex. 34: 5-7. The Lord gives His
presence was manifested above   name as Merciful and Gracious
the mercy-seat.   and Longsuffering.

[1] Ps. 97:6; 98:2.   [2] 1 John 3:4.   [3] Rom. 3:21.

CHAPTER V

THE GOLDEN CANDLESTICK

HE golden candlestick with its seven golden lamps was on the south side of the first apartment of the sanctuary. It was made of gold beaten into shape by the workman's hammer. [1] It took many a hard and skilful blow to form those delicate flowers and bowls; but the candlestick was to be made after the heavenly model to teach heavenly lessons to mankind.[2]

John, the beloved disciple, was permitted to look into the first apartment of the sanctuary in heaven, and there he beheld seven golden candlesticks. He also beheld the Saviour in the midst of the glorious candlesticks, of which the earthly one was a shadow.

Christ, in explaining to John the meaning of what he had seen, said, " The seven candlesticks which thou sawest are the seven churches." [3] The number seven in the Bible denotes a complete number. The candlestick of beaten gold with its seven

[1] Ex. 25 : 31-37.   [2] Ex. 25 : 40, margin.   [3] Rev. 1 : 12-20.

(50)

bowls for the lamps was an "example and shadow of heavenly things." [1] Its seven branches, each holding aloft a lamp, represented the church of God.

The individual that forms a part of the "church of the first-born, which are enrolled in heaven," [2] will often feel the work-man's hammer; "for we are His (God's) *workmanship,* created in Christ Jesus unto good works." [3] Then, "beloved, think it not strange concerning the fiery trial which is to try you, as

The Golden Candlestick

though some strange thing hap-pened unto you." [4] It is only the Master-workman fashioning you to become a part of the great church enrolled in heaven.

The candlestick in the type held seven lamps. The beloved disciple also had a view of the heavenly lamps, of which the earthly ones were models. Before the throne of God in heaven he saw the seven lamps of fire, "which are the seven Spirits of God." [5] The church of Christ is the candlestick to hold up the light in the midst of moral dark-

ness. The Saviour says, "Ye are the light of the world." The Spirit of the Lord is said to be the eyes of the Lord which "run to and fro throughout the whole earth, strongly to hold with them whose heart is perfect toward Him." [6] Then the brightness of our light depends upon the con-dition of our heart. The Spirit is searching throughout the earth for those whose hearts are perfect toward God, and it will "*strongly hold*" with such ones: their light will not burn dim.

[1] Heb. 8:5.
[2] Heb. 12:23, margin.
[3] Eph. 2:10.
[4] 1 Peter 4:12.
[5] Rev. 4:2, 5.
[6] 2 Chron. 16:9, margin.

The lamps in the earthly sanctuary were to burn continually. [1]
So the Christian is ever to let the Spirit of God rule in his
life, and thus shed its light abroad.

None but the high priest could perform the sacred work of
lighting the lamps in the earthly sanctuary; he trimmed and
lighted them each morning and evening. [2]   So none but our
High Priest, who was "tempted in all points like as we are," [3]
can give us the help we need. In the morning we need His
Spirit to direct us during the day; and at evening we need
it to enlighten our minds as we review the work of the day,
that we may detect the flaws and dropped threads in the warp
of our lives. The trimming and lighting of the lamps was a
beautiful type with a daily lesson for us at the present time.
It was a link in that marvelous threefold typical chain of service celebrated each morning and evening, while "the whole
multitude of the people were praying without" the sanctuary. [4]
The whole burnt-offering in the court, the incense, and the
burning lamps within the sanctuary,— all were a wonderful
type which will never lose its beauty.

Whenever an individual will fulfil in his very soul the antitype of the typical "whole" burnt-offering, that is, wholly surrender himself to God, place himself and all he has upon the
altar, to be consumed in God's service as He directs, that individual, whether he be rich or poor, learned or ignorant, will be
covered with the fragrant incense of Christ's righteousness, and
his name will be enrolled with the church of the first-born in
heaven; and here in this sin-cursed earth, as he goes to and
fro, he will be a part of the great candlestick, and from his life
will shine out the bright rays of the Spirit of God.

The question may arise in many hearts, How may I become
a light-bearer in the earth? When Zerubbabel was trying under

[1] Lev. 24 : 2.   [2] Ex. 30 : 7, 8.
[3] Heb. 4 : 15.   [4] Luke 1 : 10.

very adverse circumstances to rebuild the temple in Jerusalem, he came to a time when the difficulties appeared like mountains before him. Then the Lord sent His prophet with a message to help and encourage him. Zechariah was given a view of the golden candlesticks, and was also shown whence the oil came that supplied the lamps. He saw two olive-trees, one on the right side of the bowl and the other on the left side, which through golden pipes kept the lamps supplied with oil, that they might burn brightly. [1] The prophet asked the angel the meaning of what he saw. In reply the angel said: " This is the word of the Lord unto Zerubbabel, saying, Not by might, nor by power, but by My Spirit, saith the Lord of hosts." Then he gave a message to Zerubbabel to go forward, and said that the mountain of difficulties would

" Two olive trees . . . kept the lamps supplied with oil."

become a plain before him, and that as surely as his hands had laid the foundations of the house of the Lord, so surely would he finish it.

Zerubbabel was walking by faith in the words of the prophets who had foretold how and when Jerusalem would be rebuilt; [2] but those prophets were dead, and he now faced difficulties that he might be tempted to think the prophets never expected would arise. Then God sent a living prophet with a message of encouragement, to keep the light burning, and enable Zerubbabel to press forward and complete the work prophesied of by the dead prophets.

We can not comprehend the word of the Lord without the

[1] Zech. 4 : 1-14, margin.   [2] 2 Chron. 36 : 20-23; Jer. 25 : 12; Hosea 1 : 7.

Spirit to enlighten our minds. The light shines to the degree in which we take the word and risk our all upon it: and as we come into difficulties in following out the instruction given through the dead prophets, the Lord sends messages of strength and encouragement through the living prophet, to enable us to press forward to victory.

"These are the two sons of oil (light-givers), that stand by the Lord of the whole earth." It is the Spirit of God accompanying the word which has been committed to the people, that will give light. Whatever the prophets of God have revealed to man in the past, is light; and those who have adhered strictly to the testimony of God by His prophets, although it may be hundreds of years after the testimony was given, are spoken of favorably by the living prophet, as Zechariah spoke to Zerubbabel.

TYPE	ANTITYPE
Ex. 40 : 24. Golden candlestick in the first apartment of earthly sanctuary.	Rev. 1 : 12. John saw the seven golden candlesticks in heaven.
Ex. 25 : 37 ; 40 : 25. There were seven lamps upon the candlestick.	Rev. 4 : 2, 5. John saw seven lamps of fire before the throne of God in heaven.
Ex. 30 : 7, 8. The high priest trimmed and lighted the lamps in the earthly sanctuary.	Rev. 1 : 12-18. John saw Christ, our High Priest, in the midst of the candlesticks in heaven.
Lev. 24 : 2. The lamps were burned continually, always shedding forth light.	John 1 : 9. The Holy Spirit lightens every soul that comes into the world, whether he accepts or rejects it.

CHAPTER VI

THE TABLE OF SHOWBREAD

THE table of showbread was placed on the north side of the first apartment of the sanctuary. The table was two cubits long, a cubit and a half in width, and a cubit and a half in height. It was overlaid with pure gold, and like the altar of incense was ornamented with a crown of gold around the top. [1]

On the Sabbath day the Levites made twelve loaves, or cakes, of unleavened bread. [2] These cakes were placed on the table hot each Sabbath day, [3] arranged in two rows, or piles, six in a row, with pure frankincense on each row. [4]

During the entire week the bread lay on the table. By some translators it is called "the bread of the presence." At the end of the week it was removed and eaten by the priests. [5]

[1] Ex. 25:23-30; 40:22.   [2] 1 Chron. 9:32; Lev. 24:5.
[3] Lev. 24:8; 1 Sam. 21:3-6; Matt. 12:3, 4.   [4] Lev. 24:6, 7.   [5] Lev. 24:9.

This explains why Ahimelech the priest had no common bread on the Sabbath to give to David, as the priests were accustomed to eat the "hallowed bread" on that day. [1] It was not lawful to bake common bread upon the Sabbath; the command is very plain that all bread for Sabbath use in the homes should be baked upon the sixth day. "This is that which the Lord hath said, To-morrow is the rest of the holy Sabbath unto the Lord: bake that which ye will bake to-day, and seethe (or boil) that ye will seethe; and that which remaineth over lay up for you to be kept until the morning." [2]   But the Lord directed that the Levites should prepare the showbread every Sabbath. [3]

All the service connected with the table of showbread was done upon the Sabbath. The bread was prepared on the Sabbath, and while hot was placed upon the table. The following Sabbath it was removed, and eaten by the priests on that day.

The priests served "unto the example a n d shadow of heavenly things;" therefore there is a heavenly lesson for us in the antitype of the showbread. It was a continual offering, ever before the Lord. It taught that man was wholly dependent upon God for both temporal and spiritual food, and that both alike come to us through the One who "ever liveth to make intercession" for us before the Father. [4]

This, like all other types of the sanctuary service, met its fulfilment in Christ. He is the true bread. He said, "I am the living bread which came down from heaven; if any man eat of this bread, he shall live forever: and the bread that I will give is My flesh." Then He added, "Except ye eat the flesh of the Son of man, . . . ye have no life in you." [5]   Even the disciples could not comprehend Christ's words, and they murmured. Jesus read their thoughts, and said unto them, "It is the spirit that quickeneth; the flesh profiteth nothing:

[1] I Sam. 21:4.   [2] Ex. 16:22, 23.   [3] I Chron. 9:32.
[4] Heb. 7:25.   [5] John 6:51-53.

the *words* that I speak unto you, *they* are spirit, and *they* are life." [1] His word is the true bread, of which we are to eat.

As the bread in the presence of God was taken out from the sanctuary and eaten, so Jesus said, "The word which ye hear is not Mine, but the Father's which sent Me." [2] The Bible came direct from God. God gave it to Christ, Christ signified it by His angel unto the prophets, and the prophets gave it to the people. [3]

We often read the Bible as a mere form of godliness, or to get something to give to others; but if we would receive its life-giving power into our own souls, we must have it " hot," warm from heaven.

There is no more appropriate time to let God speak to our own souls through His

The Table of Showbread

word than on the Sabbath day, when we lay aside our worldly cares and business, and take time to study the Holy Word and let it come into our inmost heart until we hear God speak to *us,* not to another.

The priests were not only to set the hot bread upon the table on the Sabbath day, but later that same bread was to be eaten and become a part of their very being. God designed that His people should each Sabbath day gain a fresh experience in divine things, which would make them better fitted to meet the temptations of the week. The soul that never gains a deeper experience on the Sabbath than on any other day, fails to keep the Sabbath as God would have him. [4] We may have

[1] John 6 : 63.
[3] Rev. 1 : 1.
[2] John 14 : 24.
[4] Eze. 20 : 12.

a few minutes of quiet study of the word on the Sabbath day, when we hear the Lord speaking to us individually; but if the words are not incorporated into our lives, they give us no abiding strength. As the priests ate the bread prepared the Sabbath before, they assimilated it, and thus received strength for daily duties.

Peter evidently understood this truth when he admonished the church to desire the sincere milk of the word that they might grow thereby, and he said if they did this they would be " a holy priesthood." [1] Here is the secret of true Christian living. Eternal life does not come to the soul through forms and ceremonies. They are all right in their place; but eternal life results from feeding upon the true bread which comes from the presence of God,— God's Holy Word, the blessed Bible.

TYPE	ANTITYPE
Ex. 25 : 30. Showbread always before the Lord.	John 6 : 48. Christ said, " I am that bread of life."
Lev. 24 : 5. There were twelve cakes of the showbread, the number of the tribes of Israel.	I Cor. 10 : 17. In speaking of the church, Paul says, " We being many are one bread and one body."

[1] I Peter 2 : 2-5.

CHAPTER VII

ALTAR OF INCENSE AND ITS SERVICE

HE golden altar, or altar of incense, was before the veil in the first apartment of the sanctuary. It was a cubit square and two cubits high, with a horn upon each corner. The altar was made of the shittim, or acacia wood, and all overlaid with pure gold. Around the top was a beautiful crown of gold, and beneath the crown were rings, in which were staves for carrying the altar, all overlaid with pure gold. [1]

Within the crown of gold encircling the top of the altar, holy fire was kept constantly burning, [2] from which ascended the fragrant smoke of the incense placed upon it every morning and evening. The perfume pervaded the entire sanctuary, and was carried by the breeze far beyond the precincts of the court.

The incense, composed of an equal weight of four fragrant gums and resins, was prepared by divine direction. It was

[1] Ex. 30: 1-6.   [2] Ex. 30: 8.

very sacred, and the person making any like it, even for a perfume, was to be cut off from among the people. [1]

The high priest alone was to perform the sacred duty of placing incense before the Lord on the golden altar. [2]

The altar and the fragrant incense in the earthly sanctuary were an example of the work our great High Priest is performing for us. [3] Our minds should often dwell upon the work of Christ in the heavenly sanctuary. [4] Moses, when directed to build the sanctuary, was "caused to see" the heavenly model of which he was to make a "shadow." [5] John, the beloved disciple, was permitted several times in vision to behold the Saviour officiating in the heavenly sanctuary. He saw a heavenly being standing at the glorious golden altar. He beheld the incense offered upon that holy altar. How it must have thrilled his soul when he saw that precious incense added to the poor, faltering prayers of the struggling saints here on the earth: He saw those prayers, after the incense was added, ascend up before God, and they were accepted because they were made fragrant with the incense. [6] "We know not what we should pray for as we ought; but the Spirit itself maketh intercession for us with groanings which cannot be

The name of the Lord is a strong tower: the righteous runneth into it and are safe.   Prov. 18:10

[1] Ex. 30:34-38.   [2] Ex. 30:7, 8.   [3] Heb. 8:5.   [4] Heb. 3:1.
[5] Ex. 25:40, margin.   [6] Rev. 8:3, 4, margin.

uttered. And He that searcheth the hearts knoweth what is the mind of the Spirit, because He maketh intercession for the saints according to the will of God." [1] But even the Spirit could not present the prayers of sinful mortals before a pure and holy God without adding the fragrant incense.

When Jesus was preparing His disciples for His separation in person from them, He assured them, " Whatsoever ye shall ask the Father in My name, He will give it you." [2] The power in a name is the character of the individual that bears the name. The name of the precious Redeemer is honored, and every petition presented in that name is granted in the courts of heaven because Jesus lived a sinless life. He " knew no sin." The prince of this world had nothing in Jesus, [3] for He was pure and holy, without one stain of sin. It is Christ's righteousness that makes our prayers accepted before the Father.

John saw the smoke of the incense with the prayers of the saints ascend up before God. Our prayers, made fragrant by the righteousness of Christ our Saviour, are presented by the Holy Spirit before the Father. To John in vision it appeared like a cloud of smoke bearing the prayers and fragrant incense up before the throne of the Infinite One. The weakest saint who knows how to press his petitions to the throne of grace in the name of Jesus, the sinless One, has all the treasures of heaven at his command. Having the richest millionaire of earth sign his checks at earthly banks would in no way compare with the privilege of the Christian.

The name of Jesus is often added to prayers in a meaningless way. Many prayers are spoken for a mere form of worship, and rise no higher that the head of the one who offers them; but every prayer of faith reaches the ear of the God of the universe. David understood what was typified by the incense,

<hr>

[1] Rom. 8 : 26, 27.   [2] John   16 : 23.   [3] John   14 : 30.

and prayed, " Let my prayer be set forth before Thee as incense; and the lifting up of my hands as the evening sacrifice." [1]

As there was no other part of the daily ministration that brought the priest so directly into the presence of God as the offering of incense; so there is no part of our religious service that brings us so close to the Master as the pouring out of our souls in earnest prayer. Anciently, as in the antitype, the prayer of faith entered the " holy dwelling-place " of God in heaven. [2]

A lamb was burned upon the brazen altar in the court each morning and evening at the time the incense was renewed upon the altar. [3] The golden altar was an " altar of continual intercession," representing the prayers of God's people coming up before Him continually; while the brazen altar was an " altar of continual atonement," representing the putting away and destruction of sin, the only thing that separates us from God and prevents our prayers from being answered.

The morning and evening ·lamb was offered as a whole burnt-offering for the entire congregation, showing their desire to put away sin and consecrate themselves to the Lord, so that their prayers could ascend from off the altar with the fragrant incense.

In ancient Israel the people living near the temple gathered at the hour of sacrifice, and often " the whole multitude of the people were praying without at the time of incense." [4] The habit of morning and evening prayer in the home came from this typical worship. The faithful Israelite who was far from the temple would pray with his face toward the temple where the incense was ascending each morning and evening. Josephus says the incense was offered as the sun was setting in the evening, and in the morning as it was rising.

[1] Ps. 141 : 2. [2] 2 Chron. 30 : 27.
[3] Ex. 29 : 38-42. [4] Luke 1 : 10.

The type was beautiful, but the antitype far surpasses the type. In the heavenly sanctuary there is an inexhaustible supply of Christ's righteousness. In the type the incense was *always* ascending, typifying that at any time, day or night, when a struggling soul cries out for help, or gives thanks and praise for help received, his prayer is heard. In the morning, as the duties of the day seem more than human strength can bear, the burdened soul can remember that in the type a fresh supply of incense was placed on the altar each morning, and from out the antitypical heavenly sanctuary help will come for the day to the one that claims divine help in the name of Jesus.[1] In the evening, as we review the work of the day and find it marred by sin, there is blessed comfort, as we kneel confessing our sins, to know that in heaven the fragrant incense of Christ's righteousness will be added to our prayers; as in the type the cloud of incense shielded the priest,[2] so Christ's righteousness will cover the mistakes of the day; and the Father, looking upon us, will behold only the spotless robe of Christ's righteousness. If we realized more fully the privilege of prayer, we would often say with the prophet, "I will greatly rejoice in the Lord, . . . for He hath

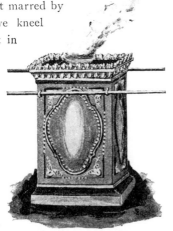

The Altar of Incense

clothed me with the garments of salvation, He hath covered me with the robe of righteousness."[3]

Not all prayers that are accepted before God are answered

---

[1] Deut. 33:25.   [2] Lev. 16:13.   [3] Isa. 61:10.

immediately, as it would not always be best for us; but every prayer to which the fragrance of Christ's righteousness has been added, is lodged on heaven's altar, and in God's good time will be answered. John saw those who officiated before the throne of God holding in their hands "vials full of incense," which, he said, were "prayers of saints." [1] These prayers had been accepted, for the *added* incense was so fragrant that John said the vials were full of incense.

In the typical work the one who attempted to use the fragrant perfume of the incense for his own use was cut off from among the people of God; there was to be no imitation of the incense. [2] No fire was to be used for burning

Let my prayer be set forth before Thee as incense; and the lifting up of my hands as the evening sacrifice. PS. 141:2

the incense except that taken from the altar before the Lord. Nadab and Abihu, while under the influence of strong drink, offered "strange fire" before the Lord, and were slain. [3] Their fate is an object-lesson of all who fail to appreciate the perfect righteousness of Christ, and appear before the Lord clothed in the "filthy rags" of their own righteousness. [4]

When the plague was smiting the hosts of Israel, Aaron the high priest, put incense on the censer and ran among the people, "and the plague was stayed." [5] The sacred incense was burned only on the golden altar and in the censers of the priests. The

[1] Rev. 5:8, margin.   [2] Ex. 30:37, 38.   [3] Lev. 10:1-10.
[4] Isa. 64.6.   [5] Num. 16:46-48.

other Levites were not allowed to burn it.[1] The priests who performed the work which typified Christ's work in a special sense, were the only ones who could burn incense before the Lord.

The horns of the golden altar were often touched with the blood of the sin-offering, thus typifying that it was Christ's death that made it possible for our prayers to be answered and for us to be clothed in His righteousness. As the fragrance of the incense was not confined to the sanctuary, but was carried in the air to the surrounding neighborhood; so in like manner, when one is clothed with Christ's righteousness, an influence will go out from him which those that come in contact with him will recognize by its fragrance as of heavenly origin.

TYPE	ANTITYPE
Ex. 30: 1-3 ; 40: 26. The golden altar was before the veil.	Rev. 8: 3. There is a golden altar in heaven before the throne of God.
Ex. 30: 7, 8. Incense was burned on the golden altar by the high priest every morning and evening.	Rev. 8: 3, 4. *Much* incense is added to the prayers of *all* saints, and they then ascend before God.
Ex. 30: 9; Lev. 10:1-9. The one who should burn incense with strange fire was to be destroyed.	Isa. 64: 6. One clothed with his own righteousness will be destroyed.

[1] Num. 16:3-35.

5

My soul waiteth for the Lord more than they that watch for the morning: I say, more than they that watch for the morning. PS. 130:6

SECTION III

The Priesthood

The Heavenly Priesthood

HIS earthly work is done,
  The Victim's blood is shed,
And Jesus now is gone
  His people's cause to plead;
He stands in heaven, their great High
  Priest,
He bears their names upon his breast.

He sprinkles with his blood
  The mercy-seat above;
He seals our brotherhood
  With his atoning love;
And justice threatens us no more,
But mercy yields her boundless store.

No temples made with hands
  His place of service is;
In heaven itself he stands,
  A heavenly priesthood his:
In him the shadows of the law
Are all fulfilled, and now withdraw.

And though awhile he be
  Hid from the eyes of men,
His people look to see
  Their great High Priest again;
In brightest glory he will come,
And take his waiting people home.

                    —*Thomas Kelly.*

CHAPTER VIII

CHRIST OUR HIGH PRIEST

THE Saviour has many titles, for He "hath by inheritance obtained a more excellent name"[1] than all the angelic host of heaven. Of the many titles bestowed upon Him, there is none more dear to humanity than the "Lamb of God"[2] and "High Priest." By virtue of these two offices He lifts poor fallen humanity up where they can share in His glorious kingdom of grace, even while in the midst of this sin-cursed earth.

In the typical service the one who realized he was a sinner must bring a lamb for a sin-offering. The priest could not officiate for him without this offering.[3] That entire service was but a great kindergarten lesson, making the way of salvation so simple that none could fail to comprehend it. When we realize that we have sinned, we remember our "Lamb," con-

[1] Heb. 1:4.　　　[2] John 1:29, 36.　　　[3] Lev. 4:27-29.

(69)

fess our sins, and in His name they are forgiven; then He
officiates as High Priest in our behalf before the Father. He
pleads the merits of His blood, and covers o u r life, stained
with sin, with the robe of His spotless righteousness, and we
stand before the Father "accepted in the Beloved." [1] How can
we fail to love Him who offered His life for us? Christ
could say of His Father, "Therefore doth My Father love
me, because I lay down My life." [2] Even the infinite love of
the Father for His Son was increased by that act.

In the type, the blood of the sin-offering was shed in the
court, and then the priest entered the sanctuary with the blood
to present it before the Lord. [3] The Saviour gave His life a
sacrifice for sin here upon the earth; and as He entered the
heavenly sanctuary as High Priest, He is called the "Forerunner." Under no circumstances, except as He enters "within
the veil" of the heavenly sanctuary, is that name applied to the
Saviour. [4]

In all monarchical forms of government the forerunner is
a familiar character. In gorgeous uniform, with waving plumes,
he rides before and announces the approach of the royal car-
riage. While he is always hailed with joy by the waiting
crowds, yet he is not the center of attraction; their eyes do
not follow him as he passes on, but are turned down the road
whence he came to get the first glimpse of the royal personage
of whom he is the forerunner.

Of the many condescensions on the part of our blessed Master,
this is one of the grandest. When He entered heaven a mighty
Conqueror over death and the grave, before the entire heavenly
host and representatives of other worlds, He entered a forerunner for *us*. He presented the "wave sheaf," those brought
forth from their graves at the time of His resurrection, as a

[1] Eph. 1:6.   [2] John 10:17.   [3] Heb. 9:12.
[4] Heb. 6:19, 20.

sample of the race He had died to redeem, [1] thus directing the attention of that wonderful assemblage down the road whence He came to watch — for royalty? — yes, for royalty made so by His precious blood. [2] It is only a company of poor, frail mortals stumbling along and often falling by the way; but when they reach the heavenly gate, they will enter "heirs of God, and joint-heirs with Christ." [3]

It meant much for us that Christ entered within the veil as our Forerunner, for all heaven is watching the church of God on earth. When tempted by the enemy to doubt God's love and

care, remember that on account of the great sacrifice made, you are so dear to the Father that "he that toucheth you toucheth the apple of His eye." [4] Heaven and earth are closely united since Christ entered within the veil as our Forerunner. The attention of every angel in glory is centered upon those striving to follow in Christ's footsteps. [5] "Are they (the angels) not *all* ministering spirits, sent forth to minister for them who shall be heirs of salvation?" [6] Why should we falter by the way, and disappoint the heavenly host who are watching for us to come over the same road that our Forerunner passed as a mighty Conqueror over death and the grave?

But let us never forget that it is a blood-stained pathway. "Who, when He was reviled, reviled not again; when He suf-

[1] Eph. 4:8, margin; Matt. 27:52, 53. [2] Rev. 1:6; 5:10.
[3] Rom. 8:17. [4] Zech. 2:8. [5] 1 Peter 2:21. [6] Heb. 1:14.

fered, He threatened not; but committed Himself to Him that judgeth righteously." [1] We can not follow in His footsteps in our own strength. For that reason " in all things it behooved Him to be made like unto His brethren, that He might be a merciful and faithful High Priest in things pertaining to God, to make reconciliation for the sins of the people. For in that He Himself hath suffered being tempted, *He is able to succor them that are tempted*. Wherefore, holy brethren, partakers of the heavenly calling, *consider* the Apostle and High Priest of our profession, Christ Jesus." [2]

In the earthly sanctuary not only the high priest but also common priests officiated, because it was impossible for one man to perform all the work; but it required the work performed by all the priests in the typical services to represent the work of our High Priest. The work of one year was taken as a type of the entire work of our High Priest. During the year " the priests (plural, both high and common) went *always* into the first tabernacle, accomplishing the service of God." This continued all the year, except *one* day; on that day, the service changed and " into the second (apartment) went the high priest alone, . . . not without blood, which he offered for himself, and for the errors of the people." [3] These priests served " unto the example and shadow of heavenly things." [4]

When Christ entered heaven, He went as the Antitype of the earthly service God had ordained, and entered upon His work within the first veil of the heavenly sanctuary. When the typical work ordained by God in the first apartment of the earthly sanctuary had fully met its Antitype, He passed through the second [5] veil into the glorious apartment of the antitypical holy of holies. There He is to perform the marvelous service which will end in the blotting out and total destruction of the

[1] I Peter 2:23. [2] Heb. 2:17, 18; 3:1. [3] Heb. 9:6,7.
[4] Heb. 8:5. [5] Heb. 9:3.

sins of the righteous, nevermore to be remembered by the re-deemed host nor by God Himself.

When Christ stands upon the sea of glass, and places the glittering crowns upon the heads of the company who have traveled the road made sacred by the foot prints of their Fore-runner, albeit with faltering step and through falling tears, and who are clad in robes made white in the blood of the Lamb, He will see of the travail of His soul and be satisfied. [1] He will rejoice over them with singing, and all heaven will ring with melody as the angels who have served under their Commander in the work of saving souls, join in singing, [2] " Blessing, and honor, and glory, and power, be unto Him that sitteth upon the throne, and unto the Lamb forever and ever." [3]

OUR HIGH PRIEST

Heb. 7 : 25.	" Is able to save to the uttermost all that come unto God by Him."
Heb. 4 : 15.	" Is touched with the feeling of our infir-mities." " Was in all points tempted like as we are, yet without sin."
Heb. 2 : 18.	" For in that He Himself hath suffered be-ing tempted, He is able to succor them that are tempted."
Heb. 2 : 17.	"He is a merciful and faithful High Priest.
Heb. 7 : 25.	" He ever liveth to make intercession for us."

[1] Isa. 53 : 11.   [2] Zech. 3 : 17.   [3] Rev. 5 : 13.

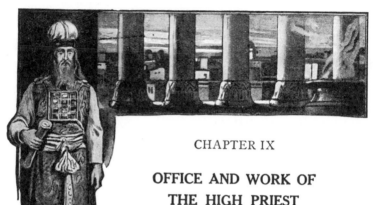

CHAPTER IX

OFFICE AND WORK OF
THE HIGH PRIEST

IN early times the patriarchs were priests over their own households, and God's original design was that the eldest son should take his father's place as priest of the family; but the plan of God was often thwarted by the sins of the eldest son. The Lord's words to Cain would indicate that he was debarred of his inherited position on account of sin: "If thou doest well, shalt thou not have the excellency? and if thou doest not well, sin lieth at the door."[1] Sin prevented Cain from having "the excellency."

On account of sin, Reuben, the first-born of Jacob, lost "the excellency of dignity, and the excellency of power," which was his inherited right.[2] When but a youth, Joseph cultivated those traits of character that gave him "the excellency" above his brethren. It is very probable that the coat of many colors given him by his father,[3] was interpreted by his brethren as indicating his accession to the priesthood.

[1] Gen. 4:7, margin.   [2] Gen. 49:3, 4; 1 Chron. 5:1, 2.   [3] Gen. 37:3, 4.

God gave His First-born for the redemption of the world; and for that reason in God's plan the first-born always inherited special privileges.   To him came a double portion of his father's estate, [1] the priesthood, and, the first-born in the descent from Isaac, the honor of being the progenitor of the Messiah.   If the first-born proved unworthy, his inheritance was given to others, as in the case of Reuben, where Judah became the progenitor of Christ, Joseph received the double portion, and Levi received the priesthood. [2]   The first-born was so often unworthy on account of sin that when the Lord brought Israel out of Egypt, He said, " I have taken the Levites from among the children of Israel instead of all the first-born . . . of Israel: therefore the Levites shall be mine." [3]   It was because the tribe of Levi stood true to God in time of a crisis, that God chose them to serve before Him; [4] and when the service of the sanctuary was established, the priesthood was given to Aaron and his sons, and the remainder of the tribe of Levi were to do the work of the sanctuary under the direction of the priests. [5] Aaron was appointed to officiate as high priest and his sons as common priests, the eldest son to take the office of high priest on Aaron's death. [6]

The consecration to the priest's office was a most imposing ceremony.   Aaron was clothed in the garments which were made for him under God's direction.   Several sacrifices were slain, and the blood of the ram of consecration was touched to the tip of the right ear, the thumb of the right hand, and the great toe of the right foot of both Aaron and his sons, signifying that their ears, hands, and feet were consecrated to the service of God.   Unleavened bread, denoting " sincerity and truth," [7] and the right shoulder of the sacrifice of consecration, were all put upon Aaron's hands and upon his sons' hands.   The priests were

[1] Deut. 21 : 17.   [2] 1 Chron. 5 : 1, 2; Num. 3 : 6, 9.   [3] Num. 3 : 12, 13.
[4] Deut. 33 : 8-11.   [5] Ex. 28 : 1.   [6] Ex. 29 : 29; Num. 20 : 25-28.   [7] 1 Cor. 5 : 8.

to typify the One of whom Isaiah said, " The government shall be upon His shoulder." [1] They were to bear the burdens of the people. The anointing oil and the blood was then sprinkled upon Aaron and his sons, typifying the blood of Christ and the Holy Spirit, which alone could fully qualify them to fill the holy office. [2]

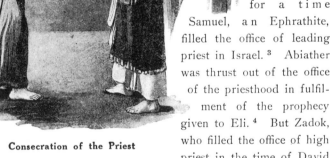

The priesthood remained unbroken in Aaron's family until the sins of Eli and his sons made it necessary to change, and for a time Samuel, an Ephrathite, filled the office of leading priest in Israel. [3] Abiather was thrust out of the office of the priesthood in fulfilment of the prophecy given to Eli. [4] But Zadok, who filled the office of high priest in the time of David

Consecration of the Priest

and Solomon, was thought by many to be a grandson of Eli. As the Israelites departed from the Lord, the priesthood became corrupt, until in the time of Christ it was bought and sold for money.

God designed that the high priest should more nearly represent Christ than any other priest. The work of every priest

[1] Isa. 9:6.
[3] 1 Sam. 1:1, 19, 20.
[2] Ex. 29:5-35.
[4] 1 Kings 2:26, 27.

was a type of Christ's work, but the common priests performed
work only in the court and the first apartment of the sanctuary,
while the high priest officiated not only in the court and the
first apartment, as well as the common priests, but went alone
into the holy of holies. [1] Aaron at times offered burnt-offerings on the brazen altar in the court. [2]

It was impossible for one man to perform all the work
of the sanctuary that typified the work of Christ, and for that
reason there was a company of common priests to assist the
high priest. It is always a rule that a higher official can fill
the offices below him. The high priest offered burnt-offerings
in the court and sin-offerings in the first apartment. Paul
speaks of the high priest offering the sin-offerings where the
blood was taken into the sanctuary. [3] In the sin-offerings for
the priests and the congregation the blood was taken within
the sanctuary. [4] It seems very fitting that the high priest should
offer the sin-offerings for the common priests and the entire
congregation. In most of the sin-offerings the flesh was eaten
in the holy place, and the blood was not taken into the sanctuary. [5] While the high priest could perform any work in the
first apartment that other priests could perform, there was a
daily service in the first apartment of the sanctuary that none
but the high priest could perform. He alone could burn incense upon the golden altar before the Lord, and trim and
light the lamps on the golden candlestick. Each morning
and evening, twice every day throughout the entire year, the
high priest officiated in the first apartment of the sanctuary. [6]

The crowning service of the whole year was on the tenth
day of the seventh month, when the high priest entered the holy
of holies alone to make atonement for the sins of the people.
Upon his breast in the stones of the breast-plate were inscribed

[1] Heb. 9:7.   [2] 1 Chron. 6:49.   Heb. 13:11.
[4] Lev. 4:3-7, 13-18.   [5] Lev. 10:17, 18.   Ex. 30:7, 8.

the names of the twelve tribes, typifying Christ our High Priest as He thinks upon us individually, and confesses our names as they come up in review before God.

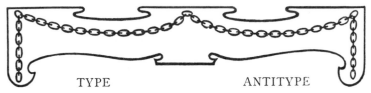

TYPE ANTITYPE

Ex. 28: 1, 2. Called of God. Heb. 3: 1-3. Appointed by God.

Ex. 29: 29. T h e priesthood Heb. 7: 23, 24. Lives forever.
passed from father to son.

Lev. 16: 1-20. The high priest Heb. 9: 14, 26. Christ atones
made the typical atonement in for sin by the sacrifice of
the end of the year's service. Himself.

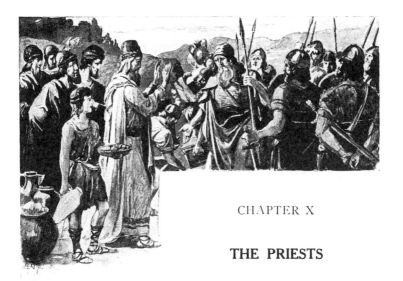

CHAPTER X

THE PRIESTS

HERE were two orders of the priesthood, the Melchizedek and the Levitical. The Melchizedek order preceded the Levitical order. In Abraham's day the priest Melchizedek was king of Salem as well as priest of the Most High God. [1] Although there is not much said in the Bible of the Melchizedek order of the priesthood, it was superior to the Levitical order, for Christ was made a priest after the order of Melchizedek. [2]

The Levitical order extended from the time Israel came out of Egypt until the cross; since that time we have the priesthood of Christ, of which all earthly priests were a type. Christ being a priest after the order of Melchizedek, we are now living under the Melchizedek order of the priesthood. There

[1] Gen. 14:17-20.　　　　[2] Heb. 6:20.

are many particulars given in regard to the Levitical order; and as all the Levitical priests served " unto the example and shadow of heavenly things," when we study the Levitical priesthood, we are really studying the priestly work of our Lord and Saviour Jesus Christ.

The Levitical priesthood was divided into twenty-four courses. [1] Each course had its chief or governor of the sanctuary. [2] This continued down to the time of Christ. [3] When the Saviour ascended to heaven, He led a multitude of captives; [4] and when John in vision was shown the first apartment of the heavenly sanctuary, with its seven lamps of fire burning before the throne of God, he saw four and twenty elders seated upon four and twenty seats, and they worshiped the Lamb, saying, " Thou . . . hast redeemed us to God by Thy blood out of every kindred, and tongue, and people, and nation; and hast made us unto our God kings and priests. " [5] In this we see the antitype of the twenty-four courses of priests. The chiefs, or elders, of each course have seats of honor, and they are kings and priests after the order of Melchizedek. The remainder of the multitude Christ took into heaven are not mentioned, but it is reasonable to suppose that they constitute the courses of which the four and twenty elders are the chiefs.

Only the descendants of Aaron were allowed to serve as priests. [6] In the type the priest who could not prove his genealogy direct from Aaron, the first high priest, was cast out of the priesthood; [7] so in the antitype, the Christian who can not prove his direct connection with Christ, the heavenly High Priest, will never become one of the " royal priesthood." [8]

God has provided for the support of all the different orders of the priesthood by the same method. " The earth is the Lord's, and the fulness thereof." [9] The silver and the gold and the

[1] 1 Chron. 24 : 1-19 ; 2 Chron. 8 : 14.   [2] 1 Chron. 24 : 6, 31.   [3] Luke 1 : 8.
[4] Eph. 4 : 8, margin.   [5] Rev. 4 : 4 ; 5 : 8-10.   [6] Num. 3 : 10.   [7] Ezra 2 : 26.
[8] 1 Peter 2 : 9 ; Rev. 20 : 15.   [9] Ps. 24 : 1.

cattle upon a thousand hills all belong to Him. [1] Man is placed as steward over the Lord's heritage, and the Lord claims one tenth of everything on the earth as His portion. " All the tithe of the land, whether of the seed of the land, or of the fruit of the tree, is the Lord's: *it is holy* unto the Lord." [2]

Of the tithe the Lord says, " I have given the children of Levi all the tenth in Israel for an inheritance, for their service which they serve, even the service of the tabernacle of the congregation." [3] The individual who selfishly uses the entire ten portions for himself, not reserving one tenth for the Lord, is guilty of robbing the Lord. " Will a man rob God? Yet ye have robbed Me. But ye say, Wherein have we robbed Thee? In tithes and offerings." [4] Abraham paid a faithful tithe to Melchizedek; [5] and Jacob promised to pay tithe of all, even if he received only food and raiment. [6] Those who belong to the great household of faith and are children of Abraham, will " do the works of Abraham." [7] They will pay a faithful tithe for the support of those who, like the Levitical priests, give their lives for the advancement of Christ's kingdom upon the earth. Just as the priest lived " of the things of the temple, . . .

A good name is rather to be chosen than great riches, and loving favor rather than silver and gold. Prov 22:1

[1] Ps. 50: 10-12. [2] Lev. 27: 30-33. [3] Num. 18: 20-24. [4] Mal. 3: 8-11.
[5] Gen. 14: 17-20. [6] Gen. 28: 20-22. [7] John 8: 39.

6

even so hath the Lord ordained that they which preach the gospel should live of the gospel." [1]

TYPE	ANTITYPE
Heb. 8 : 5. The earthly priests served " unto the example and shadow of heavenly things."	Heb. 10 : 10. " We are sanctified through the offering of the body of Jesus Christ once for all."
1 Chron. 24 : 1-19, 31. Priests were divided into twenty-four courses, with a chief over each course.	Rev. 4 : 4, 5 ; 5 : 8-10. John saw twenty-four elders in the first apartment of t h e heavenly sanctuary.
Ezra 2 : 61, 62. There was a record kept of all who had a right to officiate in the priest's office.	Rev. 20 : 15. None will be saved whose names are not found written in the book of life.

---

[1] 1 Cor. 9 : 9-14.

CHAPTER XI

THE LEVITES

 NE entire tribe of Israel was set apart for the service of the sanctuary. As we recall the last words spoken to Levi by his father Jacob as he lay on his death-bed, we might wonder that his descendants were chosen for that sacred work. When Jacob remembered the sins of Levi, he pronounced almost a curse instead of a blessing upon his son, and closed it with these words: " I will divide them in Jacob, and scatter them in Israel." [1]

Wondrous is the love of our God that can change a curse into a blessing. [2] Only a mighty God can make scarlet sins as white as snow. [3] The impulsive nature which, under the control of Satan, drives a man to commit desperate crimes, is not removed when he is converted. That same impetuosity, consecrated and under the control of Christ, makes him a valiant warrior for the Lord. Saul, the desperate persecutor, when converted, became Paul, the leading apostle.

[1] Gen. 49 : 5-7.   [2] Neh. 13 : 2.   [3] Isa. 1 : 18.

The fearless character which, under the control of Satan, led Levi to murder the Shechemites, when controled by the grace of God, enabled his descendants to take their stand boldly on the Lord's side when the mass of Israel went into idolatry. [1] God then turned the curse into a blessing; He said because they had observed His law and kept His covenant, they should "teach Jacob His judgments and Israel His law." [2]

In order that their influence for good might be more widely felt throughout Israel, the Lord, instead of giving them one portion of the land for their inheritance, as He had given the other tribes, appointed as their portion forty-eight cities scattered among all the tribes. [3] Truly they were divided in Jacob and scattered in Israel, but the curse was turned into a blessing.

Our God is "the same yesterday, and to-day, and forever." [4] When He pronounces evil against a nation or an individual because of their wickedness, if they turn from their wrong-doing, God says He "will repent of the evil" He "thought to do unto them," and as in the case of Levi, a blessing will come instead of the curse. [5]

The term "Levite" was applied to all the priests, but only the descendants of Aaron were to hold the sacred office. The remainder of the tribe were to do the service of the sanctuary under the direction of the priests. They were not allowed to officiate at the altar of burnt-offering, nor to burn incense, nor to do any of the priest's work within the veil. The Levites were to serve, or minister to, the priests; but the priests were to minister for the people before the Lord.[6]

The Levites were consecrated to the work of the sanctuary by the laying on of hands by the whole assembly of Israel, and then Aaron offered them "before the Lord for an offering of the children of Israel." [7]

[1] Ex. 32 : 26-29.   [2] Deut. 33 : 8-11.   [3] Num. 18 : 20 ; 35 : 1-8.
[4] Heb. 13 : 8.   [5] Jer. 18 : 7-10.   [6] Num. 18 : 1-7.   [7] Num. 8 : 9-14.

The Levites were chosen by the Lord instead of the first-born of Israel. [1] While journeying in the wilderness, they carried all that pertained to the tabernacle; but although they bore the sacred furniture, they were never permitted even to look upon it. [2]

After the temple was built, the Levites were assigned the work of waiting on the priests in the sanctuary service. They prepared the showbread, often led the singing, collected the tithe, and did a large amount of work in connection with the service of the Lord. [3]

In the time of David the Levites began to serve in the sanctuary at the age of twenty-five. At fifty years of age they were to "return from the warfare of the service." [4] They were not discharged; they still had an oversight of the work, but were not expected to perform arduous duties.

The work of the Levites was largely confined to the court, and thus typified the work of the gospel ministry of the present day.

TYPE	ANTITYPE
Num. 18:1-7. The Levites served under the priests in the court of the sanctuary.	Matt. 28:19, 20. Christ's ministers are to go to all the world — the antitypical court.
2 Chron. 35:3; 30:22. The Levites were teachers in Israel.	Matt. 28:19. Christ commissioned His disciples to teach all nations.

[1] Num. 8:17, 18.
[3] 1 Chron. 23:24-32.
[2] Num. 4:20.
[4] Num. 8:23-26, margin.

CHAPTER XII

GARMENTS OF THE PRIESTS

THE garments worn by the ordinary priests were of white linen, a fit emblem of the Spotless One of whom their ministry was a type. The outer robe was white, woven in one piece, and extended nearly to the feet. It was confined at the waist with a white linen girdle, embroidered in blue, purple, and scarlet. A white linen miter, or turban, covered the head. These articles, with the linen breeches which were worn by all officiating priests, completed the costume of the common priest. These garments of white linen were made for " glory and for beauty." [1]

Only the family of Aaron could wear the rich garments of the priest; but there are robes of " fine linen, clean and white,"

[1] Ex. 28 : 40-42.

in store for every overcomer. [1] Even in this life, Christ clothes His faithful ones with "the garments of salvation" and "the robe of righteousness." [2]

The pure white garments were worn by the high priest on ordinary occasions, but when he entered the most holy place to make atonement for the people, he was clad in gorgeous robes, which fitly represented our High Priest as He confesses the names of His people before the judgment-seat of the Judge of the whole earth.

The high priest always wore the long white linen robe of the common priest, but over this was a robe of blue woven in one piece, and beautifully ornamented around the skirt with golden bells and pomegranates of blue, purple, and gold. The ephod, a sleeveless garment of white linen, beautifully embroidered in gold, blue, purple, and scarlet, was worn over the blue robe. This was shorter than the other garments, and was confined at the waist by a richly embroidered girdle of the same color.

On the gold embroidered shoulders of the ephod were two onyx stones, on which were engraved the names of the twelve tribes of Israel, six names on each shoulder, thus typifying the Mighty One who bears the perplexities and burdens of His people upon His shoulders. [3]

While the robe of blue with its golden bells and the handsomely embroidered ephod were beautiful, yet the crowning feature in all the gorgeous dress of the high priest was the breastplate worn over his heart as he officiated in the holy of holies before the Lord. The breastplate was of the same material as the ephod. It was in the form of a square and measured a span. In it were set in gold twelve precious stones, arranged three in a row. On each stone was engraved the name of one of the tribes of Israel. Around these was a border of a variety

[1] Rev. 19:8.   [2] Isa. 61:10.   [3] Isa. 9:6.

of stones. The stones in the breastplate were the same as those that form the foundation of the New Jerusalem.[1] The breastplate hung from the shoulders of the ephod and was fastened at the waist by a blue cord through gold rings.

Set in the breastplate, one on either side, were two brilliant stones, called the Urim and Thummim. By means of these stones the mind of the Lord could be ascertained by the high priest. When questions were asked, if light encircled the precious stone at the right, the answer was in the affirmative; but

"Stone is an enduring substance, but far more enduring is the book of life, where the names which Christ has confessed, are written to remain forever."

if a shadow rested on the stone at the left, the answer was negative.

The breastplate being attached to the ephod, David, in calling for the priest to bring the ephod when he was undecided as to what course to pursue, was really asking for the breastplate, by which he might know the mind of the Lord.[2]

There was one other article belonging to the high priest's garments,— the miter, or bonnet.[3]   A gold plate bearing the inscription, "Holiness to Jehovah," was fastened by a blue lace to the front of the white bonnet, or turban, worn by the priests.

[1] Ex. 28 : 2-39.   [2] I Sam. 23 : 9-12.   [3] Ex. 28 : 36, 37.

No priest was allowed to wear the priestly garments except when officiating in the sanctuary or court. [1]

There is a touching significance in the high priest's wearing the names of all Israel on his shoulders and over his heart as he performed the work which typified the judgment, when the case of every one will come up in review before God. The breastplate was called "the breastplate of judgment." [2] Those names engraved on the stones were a type of the names of the overcomers, which Christ will confess before His father and the angels. Stone is an enduring substance, but far more enduring is the book of life, where the names which Christ has confessed, are written to remain forever. [3]

TYPE	ANTITYPE
Ex. 28 : 32. Garment all of one piece.	John 19 : 23. Christ's earthly garment was woven in one piece.
Ex. 28 : 15-21. The breastplate of judgment contained the names of the twelve tribes, and was worn over the heart of the high priest as he performed the work which typified the work of the judgment.	Rev. 3 : 5. As each individual name comes up in review before God in the judgment, Christ will "confess" the names of the overcomers, and their names will remain in the book of life.

[1] Eze. 44 : 19.   [2] Ex. 28 : 15.   [3] Rev. 3 : 5.

Bless the Lord,
O my soul:
and all that is
within me, bless His
holy name.

Ps. 103:1

SECTION IV

Springtime Annual Feasts

The Paschal Lamb

PASCHAL Lamb, by God appointed,
  All our sins on Thee were laid;
By Almighty Love anointed.
 Thou redemption's price hast paid.
All thy people are forgiven
 Through the virtue of thy blood;
Opened is the gate of heaven,
  Peace is made 'twixt man and God.

Jesus, hail! enthroned in glory!
 There forever to abide;
All the heavenly hosts adore thee,
 Seated at thy Father's side:
There for sinners thou art pleading;
 There thou dost our place prepare,
Ever for us interceding,
 Till in glory we appear.

Worship, honor, power, and blessing,
 Thou art worthy to receive;
Loudest praises, without ceasing,
 Meet it is for us to give;
Help, ye bright angelic spirits,
 Bring your sweetest, noblest lays;
Help to sing our Saviour's merits,
 Help to chant Immanuel's praise!
                    —*John Bakewell.*

CHAPTER XIII

THE PASSOVER

 HE Passover was the opening feast of the yearly round of religious services. It was both commemorative and typical,— commemorative of the deliverance of the children of Israel from the bondage of Egypt, and typical of the deliverance from the thralldom of sin of every individual who claims Christ as his Passover Lamb, and accepts His blood as a covering for past sins. [1]

The Passover was celebrated in the early springtime, when the opening buds and flowers proclaimed that winter was past. As the time drew near for this feast, every road leading toward Jerusalem was thronged with devout Jews wending their way toward the holy city; for every man of the children of Israel had to appear before the Lord at the time of this feast. [2] All classes mingled together in these traveling companies, which were constantly increasing as they neared the city. Shepherds, farmers, priests, and Levites, men from all walks in life, joined the throngs which entered Jerusalem from all directions. The homes in the city were thrown open to entertain them, and

(93)

[1] 1 Cor. 5:7.   [2] Deut. 16:16.

tents were pitched upon the house-tops and in the streets to shelter those attending the feast, and to provide rooms where as families and groups they might gather to eat the Passover.

Prior to the deliverance of the children of Israel from Egypt, the new year began in the autumn;[1] but when the Lord brought the Israelites out from Egyptian bondage, in the month Abib, or Nisan, He said, " This month shall be unto you the beginning of months: it shall be the first month of the year to you."[2] The month Abib corresponds with the last of March and the first of April.

On the tenth day of the month Abib, the Passover lamb was selected, and was kept separate from the rest of the flock until the fourteenth day of the month, when it was slain. There was an appointed hour for the slaying of the lamb,— " between the two evenings,"[3] or about the ninth hour of the day, which in our reckoning of time would be three o'clock in the afternoon.

The lamb was roasted entire, not one bone being broken. If the family was small, several families could join together in the feast. Unleavened bread and bitter herbs were eaten with the lamb. The unleavened bread commemorated the rapid flight from Egypt, when the children of Israel took their dough before it was leavened, " their kneading-troughs being bound up in their clothes upon their shoulders." The unleavened bread also typified the condition of the one who is covered by the blood of Christ, the antitypical Lamb. [4] To such a one the Lord says, " Let us keep the feast, not with old leaven, neither with the leaven of malice and wickedness; but with the unleavened bread of sincerity and truth."[5]

Not only was unleavened bread used in the feast, but no leaven was allowed in the homes during the entire week following the day of the Passover.

This is a very beautiful emblem of the Christian, who, while

[1] Ex. 23 : 16 ; 34 : 22, margin.   [2] Ex. 12 : 2.
[3] Ex. 12 : 6, margin.   [4] Ex. 12 : 1-46.   [5] 1 Cor. 5 : 8.

claiming to be sheltered by the blood of Christ, should not only keep his mouth from speaking evil, but his heart also should be free from the "leaven of malice and wickedness." The bitter herbs were a reminder of their cruel bondage in Egypt. The lamb was to be eaten in the night of the fourteenth day of the month. If any of the flesh remained until the morning, it was burned by fire.

When the lamb was slain, a sprig of hyssop was dipped in the blood, and with it they were to strike the two side posts and the lintel of the door of the house where the lamb was eaten. This commemorated that wonderful deliverance of the first-born of Israel when all the first-born of Egypt were slain. The Lord said, " The blood shall be to you a token upon the houses where ye are: and when I see the blood, I will pass over you,

" Every Passover lamb, . . . was a type of the Saviour."

and the plague shall not be upon you to destroy you, when I smite the land of Egypt." [1]

While the event commemorated by the blood on the lintel was wonderful, yet the event typified was far more wonderful. Just as truly as the destroying angel passed through Egypt and laid the icy hand of death upon the brow of every first-born child who was not shielded by the blood, so the second death, from which there will be no resurrection, will fall upon every one who has not been cleansed from sin by the blood of Christ. [2] There was no respect of persons; all were slain, from the heir to the throne of Egypt to the first-born of the prisoner in the dungeon. Ex-

[1] Ex. 12:13. [2] Rev. 20:14, 15.

alted station, wealth, or earthly fame will not shield one from the destroying angel of the Lord. One thing alone will shield rich and poor alike, it is the precious blood of Christ. " The blood of Jesus Christ His Son cleanseth us from all sin." " If we confess our sins, He is faithful and just to forgive us our sins, and to cleanse us from all unrighteousness." [1]

Dwelling upon the commemorative side of the Passover feast, strengthens our faith. Remembering how the Lord wrought for His afflicted people, how he heard their cries and worked miracles for their deliverance, brings a blessing to the soul; but there is also salvation for the one who dwells upon the typical part of the Passover feast, and claims the blessings there shadowed forth by type and symbol. Every Passover lamb, from the one slain on the night of the deliverance from Egypt to the time of Christ, was a type of the Saviour in a special sense. " Christ our Passover is sacrificed for us." [2]

Just as the Passover lamb had for centuries been taken from the flocks a few days before it was to be slain, and had been kept separate, a lamb marked for death; so a few days before Christ was crucified, the Sanhedrin condemned Him to death. From that day forth, as they looked upon Him, they knew that His death was determined. As the lamb was kept apart, so " Jesus therefore walked no more openly among the Jews." [3] This was only a few days before Jesus was seized by the cruel mob and condemned by false witnesses.

On the morning after that awful night of torture and agony, the Saviour was brought to Pilate's judgment hall. All night the Jews had followed Christ while He had been in the presence of their high priest; but now, when He was taken into the Roman hall of justice, the Jews " went not into the judgment hall, lest they should be defiled; but that they might eat the

[1] 1 John 1: 7, 9.   [2] 1 Cor. 5: 7.   [3] John 11: 47-54.

Passover." [1] According to their ceremonial laws of defilement, they would not be permitted to eat the Passover if they entered this place. This was the morning of the day the Saviour was crucified. It was the preparation day for the Jewish Passover, the day upon which, "between the two evenings," the lamb was to be slain; or, in other words, it was the fourteenth day of the month Abib, or Nisan, which in the year the Saviour was crucified fell upon Friday, for the day following was the Sabbath day, according to the commandment, the seventh day of the week. [2]

It was not by chance that the Saviour was crucified upon Friday, the sixth day of the week. For centuries God had ordained that the day follow- ing

"Christ our Passover is sacrificed for us."

the Passover, the fifteenth day of the month Abib, should be kept as a ceremonial sabbath, [3] thus typifying the fact that Christ, the real Passover, would be offered the day before the Sabbath. The Passover lamb was slain between the two evenings, or about the ninth hour of the day. The great antitypical Lamb, as He hung between heaven and earth an offering for sinful man, about the ninth hour,

[1] John 18 : 28.   [2] Luke 23 : 52-56.   [3] Lev. 23 : 6, 7.

7

Oh that men would praise the Lord for His goodness, and for His wonderful works to the children of men.

Ps. 107:8

cried, "It is finished," and yielded up His life an offering for sin. [1] At this hour the priests were preparing to slay the lamb at the temple, but they were arrested in their work. All nature responded to that cry of agony from the Son of God. The earth reeled to and fro, and unseen hands rent the veil of the temple from the top to the bottom, [2] showing by an unmistakable sign that type had met antitype. The shadow had met the substance which cast the shadow. No longer was man to approach God by means of offerings of animals, but he was to come boldly to a throne of grace, [3] and present his request in the precious name of "Christ our Passover."

The work typified by the Passover extends on down through the ages, and will not have fully met its antitype until the children of God are forever freed from the power of the enemy of all righteousness.

It was at midnight that the destroying angel passed throughout Egypt, and manifested his power in delivering the people of God from bondage; so it will be at midnight that God will manifest His power for the final deliverance of His people. [4] The prophet, looking down through the ages, says, "The peo-

[1] Matt. 27:46-50; John 19:30. [2] Matt. 27:50, 51. [3] Heb. 4:15, 16. [4] Ex. 12:29, 30.

ple shall be troubled at midnight, and pass away: and the mighty shall be taken away without hand." [1]

Those partaking of the Passover feast were to leave nothing of it until the morning. The morning was to bring a new experience — freedom from bondage. The soul that accepts Christ as his Passover and partakes of Him by faith, enters upon a new experience — freedom from the condemnation of the old life. When God manifests His power at midnight for the final deliverance of His people, the morning will leave none in bondage. "Prison walls are rent asunder, and God's people who have been held in bondage for their faith are set free," nevermore to feel the oppressive power of the enemy.

The destruction of Pharaoh and all his host in the Red Sea, and the song of deliverance sung by the Israelites on the other shore, were typical of the final deliverance of God's people from this earth. [2] The righteous will be caught up to meet the Lord in the air, but the wicked, like Pharaoh's host, will be left dead upon the earth, neither gathered nor buried. [3]

No stranger could partake of the Passover feast; but there were provisions made in the old Levitical service whereby a stranger, by complying with certain forms and ceremonies, could become an Israelite, and then partake of the Passover. [4] Sin debars mankind from sharing in the blessings promised the children of God, but there is a remedy for sins: "Though your sins be as scarlet, they shall be as white as snow; though they be red like crimson, they shall be as wool." [5] "If any man sin, we have an advocate with the Father, Jesus Christ the righteous." [6]

The children of Israel were surrounded by heathen nations, who, when all the men went up to attend t h e annual feasts, would seize upon their flocks and land, unless they were es-

---

[1] Job 34:20.   [2] Rev. 15:2, 3.   [3] 1 Thess. 4:16, 17; Jer. 25: 30-33
[4] Ex. 12:48.   [5] Isa. 1:18.   [6] 1 John 2:1.

pecially protected by God; for not only at the Passover, but three times in the year all the men of Israel were required to attend the feasts at Jerusalem. They went up trusting the promise, " I will . . . enlarge thy borders: neither shall any man desire thy land, when thou shalt go up to appear before the Lord thy God thrice in the year." [1] We have the same God to-day, and for the man or woman who will seek " first the kingdom of God, and His righteousness," God will " enlarge their borders," and protect their temporal interests. [2]

No longer do God's people gather at Jerusalem to eat the Passover; but faithful followers of the Lord in all nations of the earth partake of the memorial of His broken body and shed blood. To each company the words are spoken:—" As often as ye eat this bread, and drink this cup, ye do show the Lord's death till He come." [3]

There is a difference between the annual offerings, or feasts, and the ordinary offerings. The sin-offering, trespass-offering, peace-offering, or any of the ordinary offerings could be celebrated at *any time* in the year, whenever the occasion or needs of the people demanded it; but not so with the annual feasts.

All the annual feasts were prophetic as well as typical. While the Passover lamb, slain each year, was a shadow of " Christ our Passover," who was sacrificed for us, the fact that the lamb could be slain *only* on the fourteenth day of the month Abib, was a prophecy that the antitypical Passover Lamb would yield up His life for the sins of the world on the fourteenth day of Abib.

One unanswerable argument that Jesus is the Messiah, is that He died upon the cross the very day, and time of the day, that God had said the Passover lamb should be slain; and He came forth from the dead the same day of the month, that the first-fruits had been waved for centuries. God, Himself, definitely

[1] Ex. 34 : 24.   [2] Matt. 6 : 24-33.   [3] 1 Cor. 11 : 26.

fixed the date for the celebration of each of the annual offerings. The day of the year when each annual offering was to be celebrated, was a direct prophecy of the *time* when the type would meet its antitype.

TYPE   ANTITYPE

" Christ our Passover is sacrificed for us." 1 Cor. 5 : 7.

TYPE	ANTITYPE
Ex. 12 : 3-5. Lamb selected some days before it was slain.	John 11 : 47-53. Christ condemned to death by the Sanhedrin some days before the crucifixion.
Ex. 12 : 6. It was set apart, and kept separate from the flock.	John 11 : 53, 54. " Jesus therefore walked no more openly among the Jews."
Ex. 12 : 6. The Passover lamb was slain on the fourteenth day of Abib, or Nisan.	John 18 : 28; 19 : 14; 19 : 31; Luke 23 : 54-56. Jesus was crucified on the day the Jews were preparing to eat the Passover; viz., the fourteenth day of the month Abib, or Nisan.
Ex. 12 : 6, margin. The lamb was slain between the two evenings.	Mark 15 : 34-37; John 19 : 30. Jesus died upon the cross " between the two evenings," or about the ninth hour.
Ex. 12 : 46. Not a bone of the lamb was broken.	John 19 : 33-36. Not a bone of the Saviour was broken.

Ex. 12 : 7. Blood was placed on the two posts and lintel of the door.

1 John 1 : 7. "The blood of Jesus Christ His Son cleanseth us from all sin."

Ex. 12 : 8. Unleavened bread and bitter herbs were eaten with the lamb.

1 Cor. 5 : 7, 8. Unleavened bread represented freedom from malice and wickedness.

Ex. 12 : 19. No leaven was allowed in their homes for one week after the Passover feast.

1 Peter 3 : 10; 1 Thess. 5 : 23. The Christian is not only to keep his lips from speaking guile; but his whole spirit, soul, and body are to be preserved blameless.

Ex. 12 : 7, 12, 29, 42. Deliverance came at midnight after the slaying of the first-born of the Egyptians.

Job 34 : 20. "It is at midnight that God manifests His power for the deliverance of His people."

Ex. 12 : 22, 23. No shelter from the destroyer except under the blood of the Passover lamb.

Acts 4 : 12. "Neither is there salvation in any other: for there is none other name under heaven given among men, whereby we must be saved."

Ex. 12 : 10, 46. None of the lamb to be left until morning. The portion not eaten was to be burned.

Mal. 4 : 1-3; Eze. 28 : 12-19. When the righteous are delivered, ashes will be the only reminder of sin and sinners.

Ex. 12 : 43. No stranger could eat of the Passover.

Rev. 21 : 27. No sinner can share in the reward of the righteous.

Ex. 12 : 48. There was a provision made by which a stranger could eat of the Passover.

Eph. 2 : 13; Gal. 3 : 29. "But now, in Christ Jesus, ye who sometimes were far off, are made nigh by the blood of Christ."

CHAPTER XIV

THE FEAST OF UNLEAVENED BREAD

THE Feast of Unleavened Bread began with the fifteenth day of the month Abib, or Nisan, and continued seven days. [1] Unleavened bread was eaten with the Passover lamb; but the Feast of Unleavened Bread followed the Passover, although at times the term "Feast of Unleavened Bread" also included the Passover. Many offerings were offered upon each one of the seven days, and among them seven lambs. The first and last days of the feast were kept as ceremonial sabbaths, but the first one of these sabbaths was reckoned the more important, being spoken of as *the* Sabbath. [2]

"The whole Jewish economy is a compacted prophecy of the gospel," and every service commanded by God in the Jewish economy was either a shadow of the service of our High

[1] Num. 28:17. [2] Lev. 23:11, 15.

(103)

Priest in the heavenly sanctuary, or of the service enjoined upon the earthly congregation for whom he is officiating. Therefore there was a special significance attached to the fact that for centuries the day following the Passover was kept as a sabbath.

In the previous chapter we have shown that it was not by chance that in the year the Saviour was crucified the Passover came on Friday, the sixth day of the week. Neither was it by chance that the ceremonial sabbath, the fifteenth day of Abib, came upon the seventh-day Sabbath of the Lord. It was type meeting antitype. The beloved disciple John said, " That Sabbath was a high day," [1] which term was used whenever the ceremonial annual sabbath came upon the weekly Sabbath of the Lord.

Four thousand years before, on the first sixth day of time, God and Christ finished the work of creation. God pronounced the finished work very good, and " He rested on the seventh day from all His work which He had made. And God blessed the seventh day, and sanctified it: because that in it He had rested from all His work which God created and made." [2] About twenty-five hundred years later, God, amid t h e awful grandeur of Sinai, commanded His people to " remember the Sabbath day to keep it holy;" [3] for upon that day — the seventh day — He rested from the work of creation.

It was a mighty work to speak this world into existence, to clothe it with verdure and beauty, to supply it with animal life, to people it with human beings made in the image of God; but it is a far greater work to take the earth marred by sin, its inhabitants sunken in iniquity, and re-create them, bringing them really to a higher state of perfection than when they first came from the hand of the Creator. This is the work undertaken by the Son of God; and when He cried upon Calvary, " It is

[1] John 19:31.   [2] Gen. 2:2,3.   [3] Ex. 20:1-17.

finished," He spoke to the Father, announcing the fact that He had complied with the requirements of the law, He had lived a sinless life, had shed His blood as a ransom for the world, and now the way was opened whereby every son and daughter of Adam could be saved if they would accept the offered pardon.

As the westering sun was heralding to the world the approach of the holy Sabbath of the Lord, from the cross on Calvary the Son of God proclaimed the work of redemption finished. That work was to affect the entire creation, and although wicked men understood not the meaning of those mystic words, " It is finished," all nature responded, and, as it were, leaped for joy; even the solid rocks were rent asunder. God designed that this stupendous event should be recognized by humanity; and as those living and even gazing upon the scene were unconscious of its significance, sleeping saints were awakened from their graves to proclaim the glad news. [1]

The work of redemption was completed on the sixth day, and as God rested after the work of creation, so Jesus rested in Joseph's tomb during the sacred hours of that holy Sabbath. His followers rested also; for He had ever taught them obedience to His Father's holy law. He had forbidden any ever to think that even a jot or tittle of the law of God could be changed. [2] For four thousand years the Sabbath had been observed as a memorial of creation; but after the Saviour died upon the cross it was doubly blessed, being a memorial of redemption as well as of creation.

[1] Matt. 27:50-53.   [2] Matt. 5:17, 18.

The Sabbath, like a great bridge, spans all time. The first pier upholding this great institution was placed in Eden, when, according to the account given in Gen. 2 : 2, 3, God and unfallen man rested through the sacred hours of the Sabbath. The second pier of the bridge was founded amid the thunders of Sinai, when God, in proclaiming the fourth commandment as found in Ex. 20 : 8-11, gave the fact that He had rested upon the seventh day from the work of creation, as the reason why man should keep it holy. The third pier of the Sabbath bridge was hallowed by the blood of Calvary. While the Son of the mighty God rested in the tomb from the work of redemption, it is recorded in Luke 23 : 54-56 that Jesus' followers " rested on the Sabbath day according to the commandment." The fourth pier of this wonderful bridge will be laid in the earth made new. In Isa. 63 : 22, 23, we are told that after the last trace of the curse of sin is removed from the earth, all flesh will from Sabbath to Sabbath come to worship before the Lord. As long as the new heavens and the new earth remain, so long will the redeemed of the Lord love to commemorate the Sabbath as a memorial of the finished work of Christ in the redemption of this fallen world, as well as a memorial of its creation.

The second day of the Feast of Unleavened Bread was the offering of first-fruits. This was a very important service, and will be dwelt upon separately from the rest of the feast. During the seven days following the Passover, the people ate unleavened bread. Seven, denoting a complete number, was a fitting type of the life that should be lived by the one who claims Christ as his Passover, and has the blessed assurance that his sins are covered by the blood of the Saviour. Leaven is a type of " malice and wickedness "; unleavened bread represents " sincerity and truth." He whose past sins are hidden, [1]

[1] Rom. 4 : 7, 8.

and who realizes what it is to have the condemnation of his old life lifted from him, enters into a new life, and should not return to his life of sin, but live in all "sincerity and truth." All this was symbolized by the seven days' Feast of Unleavened Bread, following the Passover.

TYPE	ANTITYPE
Lev. 23 : 6, 7. The day following the Passover, the fifteenth day of Abib, was a ceremonial sabbath.	Luke 23 : 54-56; John 19 : 31. The fifteenth day of Abib, in the year the Saviour was crucified, was the seventh-day Sabbath of the Lord.
Deut. 16 : 4. "There shall be no leavened bread seen with thee in all thy coast seven days."	1 Cor. 5 : 7. "Purge out therefore the old leaven, that ye may be a new lump, as ye are unleavened. For even Christ our Passover is sacrificed for us."
Deut. 16 : 3. "Seven days shalt thou eat unleavened bread, . . . that thou mayest remember the day when thou camest forth out of the land of Egypt all the days of thy life."	1 Cor. 5 : 8. "Let us keep the feast, not with old leaven, neither with the leaven of malice and wickedness; but with the unleavened bread of sincerity and truth."

CHAPTER XV

THE OFFERING OF THE FIRST-FRUITS

HEN the waving fields of golden grain proclaimed that the time of harvest had come, the service of offering the first-fruits before the Lord was performed in the temple.

As the children of Israel journeyed toward Jerusalem to attend the Passover, on every side could be seen fields of yellow barley, the heads heavy with ripened grain bending in the breeze. But not a sickle could be put into the grain, or even kernels gathered to be eaten until the first-fruits had been presented before the Lord.

The offering of first-fruits came on the third day of the Passover feast. The fourteenth day of the month Abib, or Nisan, the Passover was eaten, the fifteenth day was the Sabbath, and upon

(108)

the sixteenth day, or as the Bible states it, " On the morrow after the Sabbath," the first-fruits were waved before the Lord [1]

It was a beautiful service. The priest clad in his sacred robes, with a handful of yellow heads of ripened grain, entered the temple. The glow of burnished gold from walls and furniture blended with the tints of the golden heads of grain. The priest paused in front of the golden altar, and waved the grain before the Lord. Those first heads were a pledge of the bountiful harvest to be gathered, and the waving indicated thanksgiving and praise to the Lord of the harvest.

The waving of the first-fruits was the principal service of the day, but a lamb was also offered as a burnt-offering. No portion of the first-fruits were ever burned in the fire, for they were a type of resurrected beings clad in immortality, nevermore subject to death or decay.

For centuries God had met with His people in the temple, and accepted their offerings of praise and thanksgiving; but a change came. When Christ died on Calvary and the veil of the temple was rent asunder, the virtue of the temple service came to an end. The Jews slew their paschal lambs as formerly, but the service was only a mockery; for that year, upon the fourteenth day of the month Abib, " Christ our Passover was sacrificed for us." The Jews kept the empty form of the Sabbath on the day following the Passover; but it was the rest experienced by Jesus and His followers that was accepted of God. On the sixteenth day of the month, in the year the Saviour died, the Jews in the temple God had forsaken went through the empty form of offering the heads of grain, while Christ, the antitype, arose from the dead, and became " the first-fruits of them that slept." [2] Type had met antitype.

Every field of ripened grain gathered into the garner, is

[1] Lev. 23 : 5-11.   [2] 1 Cor. 15 : 20.

but a reminder of the great final harvest, when the Lord of the harvest, with His band of angel reapers, will come to gather the spiritual harvest of the world. Just as the first handful of grain was a pledge of the coming harvest, so the resurrection of Christ was a pledge of the resurrection of the righteous; " for if we believe that Jesus died and rose again, *even* so them also which sleep in Jesus will God bring with Him." [1]

The priest did not enter the temple with only one head of grain, he waved a handful before the Lord; neither did Jesus come forth from the grave alone, for " many bodies of the

**" Every field of ripened grain gathered into the garner, is but a re-
minder of the great final harvest."**

saints which slept arose, and came out of the graves after His resurrection." [2]   While the Jews were preparing to perform the empty service of the offering of first-fruits in the temple, and the Roman soldiers were telling the people that the disciples had stolen the body of Jesus, these resurrected saints went through the streets of the city, proclaiming that Christ had indeed risen. [3]

It is a sad fact that even the disciples who loved their Lord were so blinded that they could not recognize the fact that

[1] I Thess. 4:14.   [2] Matt. 27:52, 53.   [3] Matt. 28:11-15.

the time had come for the appearance of the great Antitype of the service they had yearly celebrated all their lives; and even when they listened to the announcement of His resurrection, it seemed to them as an idle tale, and they believed it not. [1] But God never lacks for agents. When living human beings are dumb, He awakens sleeping saints to perform His appointed work. In the type the grain was waved in the temple, and to fulfil the antitype Christ must present Himself and the company who had risen with Him before God in the first apartment of the heavenly temple.

In the early morning of the resurrection day, when Jesus appeared to Mary, she fell at His feet to worship Him, but Jesus said to her, " Touch Me not; for *I am not yet* ascended to My Father: but go to My brethren, and say unto them, I ascend unto My Father, and your Father; and to My God, and your God." [2] In these words Jesus notified His followers of the great event to take place in heaven, hoping that on earth there might be an answering chord to the wonderful rejoicing in heaven; but just as they had slept in the garden on the night of Christ's agony, and failed to give Him their sympathy, [3] so now, blinded by unbelief, they failed to share the joy of the Saviour's great triumph. Later on the same day Jesus appeared to His followers, and allowed them to hold Him by the feet and worship Him, [4] showing that in the meantime He had ascended to His Father.

Paul tells us that when Christ ascended up on high, " He led a multitude of captives." [5] In speaking of them in Rom. 8: 29, 30, he tells how this company of resurrected saints, who came forth from their graves with Christ, were chosen. They were " predestinated," then " called," " and whom He called, them He also justified: and whom He justified, them He also

[1] Luke 24: 10, 11.   [2] John 20: 17.   [3] Matt. 26: 40-44.
[4] Matt. 28: 9.   [5] Eph. 4: 8, margin.

glorified." This was done that "He might be the first-born among many brethren." This company was composed of individuals chosen from every age, from that of Adam down to the time of Christ. They were no longer subject to death, but ascended with Christ as trophies of His power to awaken all that sleep in their graves. As the handful of grain in the typical service was a pledge of the coming harvest, so these saints were a pledge of the innumerable company that Christ will awaken from the dust of the earth when He comes the second time as King of kings and Lord of lords. [1]

Little did the inhabitants of earth dream of the wonderful antitypical offering of first-fruits that was being celebrated in the heavenly temple at the time the Jews were carrying out the empty forms in the temple on earth.

That was a wonderful congregation in the heavenly courts. All the hosts of heaven and representatives from the unfallen worlds were assembled to greet the mighty Conqueror as He returned from the most terrible war ever waged and the greatest victory ever won. Earthly battles that simply gain dominion over a small portion of the earth for a brief span of years, are as nothing compared with the war that raged between Christ and Satan here upon this earth. Christ returned to heaven bearing the scars of that terrible struggle in the prints of the nails in His hands and feet and the wound in His side. [2]

Words fail to describe the scene as the heavenly host with one accord fall prostrate at His feet in adoration; but He waves them back, He bids them wait. Jesus has entered heaven as " the first-born among many brethren," and He will not receive the worship of the angels until the Father has accepted the first-fruits of the harvest to be gathered from the world He has died to redeem. [3] He pleads before the Father, " I will that they also,

[1] John 5 : 28, 29.   [2] Isa. 49 : 16.   [3] Matt. 13 : 38-43.

"Let all the angels of God worship Him."

whom Thou h a s t given Me, be with Me where I am." He does not plead in vain. The great antitype of the service celebrated for centuries is fully met. The Father accepts the first-fruits as a pledge that all the redeemed host will be received by Him. Then the decree goes forth, " Let all the angels of God worship Him."

We wonder how Christ could ever leave the glories of heaven to return to the earth, where He had met only ignominy and reproach.   But marvelous is the power of love! His sorrowing followers on earth were so dear to His heart that the worship of all heaven could not keep Him from them, and He returned to comfort and cheer their hearts.

The first three days of the Passover feast typified wonderful events in the work of our Saviour. The first day typified His broken body and shed blood; and the day before the type met antitype, Christ gathered His disciples together and instituted the touching memorial service of the Lord's supper, to commemorate His death and suffering until He comes a second time. [1]

Every weekly Sabbath of the Lord is a memorial of that Sabbath on which Jesus rested in the tomb, after He had finished His work on earth for the redemption of a lost race.

God has not left His church without a memorial of the great antitype of the offering of the first-fruits. He has given them baptism to commemorate this glorious event. As Christ

---

[1] Matt. 26 : 26-29.

8

was laid in the tomb, so the candidate for baptism is laid in the watery grave. "We are buried with Him by baptism into death: that like as Christ was raised up from the dead by the glory of the Father, even so we also should walk in newness of life." As the first-fruits of the resurrection taken to heaven by Christ were a pledge of the final resurrection, so rising from the watery grave of baptism is a pledge of the resurrection to the faithful child of God; "for if we have been planted together in the likeness of His death, we shall be also in the likeness of His resurrection." [1]

TYPE   ANTITYPE

Christ the First-fruits.   1 Cor. 15 : 23.

Lev. 23 : 5-11. The first-fruits were offered the third day after the Passover.	1 Cor. 15 : 20; Luke 23 : 21-23. Christ arose on the third day, and became the first-fruits.
Lev. 23 :10, margin. The priest waved a handful of grain in the head or an omer of kernels.	Rom. 8 : 29; Matt. 27 : 52, 53. Many saints arose with Christ. He was the first-born among many brethren.

---

[1] Rom. 6 : 3-5.

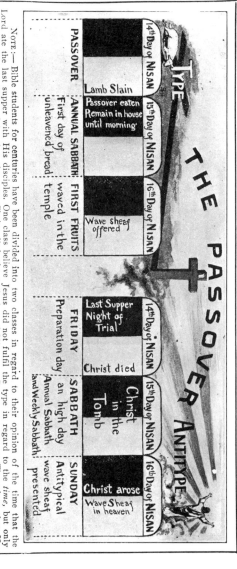

THE PASSOVER

TYPE

14th Day of NISAN	15th Day of NISAN	16th Day of NISAN
PASSOVER	ANNUAL SABBATH	FIRST FRUITS
Lamb Slain	Passover eaten Remain in house until morning'	Wave sheaf offered
	First day of unleavened bread	waved in the temple

ANTITYPE

14th Day of NISAN	15th Day of NISAN	16th Day of NISAN
FRIDAY	SABBATH	SUNDAY
Last Supper Night of Trial	Christ in the Tomb	Christ arose
Christ died		Wave Sheaf in heaven
Preparation day	an high day Annual Sabbath and Weekly Sabbath	Antitypical wave sheaf presented

Note:— Bible students for centuries have been divided into two classes in regard to their opinion of the time that the Lord ate the last supper with His disciples. One class believe Jesus did not fulfil the type in regard to the *time*, but only as to the event. They claim that the year Christ died, the 14th day of Nisan, or Passover, came on Thursday; that He was crucified on Friday, the annual sabbath, the 15th day of Nisan; and arose from the dead on the 17th day of Nisan. In support of this position, they quote the following texts: Matt. 26: 17; Mark 14: 1, 12; Luke 22: 7.

The other class believe that, when God decreed certain offerings should be offered on a definite day of the month, the type would meet antitype at that *specified time.* "These types were fulfilled not only as to *the event,* but *as to the time.*"—*Great Controversy, p.* 399. In fulfilment of this Christ was crucified on Friday, the 14th day of Nisan, and died on the cross about the ninth hour.—"between the two evenings"—at the very time the Passover lamb had been slain for centuries. The previous evening He had eaten the last supper with His disciples. The Saviour rested in the tomb on the Sabbath, the 15th day of Nisan, which had been kept as an annual sabbath in type of this event. "Christ was the antitype of the wave-sheaf, and His resurrection took place on *the very day* when the wave-sheaf was to be presented before the Lord." —*Desire of Ages, large edition, p.* 785. This was Sunday, the 16th day of Nisan. In support of this position the following texts are quoted: John 13: 1, 2; 18: 28; 19: 14; 13: 29; 19: 31.

PENTECOST

 ENTECOST, so called because it was held fifty days after the waving of first-fruits,[1] was the last of the annual feasts held in the first half of the year.[2] This feast was called the Feast of Weeks, on account of seven weeks intervening between it and the Passover feast.[3] It was also called the Feast of Harvest, as it came at the close of the harvest.[4] The Feast of Weeks was one of the three principal annual feasts, when all the men of Israel were required to appear before the Lord in Jerusalem.

As the children of Israel journeyed toward Jerusalem to attend this feast, on all sides could be seen the stubble from which had been gathered the ripened grain that lay all ready to be trodden out upon the threshing-floors.

At the time of the Passover feast there was uncertainty in regard to the coming harvest, as drought or storm might blight it before it was gathered; but now there was no uncertainty.

[1] Lev. 23:16.
[2] Acts 2:1.
[3] Deut. 16:9, 10.
[4] Ex. 23:14-16.

(116)

The fruit of the harvest was in their possession, to be used for their pleasure and the advancement of the work of the Lord. And none were to appear before the Lord empty. They were not simply to bring a few heads of grain, as in the springtime; but they were to bring a freewill-offering according as the Lord had blessed them. [1]

This feast was sometimes called the Day of the First-fruits [2] because the children of Israel were expected to make liberal offerings to the Lord at this time. It was a season of great rejoicing for the entire family, in which the Levites and the poor and afflicted were to join.

The services of the Feast of Weeks, or Pentecost, occupied but one day. Many offerings were presented at the temple, among them two loaves of leavened bread, which were waved before the Lord. The Feast of Weeks was observed as an annual sabbath, and was a holy convocation. [3]

When Christ ascended from the earth, He bade His disciples teach all nations. They were to carry the gospel to the entire world. The disciples saw only a mere handful of believers as the result of Christ's three years of toil and sacrifice. But when Pentecost had fully come, or in other words, when the seed which the Son of God Himself had sown during those three and a half years of weary toil, had sprung up, then came the harvest. [4]

The disciples were ignorant of the results of the Saviour's life, work, and sacrifice upon the minds of the people. In explaining to them the parable of the tares and the wheat, Christ had said, " He that soweth the good seed is the Son of man," but they comprehended it not. As the Saviour went from city to hamlet, He was constantly sowing the " good seed." The harvest of souls gathered from this seed was to be presented at the antitypical Feast of Harvest. For centuries the children of

[1] Deut. 16: 10.
[3] Lev. 23: 15-21.
[2] Num. 28: 26.
[4] Acts 2: 41.

Israel had celebrated this feast, bringing offerings from their harvest of grain. Of each one God had said, At the Feast of Harvest thou shalt present "the first-fruits of *thy labors, which thou hast sown* in the field." [1] The antitype came when the Son of man presented "the first-fruits" of His labor, which He had sown in the field.

There was a work for the disciples to do in order that they might be ready for the great antitypical Feast of Harvest. They

"They needed to study the Scriptures, . . . that they might receive the outpouring of the Holy Spirit."

needed to study the Scriptures, to put aside every difference, and become of one accord, that they might receive the outpouring of the Holy Spirit, which would enable them to know how to care for the great harvest of three thousand souls that was awaiting them as the result of the Saviour's ministry. They also needed this special outpouring of the Spirit to prepare them to carry forward the wonderful work begun on the day of Pentecost, until

[1] Ex. 23 : 16.

every creature under heaven should hear the glad news of salvation. [1]

In Palestine there was an early rain and a latter rain, which came in time to ripen the harvest. The prophet Joel, in speaking of the work of God in the last days, uses the terms " former " and " latter rain " to represent the outpouring of God's Spirit. And in the following words he gives the assurance that in the closing work of the gospel in the earth God will again pour out His Spirit: " He hath given you the former rain moderately, and He will cause to come down for you the rain, the former rain, and the latter rain, . . . and the floors shall be full of wheat." [2] This great harvest of souls at the antitypical Feast of Harvest was only a beginning of the greater harvest that will be gathered before the end of the world.

In the type the children of Israel brought liberal offerings to the Lord at the Feast of Harvest. Those who entered into the spirit of the antitypical Feast of Harvest, or Pentecost, " sold their possessions and goods," and gave the proceeds to help in carrying forward the work of the Lord. These offerings enabled the disciples to extend the work rapidly, so that within about thirty-four years they could say that every creature under heaven had heard the gospel. [3] Those who enter into the spirit of the latter rain will, like the early disciples, lay all upon the altar to be used by the Lord in the great closing work.

As the seed sown by the Son of man during His earthly ministry brought a harvest of souls at Pentecost, or the early rain, so the good seed sown by Christ's ambassadors who faithfully scatter the printed page filled with the gospel message, and by voice and life teach the saving truth, will yield a bountiful harvest in the time of the latter rain, when God's Spirit is poured out upon all flesh. Then will be gathered the fruit of what each one has sown in the field. " He which soweth spar-

[1] Acts 1 : 14-26.　　　[2] Joel 2 : 23, 24.　　　[3] Col. 1 : 23.

ingly shall reap also sparingly, and he which soweth bountifully shall reap also bountifully," [1] is the divine promise.

TYPE	ANTITYPE
Lev. 23: 16. This feast was held seven weeks, or fifty days, from the offerings of first-fruits.	Acts 2: 1. The day of Pentecost had *fully* come, that is, the full seven weeks had passed.
Deut. 16: 16. All the men of the children of Israel were to appear before the Lord at Jerusalem at the time of this feast.	Acts 2: 7-11. Men from all parts of the then known world were gathered at Jerusalem at the time of Pentecost.
Ex. 23: 16. The Feast of Harvest indicated " the first-fruits of t h y labors which thou hast sown in the field."	Acts 2: 41. The antitype of the first-fruits was three thousand souls, the spiritual harvest gathered as the result of Christ's personal work.
Deut. 16: 11, 12. Those celebrating this feast in the type were to " rejoice before the Lord " and remember their freedom f r o m Egyptian bondage.	Acts 2: 41, 46. Those that shared in the antitypical Feast o f Harvest made it a time of rejoicing on account of their freedom from the bondage of sin.
Deut. 16: 10. The children of Israel were to make liberal offerings at this feast, according as God had blessed them.	Acts 2: 44, 45. At the antitypical feast " all that believed " sold their possessions and goods and gave them to the Lord's work.

[1] 2 Cor. 9: 6.

SECTION V

Various Offerings

The Perfect Sacrifice

LORD, we are vile, and full of sin,
We're born unholy and unclean;
Sprung from the man whose guilty fall
Corrupts his race, and taints us all.

Behold, we fall before thy face;
Our only refuge is thy grace:
No outward forms can make us clean;
The leprosy lies deep within.

Nor bleeding bird, nor bleeding beast,
Nor hyssop branch, nor earthly priest,
Nor running brook, nor flood, nor sea,
Can wash the dismal stain away.

Jesus, thy blood, thy blood alone,
Hath power sufficient to atone;
Thy blood can make us white as snow;
No other tide can cleanse us so.

—Isaac Watts.

CHAPTER XVII

THE SIN-OFFERING

I N none of the types was the individual worshiper
brought into so close touch with the sanctuary service
as in the sin-offering. There is no part of religious
worship that brings the individual worshiper into such
close touch with the Lord as when he kneels at the Saviour's
feet, confessing his sins, and knowing the strength of the promise,
" If we confess our sins, He is faithful and just to forgive us our
sins, and to cleanse us from all unrighteousness." It is then that
the repentant sinner touches the hem of the Master's garment, and
receives His healing power in the soul.

Sin is the transgression of the law of God. The one who had
" done somewhat against any of the commandments of the Lord "

(123)

was guilty of sin; and in order to be free from sin, he must bring an offering, that by seeing the innocent victim die for his sins he might more fully comprehend how the innocent Lamb of God could offer His life for the sins of the world. If the sinner was a priest, filling that holy office where the influence of his wrong course would cause others to stumble, then he was to bring a bullock, an expensive animal, as a sin-offering; but if he was one of the common people, he could bring a kid or a lamb. The value of the animal to be offered was determined by the position held by the transgressor.

The sin-offering was brought into the court of the sanctuary, to the door of the tabernacle of the congregation. [1] The sinner, with his hands laid upon the head of the lamb, confessed over it all his sins, and then with his own hand he killed it. [2] Sometimes the blood was taken into the first apartment of the sanctuary by the officiating priest, who dipped his finger in the blood and sprinkled it before the Lord. The horns of the golden altar, the altar of incense, were also touched with the blood. The priest then came out into the court, and poured all the blood at the base of the altar of burnt-offering. [3] The bodies of the animals whose blood was taken into the sanctuary, were burned without the camp. [4] "Wherefore Jesus also, that He might sanctify the people with His own blood, suffered without the gate." [5]

The sinner, by confessing his sins over the lamb, in type and shadow transferred them to the lamb. The life of the lamb was then taken instead of the life of the sinner, typifying the death of the Lamb of God, who would offer His life for the sins of the world. The blood of the animal was powerless to remove sin, [6] but by shedding its blood the penitent revealed his faith in the divine offering of the Son of God. Every

---

[1] Lev. 4 : 1-35.　　[2] Lev. 4 : 29; Num. 5 : 7.　　[3] Lev. 4 : 7, 18, 25, 30.
[4] Lev. 6 : 30.　　[5] Heb. 13 : 12.　　[6] Heb. 10 : 4.

sin-offering was to be without blemish, thus typifying the perfect sacrifice of the Saviour. [1]

In some offerings the blood was not taken into the sanctuary, but in every sin-offering all the blood was poured out at the base of the altar of burnt-offering in the court. When the blood was not taken into the first apartment of the sanctuary, a portion of the flesh of the sin-offering was eaten by the priest in the holy place. [2]

As the priest assimilated the flesh of the sin-offering, and it thus became a part of his own body; and as he performed the work of the sanctuary, he strikingly typified how " Christ bare our sins in His own body on the tree," [3] and then entered the heavenly sanctuary with that same body to appear in the presence of God for us.

The priest ate only the flesh of the sin-offering when the blood was not taken within the sanctuary. The command in regard to this was very plain: " No sin-offering, whereof any of the blood is brought into the tabernacle of the congregation to reconcile withal in the holy place, shall be eaten: it shall be burnt in the fire." [4] To violate this command would ignore the significance of the type. The priest entering into the sanctuary to present the blood of the sin-offering before the Lord, was a forcible symbol of Christ who, by His *own* blood, entered into the heavenly sanctuary, " having obtained eternal redemption for us." [5] By the blood and by the flesh the confessed sins of the sinner were in type transferred to the sanctuary. They were hid from view, for no human eyes, except the eyes of those who officiated as priests, gazed within the sanctuary.

The type was beautiful, but how much more beautiful the antitype! When the sinner lays his sins on Christ, " the Lamb

[1] I Peter 1:19.   [2] Lev. 10:18.   [3] I Peter 2:24.
[4] Lev. 6:30.   [5] Heb. 9:11, 12.

of God, which taketh away the sin of the world," those sins are hidden, covered by the blood of Christ.[1] They are all recorded in the books in heaven;[2] but the blood of the Saviour covers them, and if he who sinned is faithful to God, they will never be revealed, but will finally be destroyed in the fires of the last day. The most wonderful part is that God Himself says He will cast them behind His back[3] and will not remember them.[4] Why need any one carry the burden of sins when we have such a merciful Saviour waiting to receive them?

In every sin-offering two things were essential on the part of the sinner: first, to realize his own sinfulness before God, and to prize pardon sufficiently to make a sacrifice to obtain it; second, to see by faith beyond his offering, the Son of God through whom he is to receive his pardon, " for it is not possible that the blood of bulls and of goats should take away sins."[5] The blood of Christ alone can atone for sin.

After the blood was presented before the Lord, there was yet an important work for the sinner to perform. With his own hands he was to remove all the fat from the different organs of the animal offered as a sin-offering,[6] and give it to the priest, who burned it upon the brazen altar. At first thought this might seem a strange ceremony, but when we remember that the fat represented sin,[7] we see that it is a fitting ceremony.

It was evidently viewing this service in the sanctuary that saved David from backsliding. He had beheld the prosperity of the wicked, and was envious of them, until his " steps had well-nigh slipped;" but when he went into the sanctuary, then he understood the end of the wicked.[8] We can imagine him watching the sinner separating the fat and the priest placing it upon the great altar, and presently nothing remained but ashes. In it he saw ashes only as the final end of all who would not separate from

[1] Rom. 4:7, 8.   [2] Jer. 2:22.   [3] Isa. 38:17.   [4] Isa. 43:25.
[5] Heb. 10:4.   [6] Lev. 7:30, 31.   [7] Ps. 37:20; Isa. 43:23, 24.   [8] Ps. 73:2-17.

sin;[1] for if the sin was a part of themselves, then when the sin was burned, they would be burned with it. The only reason God will ever destroy a sinner is

"Why need any one carry the burden of sins when we have such a merciful Saviour waiting to receive them?"

because the sinner keeps sin in his own character, and will not separate from it.

[1] Mal. 4:1-3.

This was an impressive type, the priest waiting for the sinner to separate the fat from the offering, ready to take it as soon as it was offered to him. So Christ, our great High Priest, is waiting for each sinner to confess his sins and give them to Him, that He in return can clothe the sinner with His own robe of righteousness;[1] and consume his sins in the fires of the last day. Paul evidently refers to this part of the sanctuary service in Heb. 4: 12.

The burning of the fat was "a sweet savor unto the Lord."[2] There are few odors more disagreeable than that of burning fat and yet it is sweet to the Lord, for it typified the sin consumed and the sinner saved. God takes no pleasure in the death of the wicked;[3] but He delights in the destruction of sin separated from the sinner. When the redeemed of the Lord from within the shelter of the New Jerusalem

"The blood was all poured out at the base of the altar of burnt-offering."

behold the fires of the last day consuming all the sins they have committed, it will be indeed a sweet savor to them. [4]

An individual who was too poor to offer a lamb for a sin-offering could bring two pigeons; and if he was so poor that he did not possess two pigeons, then he could catch two of the wild turtle doves, and offer them for a sin-offering; but if he was too feeble to capture the wild doves, the Lord made provision that he should be allowed to bring a small portion of fine flour, and the priest

[1] Isa. 61: 10.   [2] Lev. 4: 31.   [3] Eze. 33: 11.   [4] Rev. 20: 8, 9.

would present the crushed grain as a type of the broken body of
the Saviour. Of this one it was said, " His sin shall be forgiven
him," just the same as of the one that was able to bring a bullock.
The handful of flour burned corresponded to the burning of the
fat, in type of the final destruction of sin; and the remainder was
eaten by the priest; thus typifying Christ's bearing the sins.[1]

In every sin-offering where animals or birds were offered, the
blood was all poured out at the base of the altar of burnt-offering in the court of the sanctuary. When we remember how particular the Lord was that everything about the camp should be
kept in a sanitary condition,[2] we can see at a glance that it must
have required much labor to keep the court clean. Therefore the
Lord would not have directed that all the blood be poured on the
ground at the base of the altar if it had not contained a very
important lesson.

The first sin ever committed in the earth affected the earth as
well as the sinner. The Lord said to Adam, " Cursed is the ground
for thy sake."[3] When the first murder was committed, the
Lord said to Cain, " Now art thou cursed from the earth." He
also said that from that time the earth would not always yield
her increase; there would be failure of crops, and barrenness.[4]

The curse of sin rests heavier and heavier upon the earth.[5]
There is only one thing in all the universe of God that can
remove this curse. " The land can not be cleansed of the blood
that is shed therein, but by the blood of him that shed it."[6] It
must be one of humanity, of the same family that shed the blood.
For that reason Christ partook of humanity, became our Elder
Brother,[7] that He might remove the curse of sin from the earth
as well as from the sinner. By His death upon Calvary, Christ
purchased the earth, thus redeeming it as well as its inhabitants.[8]

Since it is the sins of mankind that defile the earth, in every

[1] Lev. 5 : 7-13.   [2] Deut. 23 : 14.   [3] Gen. 3 : 17.   [4] Gen. 4 : 11, 12.
[5] Isa. 24 : 5, 6.   [6] Num. 35 : 33.   [7] Heb. 2 : 11.   [8] Eph. 1 : 14.

9

sin-offering, after the offering had been made for the sinner, the remainder of the blood was poured out on the ground at the base of the brazen altar in the court, as a type of the precious blood of Christ, which would remove every taint of sin from this earth, and clothe it in Eden beauty. [1]

TYPE   ANTITYPE

" Behold the lamb of God, which taketh away
the sin of the world." John 1 : 29.

Lev. 4 : 3, 23, 28. The animal to be without blemish.

1 Peter 1 : 19. Christ was " without blemish a n d without spot."

Lev. 4 : 4, 14. The offering was to be brought before the Lord to the door of the sanctuary.

Heb. 4 : 15, 16. " Let us therefore come boldly unto the throne of grace, that we may obtain mercy, and find grace to help in time of need."

Lev. 4 : 4; Num. 5 : 7. The sinner laid his hand on the head of the offering, thus acknowledging his sins.

1 John 1 : 9. " If we confess our sins, He is faithful and just to forgive us our sins."

Lev. 4 : 29. The sinner slew the sin-offering; he took the life of the lamb with his own hands.

Isa. 53 : 10. Christ's soul was made an offering f o r sin. Criminals often lived for days upon the cross; it was the awful burden of the sins of the world that slew Christ.

[1] Rev. 21 : 1.

Lev. 4: 5-7, 17, 18. In some offerings the blood was taken into the sanctuary and sprinkled before the Lord.

Lev. 10: 16-18. When the blood was not taken into the sanctuary, a portion of the flesh was eaten by the priest in the holy place; thus in type the priest bore " the iniquity of the congregation, to make atonement for them before the Lord."

Lev. 4: 31; 7: 30. The sinner with his own hands was to separate all the fat from the sin-offering, the fat typifying sin. Ps. 37: 20.

Lev. 4: 31. The fat is all burned to ashes in the court of the sanctuary.

Lev. 4: 7, 18, 25, 30. The blood of every sin-offering was poured on the ground at the bottom of the brazen altar in the court.

Heb. 9: 12. " By His own blood He [Christ] entered in once into the holy place, having obtained eternal redemption for us."

1 Peter 2: 24. This was a type of the One " who His own self bare our sins in His own body on the tree, that we, being dead to sins, should live unto righteousness: by whose stripes ye were healed."

Isa. 1: 16. We are not only to confess past sins, but we are to examine our own hearts and put away evil habits. " Cease to do evil."

Mal. 4: 1-3. All sin and sinners will be burned to ashes on the earth.

Eph. 1: 14. Christ purchased the earth as well as its inhabitants by His death on the cross.

CHAPTER XVIII

THE BURNT-OFFERING

THE whole burnt-offering had its origin at the gate of the garden of Eden, [1] and extended to the cross; and it will never lose its significance as long as mankind is subject to temptation and sin. The entire sacrifice was laid upon the altar and burned, [2] typifying not only a surrender of sin, but a consecration of the entire life to the service of God.

Wherever the people of God sojourned during the patriarchal age, rude altars of stone were erected, upon which to offer their whole burnt-offerings. [3] After the long period of Egyptian bondage, Israel was so prone to idolatry that the Lord had the brazen altar built in the court of the tabernacle, and instead of burnt-offerings being offered anywhere by the father of the household, they were brought to the sanctuary and offered by the priests

[1] Gen. 4:4; 8:20.   [2] Lev. 1:2-9.   [3] Gen. 12:7, 8; 13:4, 18; 35:3.

(132)

of divine appointment.[1] There were special occasions when burnt-offerings were offered in other places than the sanctuary, as the sacrifice offered by David on the threshing-floor of Ornan,[2] and the memorable sacrifice offered by Elijah upon Mount Carmel.[3]

The accounts of the burnt-offerings in the Bible are a history of wonderful victories when individuals drew near to God by putting away their sins and surrendering their lives and all they possessed to the service of the Lord. Abraham's great test of faith was a burnt-offering upon Mount Moriah.[4] Gideon's wonderful victories dated from the whole burnt-offerings offered before the Lord when he, by those offerings, showed he surrendered all to the Lord to be consumed on the altar as the Lord directed.[5]

The whole burnt-offering was a type of the full consecration that must come into every life that God can use to His glory. Paul urged the fulfilling of the antitype in the following words: "I beseech you therefore, brethren, by the mercies of God, that *ye present your bodies a living sacrifice,* holy, acceptable unto God, which is your reasonable service."[6] The offering of the most costly animal was only an abomination to the Lord unless it was accompanied by the surrender of the heart and life of the one who offered it.[7]

This principle was beautifully illustrated in the Saviour's passing by as of little value the large gifts of the rich who offered only for display, and stating that in the valuation of heaven the two mites which the poor widow gave with a heart full of love, were of more value than all the wealth given for vain display.[8] The Lord regards the gifts and offerings made by His people to carry forward His work on the earth, as "an odor of a sweet smell, a sacrifice acceptable, well pleasing to God," and He

---

[1] Deut. 12:5, 6.   [2] 2 Sam. 24:18-25.   [3] 1 Kings 18:31-38.   [4] Gen. 22:2-13.
[5] Judges 6:21-28.   [6] Rom. 12:1.   [7] Isa. 1:10, 11: Amos 5:22   [8] Mark 12:41-44.

pledges to supply all their needs. [1] " Behold, to obey is better than sacrifice, and to hearken than the fat of rams." [2]

The whole burnt-offering was offered as an atonement for sin. [3] The individual making the offering laid his hands on the head of the animal, confessing his sins; [4] and then, if it was from the flock or the herd, with his own hands he took its life. If the burnt-offering was a bird, the priest killed the offering. The blood was sprinkled round about upon the brazen altar, in type of the cleansing blood of Christ, and then the offering was burned upon the altar.

Every morning and evening a lamb was offered at the sanctuary as a whole burnt-offering. [5] Each Sabbath day four lambs were offered, two in the morning and two in the evening. [6] These sacrifices typified a reconsecration of the whole congregation each morning and evening to the service of God.

Since the shadow has met the substance, it would be hollow mockery to offer burnt-offerings morning and evening now; but the type has lost none of its significance, and contains lessons for us; for " to love Him [God] with all the heart, and with all the understanding, and with all the soul, and with all the strength, and to love his neighbor as himself, is *more than all whole burnt-offerings* and sacrifices." [7]

The heart filled with love to God and our fellow-men is an offering always acceptable to God. In order to keep the heart in this condition, it must be filled with the life-giving Word of God. [8] The Lord regards a " knowledge of God more than burnt-offerings." [9] The individual who will sacrifice selfish interests and pleasures sufficiently to take time morning and evening to study God's word, will experience that love in the heart which always has been and ever will be far more acceptable to God than " whole burnt-offerings and sacrifices."

[1] Phil. 4: 16-19.   [2] I Sam. 15: 22.   [3] Lev. 9: 7.
[4] Lev. 1: 4; Num. 8: 12.   [5] Ex. 29: 38-42.   [6] Num. 28: 9, 10.
[7] Mark 12: 33.   [8] Ps. 119: 11.   [9] Hosea 6: 6.

TYPE	ANTITYPE
Lev. 1 : 9. Sacrifice given to God was accepted as " a sweet savor unto the Lord."	Eph. 5 : 2. Christ has given Himself for us " an offering and a sacrifice to God for a sweetsmelling savor."
Ex. 29 : 38-43. God met with His people as they offered their whole burnt-offerings, and they were sanctified by His presence.	Heb. 10 : 8-10. " We are sanctified, through the offering of the body of Jesus Christ once for all."
Lev. 1 : 2-9, 13, 17. The entire body was consumed on the altar, " an offering made by fire, of a sweet savor unto the Lord."	Rom. 12 : 1. " I beseech you therefore, brethren, by the mercies of God, that ye present your bodies a living sacrifice, holy, acceptable unto God."

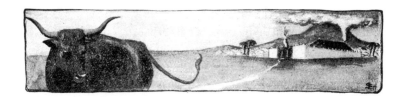

CHAPTER XIX

THE DRINK-OFFERING

THE drink-offering was celebrated long before the sanctuary service was instituted at Sinai. After the Lord appeared to Jacob at Bethel and said, "Thy name shall be called no more Jacob [a supplanter],[1] but Israel [a prince of God]" "shall be thy name,"[2] Jacob felt so grateful to the Lord that he set up a pillar in the place where He talked with him, and poured out a drink-offering thereon,[3] showing his willingness to pour out his life, if necessary, for the cause of God. The drink-offering was wine, but was never drunk by either priest or people; it was poured out before the Lord. No doubt wine was chosen for the drink-offering for the same reason that it was used in the celebration of the Lord's supper, as an emblem of the life of Christ,[4] who "poured out His soul unto death," to redeem a lost race.[5]

The drink-offering, like the meat-offering, was offered with

[1] Gen. 27 : 36, margin.   [2] Gen. 32 : 28, margin.   [3] Gen. 35 : 10-14.
[4] Lev. 17 : 11; Matt. 26 : 27, 28.   [5] Isa. 53 : 12.

burnt-offerings, for " an offering made by fire, of a sweet savor unto the Lord." [1] When Israel departed from the Lord, the drink-offering was often used in their idolatrous worship. [2] Drink-offerings were never poured on the altar of incense, [3] but always in the court, for they typified things which transpired in the antitypical court — the earth.

The pouring out of the drink-offering was no doubt an emblem of the pouring out of the Holy Spirit. [4] Paul used the beautiful type of pouring the drink-offering upon the burnt-offering, and the consuming of all upon the altar, as an illustration of his life fully surrendered to God's service. "Holding forth the life;" he said, "that I in the day of Christ,

Open Thou mine eyes, that I may behold wondrous things out of Thy Law.
Ps. 119: 18

word of may rejoice that I have

not run in vain. . . . Yea, and *if I be poured forth upon the sacrifice* and service of your faith, I joy; and rejoice with you all." [5]

When the three mighty warriors for the love they bore David risked their lives to bring him a drink from the well of Bethlehem, David considered the water too sacred to drink, for they had " put their lives in jeopardy " to obtain it; therefore he " poured it out to the Lord." [6]

The drink-offering was a type of Christ's life poured out for us, and the antitype can be repeated in the life of every one

[1] Num. 15 : 10.
[2] Jer. 7 : 18; 44 : 17-19.
[3] Ex. 30 : 9.
[4] Joel 2 : 28; Isa. 44 : 3.
[5] Phil. 2 : 16, 17, margin.
[6] 1 Chron. 11 : 17-19.

who, like Paul, rejoices in being poured forth upon the sacrifice and consumed upon the altar.

The drink-offering is no doubt referred to in Judges 9: 13 where wine is said to " cheer God and man." It is not the wine drunk at the table with friends, but wine used at the altar.

The wine of the drink-offering truly gladdened the heart of God and man; for like the water of Bethlehem poured out by David, it represented, when offered in sincerity, the pouring out of the heart or life of the sinner before God.

When Hannah gave Samuel to the sanctuary, she brought a bottle of wine with the animal for a burnt-offering. It was after she had expressed the full surrender of her only son to the Lord by her burnt-offering and the wine of the drink-offering, that she could fill the temple court with her voice of praise and thanksgiving. [1]

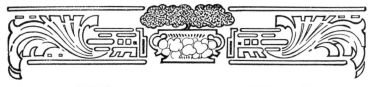

TYPE	ANTITYPE
Gen. 35 : 14. The drink-offering was poured out before the Lord.	Isa. 53 : 12. Christ " poured out His soul unto death."
Num. 15 : 10. It was poured over the burnt-offering on the altar, and consumed. The burning was a sweet savor, acceptable to God.	Phil. 2 : 16, 17, margin. The one who fully surrenders his life for the Lord's service, pours his life upon the sacrifice of Christ, to be spent for the glory of God, as His life was spent.

[1] 1 Sam. 1 : 24; 2 : 1-10.

CHAPTER XX

THE MEAT-OFFERING

DANIEL prophesied that Christ would "cause the *sacrifice* and *oblation* to cease." [1] Here reference is made to the two great divisions of offerings: *sacrifices with,* and *sacrifices without blood.* The meat-offerings belonged to the last class. There was neither flesh nor blood in the meat-offering. The original meaning of the word "meat" as first used in the Bible is "food"; [2] and in this sense the term is used in connection with this offering. The meat-offering consisted of flour, oil, and frankincense. [3] In some cases the flour was baked into unleavened cakes, or wafers, before being offered. The bread of the meat-offering was never to be made with leaven. Every meat-offering was seasoned with salt. This offering was

[1] Dan. 9: 27.   [2] Gen. 1: 29.   [3] Lev. 2: 1.

spoken of as " a thing most holy of the offerings of the Lord made by fire." [1]

No leaven or honey was allowed in any of the meat-offerings; for leaven indicated " malice and wickedness," [2] and honey turns sour and leads to fermentation.

The qualities of salt are directly opposite. Salt removes and prevents corruption; it is also an emblem of friendship. " The salt of the covenant " was never to be omitted from the meat-offering, thus reminding God's people of His protecting care and promise to save, and that only the righteousness of Christ could make the service acceptable to God.

"A portion of the meat-offering was burned on the brazen altar."

A portion of the meat-offering was burned on the brazen altar, whether it was flour or unleavened cakes; also a portion of the oil, and *all* the frankincense; [3] and the remainder was eaten by the priest in the court. [4] If a priest offered a meat-offering, no portion was eaten, but the entire offering was burned on the brazen altar. [5] The high priest offered a meat-offering every day.

Wherever flour or cakes were offered in connection with any other offering, it was called a meat-offering. The offering for the sinner too poor to bring even a wild turtle-dove was a meat-offering or trespass-offering. There was no oil or frankincense in this offering. [6] In the offering for jealousy, the oil and frankincense were also left out. No frankincense was ever added to the meat-offerings that brought " iniquity to remembrance." [7]

The meat-offering was a very common offering and was

[1] Lev. 2 : 4-13; 6 : 17.   [2] I Cor. 5 : 8.   [3] Lev. 6 : 15.   [4] Lev. 6 : 16, 17.
[5] Lev. 6 : 20-22.   [6] Lev. 5 : 11.   [7] Num. 5 : 15.

united with all burnt-offerings. [1] It was offered every morning and evening on the brazen altar, in connection with the morning and evening burnt-offering. [2]

The meat-offering of first-fruits was "green ears of corn dried by the fire, even corn beaten out of full ears." [3] We quote from Andrew A. Bonar in regard to the significance of the green ears, "A peculiar typical circumstance attends these. These are *'ears of corn,'* a figure of Christ; [4] and *'ears of the best kind,'* for so the Hebrew intimates. *They are 'dried by the fire,'* to represent Jesus feeling the wrath of His Father, as when He said, 'My strength is dried up,' *i.e.,* the whole force of my being is dried up; [5] 'I am withered like grass.' [6]

"What an affecting picture of the Man of Sorrow! How like the very life! The best ears of the finest corn in the plains of Israel are plucked while yet green; and instead of being left to ripen in the cool breeze, and under a genial sun, are withered up by the scorching fire. It was thus that the only pure humanity that ever walked on the plains of earth was wasted away during three-and-thirty years by the heat of wrath He had never deserved. While obeying night and day, with all His soul and strength, the burning wrath of God was drying up His frame. *'Beaten out of full ears,'* represents the bruises and strokes whereby He was prepared for the altar. 'Though He were a Son, yet learned He obedience by the things which He suffered.' [7] It is after this preparation that He is a perfect meat-offering, fully devoted, body and substance, to the Lord.

"In all this He is *'First-fruits,'* intimating that many more shall follow. *He* the first-fruits, then all that are His in like manner. We must be conformed to Jesus in all things; and here it is taught us that we must be conformed to Him in self-dedication — self-renunciation. We must please the Father; as

[1] Num. 15 : 3-12.   [2] Ex. 29 : 39-42.   [3] Lev. 2 : 14-16.   [4] John 12 : 24.
[5] Ps. 22 : 15.   [6] Ps. 102 : 4.   [7] Heb. 5 : 8.

He left us an example, saying, ' I do always those things that please Him,' [1] even under the blackest sky."

The meat-offering typified the full surrender of all we have, and all we are, to the Lord. This offering was always presented along with some animal sacrifice, thus showing the connection between pardon of sin and consecration to the Lord. It is after an individual's sins are forgiven that he lays all upon the altar to be consumed in God's service.

In the meat-offering, like the sin-offering, provision was made for the poor. The wealthy class baked their meat-offerings in an oven; the individual in moderate circumstances, on the " fire plate"; while the cakes baked by the poor in the " frying pan," were equally acceptable. [2]

TYPE	ANTITYPE
Lev. 2: 1-3. It was " a thing most holy of the offerings of the Lord made by fire."	Rom. 12: 1. " Present your bodies a living sacrifice, holy, acceptable unto God."
Lev. 2: 9. The meat-offering was " a sweet savor unto the Lord."	Phil. 4: 18. When God's people make sacrifices for Him, it is " an odor of a sweet smell, . . . well pleasing to God."
Lev. 2: 13. " Every oblation of thy meat-offering shalt thou season with salt; . . . with all thine offerings thou shalt offer salt."	Mark 9: 50. " Have salt in yourselves." Col. 4: 6. " Let your speech be alway with grace, seasoned with salt."

[1] John 8: 29.

[2] Lev. 2: 4-8, margin.

CHAPTER XXI

THE TRESPASS-OFFERING

THE trespass-offering was a sin-offering, and many Bible students make no distinction between it and the regular sin-offering. In some places the terms "sin-offering" and "trespass-offering" seem to be used synonymously, as in Lev. 5 : 1-13, but in other places they are spoken of as being two separate offerings. [1]

A close study of the passages that speak directly of the trespass-offering, shows that it was offered more especially for sins "in the holy things of the Lord," [2] as when a person had trespassed by not following God's instructions in regard to the holy things. He may have withheld his tithe, [3] eaten the first-fruits, [4] or sheared the first-born sheep; [5] whatever the trespass, he was to bring a ram for an offering. [6] This offering was disposed of much the same as the ordinary sin-offering, except that the blood was sprinkled "round about upon the altar," instead of touching the horns with the blood as in the sin-offering. [7]

It would seem from this that the trespass-offering did not

[1] Eze. 46 : 20.   [2] Lev. 5 : 15.   [3] Lev. 27 : 31.   [4] Ex. 34 : 26.
[5] Deut. 15 : 19.   [6] Lev. 5 : 18; 6 : 6.   [7] Lev. 7 : 1-7.

always represent sins as public as the common sin-offering represented, but was often used for sins known only to the individual himself. If the person had taken any of the holy things for his own use, had been dishonest in his dealings with his neighbor, or had appropriated articles that had been lost, etc., he was not only to restore the full value, but was to add one fifth to the estimation by the priest. [1]

The restitution was always made to the one wronged. If the individual had dealt dishonestly with the holy things of the Lord, the restitution was made to the priest as the representative of the Lord. If he had wronged his fellow-men and the one wronged had died, then the restitution was made to his kinsman; but if there was no kinsman, the restitution was made to the Lord. [2]

There was no virtue in offering the ram for a trespass-offering, unless the restitution was made in full for the wrong done. One special object of the trespass-offering was to atone for dishonest dealings with either God or man, and always required the restitution of the wrong besides the ram for the offering. It taught very clearly that wherein we have dealt falsely with God or man, simply confessing the sin and bringing an offering will not suffice; we must make amends for the wrong.

Zacchæus understood the law of the trespass-offering, and as soon as he surrendered his life to Christ, he was ready to go even beyond the requirements of the law, and restore " fourfold " to all whom he had wronged. [3]

The trespass-offering was a more complete offering than the ordinary sin-offering; besides atoning for the sin, it also, in figure, covered the result of the sin. The prophet Isaiah used the trespass-offering as a special type of Christ. He was truly the antitypical trespass-offering when He shed His blood, not only to free

[1] Lev. 5 : 16; 6 : 5.   [2] Num. 5 : 7, 8.   [3] Luke 19 : 8.

the souls of men from guilt, but to remove forever the last trace of sin from the universe of God.

We quote Isa. 53: 10 from the Jewish translator Leeser, as follows: "The Lord was pleased to crush him through disease: *when* (now) *His soul hath brought the trespass-offering, then shall He see* (His) *seed, live many days,* and the pleasure of the Lord shall prosper in His hand."

There are many precious promises to the one who will present his trespass-offerings to the Lord. He who would be victorious in God cannot be content with merely confessing his sin to God; he must make reconciliation and restoration. This is taught in the Saviour's words, "If thou bring thy gift to the altar, and there rememberest *that thy brother hath ought against* thee; leave there thy gift before the altar, and go thy way; *first be reconciled to thy brother,* and then come and offer thy gift." [1]

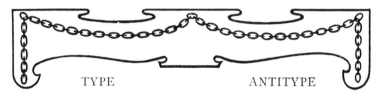

TYPE   ANTITYPE

Lev. 5: 15, 16. The trespass-offering atoned for the result of the sin as well as for the sin.

Isa. 53: 10-12. The death of Christ, the great trespass-offering, not only atones for sin, but destroys all the effect of sin.

Lev. 6: 1-7. The sacrifice without the restitution was not accepted.

Matt. 5: 23-26. Our prayers are of no avail if we cherish evil in our hearts.

[1] Matt. 5: 23, 24.

10

CHAPTER XXII

THE OFFERING OF THE RED HEIFER

HE life of every sacrifice, from the first one offered at the gate of Eden down to the cross, was a type of Christ; but the offering of the red heifer is different in many respects from all others. It was an occasional sacrifice, offered when needed, to purify from ceremonial uncleanness those who for any reason had touched the dead. [1]

The heifer was to be red, without one spot, thus in a special manner typifying the blood of Christ. It was to be without blemish, thus representing Him "who knew no sin." [2] It was to be one that had never been broken to bear the yoke; it must be a heifer that had always been free, never forced to do anything.

[1] Deut. 21 : 1-9.   [2] 2 Cor. 5 : 21.

(146)

This was symbolic of the Son of God, who came of His own free will and died for us. Christ was above all law, no yoke was upon Him. [1] While enduring the agony of Gethsemane, He could have wiped the bloody sweat from His brow and returned to His rightful place in heaven, and left the world to perish. There was no power, only that of supreme heavenly love, that forced Christ toward the cross of Calvary. [2] He came a voluntary offering, from choice. He offered Himself for the sins of the world, and the Father's love for the fallen race was so great that, much as He loved His only Son, He accepted the offered life. Angels are amenable to the law of God, therefore their life could not have atoned for the transgression of the law. Christ alone was free from the claims of the law, the only one who could redeem the lost race.

The offering of the red heifer was a very imposing ceremony. The heifer was not taken to the temple, like most other offerings, but to a rough valley without the camp, that had never been cultivated or sown. The priest, clothed in the pure white garment of the priesthood, led the heifer, and was accompanied by the elders of the city and the Levites. Cedar wood, hyssop, and scarlet were also carried to the place of offering.

When the procession reached the rough valley, they paused, and the elders came forward and killed the heifer. The priest then took the blood, and with his face toward the temple, sprinkled the blood with his finger toward the temple seven times.

If a person had been found dead in the field and it was not known who had taken the life, then the elders of the city next to where the slain man had been found, came forward and washed their hands over the body of the heifer as they offered a prayer to God requesting that the Lord would not lay innocent blood upon them. [3] After this the heifer's entire body, including the

[1] John 10 : 18.   [2] John 3 : 16.   [3] Deut. 21 : 1-9.

blood, was burned. As the flames mounted up, the priest stepped near and cast some of the cedar wood, hyssop, and scarlet into the midst of the fire. [1]

The red heifer was offered without the camp, typifying that Christ suffered, not for the Hebrew race alone, but for the whole world. If every offering had been slain within the court of the sanctuary, some might have taught that Christ died only for His own people, the Hebrew race; but the red heifer was offered without the camp, [2] symbolizing the fact that Christ died for all nations tribes, and people.

The condescension and love of the Lord is wonderful. Lest some poor, forlorn, discouraged soul should think he was not worthy to accept the offered sacrifice, the red heifer was not only taken without the camp, but to a rough valley, so rocky and utterly worthless that it had never even been plowed. No one had ever attempted to cultivate it; and yet here was the place chosen to sprinkle the blood of that special offering which typified Christ in a particular sense. It typified Him as one who is above law.

It does not matter if Satan has so marred the image of the Creator in man that there can scarcely a trace be seen of anything but the attributes of Satan; yet Christ with His mighty arm can raise such a one up to sit with Him on His throne. The whole life may be wasted and be, like the rough valley, of no account; but if such a one will turn his eyes toward the heavenly sanctuary, and plead for mercy by confessing his sins, the precious blood of Christ, of which the blood of the red heifer was a symbol, will be sprinkled over his wasted life, as verily as the blood of the heifer was sprinkled over the rough stones of the valley; and Christ will say to the repentant one as He did to the thief on the cross, who had wasted his life, " Thou shalt be with Me in paradise." [3]

[1] Num. 19 : 1-8.　　　　[2] Heb. 13 : 12, 13.　　　　[3] Luke 23 : 38-43.

There are none so sunken in sin or in heathen darkness but that hope and salvation are held out to them through the typical offering of the red heifer. This sacrifice was a shadow of heavenly things. Now type has met antitype. Christ has suffered without the camp for the sins of the whole world. There are none so sunken but that He can lift them up. It may look impossible to man; the customs and habits of the world may condemn a person, and say he is lost; but Christ is above all law. He can save to the uttermost all who come unto God by Him.[1] The cedar wood, hyssop, and scarlet cast into the fire were typical of the purifying of the earth and all vegetation from every trace of sin by the blood of Christ.[2]

Purge me with hyssop, and I shall be clean, wash me, and I shall be whiter than snow.

After the body of the heifer was burned to ashes, a person who was not contaminated by touching the dead, gathered up the ashes and placed them in a clean place, and they were kept to be used for purifying those who touched the dead.[3] If a person died in a tent or house, the house and all who touched the dead body were counted unclean until purified. This was to impress the people with the

[1] Heb. 7:25.   [2] Isa. 65:17-19.   [3] Num. 19:9, 10.

terrible nature of sin. It taught them that death came as the result of sin, and was a representation of sin. [1] Some of the ashes were placed in pure running water, and a person who was ceremonially clean dipped a b u n c h of hyssop and cedar in the ashes and water, and sprinkled the tent, the articles within the tent, and the people. This was repeated several times until all were purified. [2]

In like manner, Christ, after He shed His blood for sinful man, entered the first apartment of the heavenly sanctuary to present His blood before the Father, to cleanse man from the defilement of sin. [3]

The cedar and hyssop used to sprinkle the purifying water denoted that the person upon whom it fell was cleansed from all earthly moral defilement. The thoroughness of the work was typified by its being repeated several times.

David evidently had this ceremony in mind when he prayed, " Purge me with hyssop, and I shall be clean: wash me, and I shall be whiter than snow." [4] Paul's mind was led from type to antitype when he wrote to his Hebrew brethren, " If the blood of bulls and of goats, and the ashes of a heifer sprinkling the unclean, sanctifieth to the purifying of the flesh: how much more shall the blood of Christ, who through the eternal Spirit offered Himself without spot to God, purge your conscience from dead works to serve the living God." [5]

Many people read their Bibles and pass over these beautiful types as ceremonies peculiar to the Jews, and meaning nothing to Christians. They consider the Old Testament of little value. But the Lord through Moses gave that wonderful galaxy of types and symbols contained in the sanctuary service and the Levitical laws; and Moses was so fearful lest the people might think *he* had given them the service, that over two hundred times we find him

[1] Jas. 1 : 14, 15.　　[2] Num. 19 : 18, 19.　　[3] Heb. 9 : 11, 12.
[4] Ps. 51 : 7.　　[5] Heb. 9 : 13, 14.

assuring them that God *Himself* was the Author of them, by such expressions as " The Lord said," or " The Lord commanded." He desired all to know that God had given that marvelous system of types and shadows, not only throwing light from Eden to the cross, but revealing to sinful man the work of Christ from the cross to the end of time. These typical ceremonies, like a great reflector, throw light upon the ministry of Christ that cannot be obtained in any other portion of the Scriptures. The Saviour taught that a study of the writings of Moses would strengthen faith in Him. " Had ye believed Moses," He said, " ye would have believed Me: for he wrote of Me. But if ye believe not his writings, how shall ye believe My words?" [1]

TYPE	ANTITYPE
Num. 19: 2. A red heifer without spot.	Heb. 9: 13, 14. Christ offered Himself without spot to God.
Num. 19: 2. There was to be no blemish in the animal.	John 15: 10; 2 Cor. 5: 21. Christ never disobeyed the law of God. He " knew no sin."
Num. 19: 2. One that had never borne the yoke, never been forced to do anything.	John 10: 15. " As the Father knoweth Me, even so know I the Father: and I lay down My life for the sheep."

[1] John 5: 46, 47.

Num. 19:3; Deut. 21:4. The red heifer was slain without the camp, in a rough valley, that had never been cultivated.

Num. 19:5, 6. Heifer and cedar wood, hyssop, and scarlet, were burned in the fire.

Num. 19: 17-19. Those ceremonially unclean were cleansed by being sprinkled with the ashes.

Heb. 13:12; John 10:16. "Wherefore Jesus also, that He might sanctify the people with His own blood, suffered without the gate."

2 Peter 3:7. The earth is "reserved unto fire against the day of judgment and perdition of ungodly men."

1 Cor. 6:11. "Ye are washed, but ye are sanctified, but ye are justified in the name of the Lord Jesus."

CHAPTER XXIII

THE PEACE-OFFERING

THE whole world is seeking peace. Nations are fighting for it, and thousands of men are selling their souls to obtain riches in the vain hope that riches will bring them peace and happiness. But there is no real, abiding peace except that which comes from the great Prince of Peace; and it is never received as the reward of war and bloodshed nor the grasping greed of the world. The last legacy the Saviour gave His disciples was a legacy of peace. " Peace I leave with you, My peace I give unto you: *not as the world giveth,* give I unto you." [1]

The abiding peace of God in the heart is not obtained in the

[1] John 14 : 27.

(153)

pursuit of worldly fame or riches. The peace-offering in the Levitical service beautifully taught, in type and shadow, how to obtain this coveted treasure.

In many respects the peace-offering was different from all the other offerings. It was the only offering, except the Passover, in which the people could eat of the flesh. Unlike the Passover, it was not confined to only one day of the year, but could be celebrated at any time.

The animals for peace-offerings were chosen from the herd or the flock. They were to be without blemish, for no deformed animal could fitly represent the Prince of Peace. [1] The peace-offerings were made in token of thanksgiving, to confirm a vow or contract, and as voluntary offerings. [2] It was a peace-offering with which Moses confirmed the old covenant with Israel. [3] In times of special rejoicing, as we read in the Old Testament, the peace-offering was celebrated. When David brought the ark into Jerusalem, he offered peace-offerings and " dealt to every one of Israel, both man and woman, to every one a loaf of bread, and a good piece of flesh." [4]

The peace-offering was often associated with the other offerings; and wherever, except in the Passover feast, the people ate of the flesh, it was the peace-offering that was celebrated.

The individual who offered the peace-offering laid his hands on the head of the animal, and then slew it. Afterward he separated all the fat from the different organs of the body, and the priest burned the fat upon the altar of burnt-offering. [5] Not only was the fat given to the priest, but also the breast, the right shoulder, and the " two cheeks " of every offering.

The separation and burning of the fat typified the only way real peace can be obtained; viz., by delivering all our sins to the rightful owner. [6] The Prince of Peace, the blessed Saviour,

[1] Lev. 3 : 1.
[2] Lev. 7 : 12, 16.
[3] Ex. 24 : 5-8.
[4] 1 Chron. 16 : 1-3.
[5] Lev. 7 : 29-34.
[6] Ps. 37 : 20; Isa. 43 : 24.

" gave Himself for our sins. "[1] He purchased them that He might destroy sin and give us peace. This was fittingly typified by the priest " who served unto the example and shadow

of heavenly things," taking t h e fat from t h e hands of the one making the peace-offer- ing, and burn- ing it upon the a l t a r. The priest w a v e d the breast and t h e shoulder b e f o r e the Lord, then they were eaten by the priest as his portion of the peace-offering.

The disposi- tion of the fat, the breast, and the right shoul- der reveal the secret of o b - taining peace. The one who

" He shall gather the lambs with His arm, and carry them in His bosom."

obtains peace must separate from sin, and then lean, like the beloved disciple, upon the bosom of the Saviour. When Christ told

[1] Gal. 1 : 3, 4.

His twelve disciples that one of them would betray Him, they were afraid to ask Him who it was. They hardly knew their true relationship to the Saviour; but John, leaning upon His bosom, could look up into His face and say, " Who is it, Lord?" He felt confident that he would never betray his Lord.

The prophet Isaiah understood the meaning in the presentation of the breast of every peace-offering to the priest, for in writing of the Saviour he says, " He shall feed His flock like a shepherd: He shall gather the Lambs with His arm, and *carry them in His bosom*." [1]   The child of God to-day, who, like John the beloved disciple, leans on the bosom of his Lord, enjoys the real peace of God of which the peace-offering was only a type.

In the antitype of the priest receiving the right shoulder of *every* peace-offering, there is strength and blessing. We quote from the prophet Isaiah, who loved to write of the Saviour: " Unto *us* a child is born, unto *us* a son is given: and the government shall be upon *His shoulder:* and His name shall be called Wonderful, Counselor, The mighty God, The Everlasting Father, *The Prince of Peace.* Of the increase of His government and *peace there shall be no end.*" [2]

Notice, it is the one who realizes that Christ is his personal Saviour, and who lets the government of his affairs rest upon His shoulder, that receives never-ending peace. The reason we so often fail to receive abiding peace when we come to God is because we go no farther than if the individual in the type had given the priest no other portion than the fat. We confess our sins to Christ, and He takes them, but we give our confidence to worldly friends; we do not lean upon the bosom of the Lord, and make Him our confidant in everything, and trust Him to clear the way before us, as the shepherd cares for his lambs. We do not let the government of our affairs rest upon His strong

[1] Isa. 40: 11.   [2] Isa. 9: 6, 7.

and mighty shoulder. We fear to trust Him to manage our temporal affairs for us; and consequently, even after we have confessed our sins and been forgiven, we are soon entangled again with the perplexities and troubles of our every-day duties. Instead of having the peace of which there is no end, we have troubles without end. When we deliver the key, or control, of all our affairs to Christ, we shall find that He will open doors before us which no earthly power can shut, and ways He would not have us travel, and no power of earth can open them to entrap our feet. [1]

"We confess our sins to Christ . . . but we give our confidence to worldly friends."

After Samuel had anointed Saul to be king over Israel, he brought him to his house, and "said unto the cook, Bring the portion which I gave thee, of which I said unto thee, Set it by thee. And the cook took up the shoulder, and that which was upon it, and set it before Saul," and Samuel bade him eat of it. [2] If Saul had comprehended the wonderful lesson typified by this act of Samuel, he would have placed the government of the kingdom upon the shoulder of the great Prince of Peace, and not have made shipwreck of his life work.

There was another feature of the typical peace-offering which every one should consider who wishes to experience the abiding peace of the antitypical peace-offering. The two cheeks of each peace-offering were given to the priest. [3] The great antitypical

[1] Isa. 22:22. [2] 1 Sam. 9:23, 24. [3] Deut. 18:3.

Prince of Peace could say, " I gave . . . my cheeks to them
that plucked off the hair: I hid not My face from shame and
spitting." [1]   And to the one who would enjoy the peace that the
world can neither give nor take away, He says, " I say unto you,
That ye resist not evil: but whosoever shall smite thee on thy
right cheek turn to him the other also." [2]   Job, who the Lord
said was " a perfect and an upright man," could say, " They have
smitten me upon the cheek reproachfully." [3]   The child of God is
often asked to bear reproach and
shame for Christ's sake.

" Three angels visited the patriarch."

Unleavened cakes
anointed with oil
were eaten with the
peace-offering. The
unleavened bread in-
dicated sincerity and
truth, [4] and oil is
used as an emblem
of the Holy Spirit,
which brings peace
to the heart.
Leavened bread was
also eaten with the
peace-offerings of
thanksgiving, and
was a token of joy-
fulness.

After Abraham
had received the promise that Sarah should have a son, three
angels visited the patriarch as " he sat in the tent door in the
heat of the day," no doubt pondering on the promise; and

[1] Isa. 50:6.   [2] Matt. 5:39.
[3] Job 1:8; 16:10.   [4] 1 Cor. 5:8.

in token of thanksgiving he at once prepared a peace-offering for them of unleavened bread and flesh; and they ate of it, and immediately confirmed again to Abraham the promise of a son.[1]   It might have been on account of the perversion of the peace-offering and losing sight of its significance, that the children of Israel formed the habit of continually eating flesh.

There was one rigid restriction in the eating of the peace-offering. The flesh was all to be eaten upon either the first or the second day. The command was very plain: " If any of the flesh of the sacrifice of his peace-offerings be eaten at all on the third day, it shall not be accepted, neither shall it be imputed unto him that offereth it: it shall be an abomination, and the soul that eateth of it shall bear his iniquity."[2]

This offering, which could be offered by rich and poor alike at any time of the year and as often as they chose, was a significant type of the resurrection of the Prince of Peace. The Jewish economy of types and shadows is truly a " compacted prophecy of the gospel."

The Passover and waving of first-fruits on the third day taught the resurrection; but the priest alone entered the temple, and waved the handful of grain, in type of the resurrection of Christ; while in the peace-offering every child of God was given opportunity to show his faith in the resurrection of Christ.

If one ate of the flesh upon the third day, it indicated that he counted the Antitype of his peace-offering still dead upon that day. On the other hand, the one who refused to eat the flesh upon the third day, and burned in the fire all that was left, showed his faith in a risen Saviour.

In the warm country of Palestine the body would begin to decay upon the third day. Of Lazarus Martha said, " By this

[1] Gen. 18: 1-10.   [2] Lev. 7: 18.

time he stinketh: for he hath been dead four days." [1] But the psalmist, in prophesying of the resurrection of Christ, said, " Neither wilt Thou suffer Thine Holy One to see corruption." [2] David knew the Saviour would live the third day. Those who lived near the Lord saw the light that was reflected from the typical service.

It was upon this truth in regard to the resurrection of Christ as taught by David and typified in the peace-offering, that Peter based his strongest argument on the day of Pentecost. [3] Paul evidently referred to the types of the Passover and the peace-offering when he taught that " Christ died for our sins *according to the Scriptures;* and that He was buried, and that He rose again the third day *according to the Scriptures.*" [4] The eyes of even the disciples were so blinded by sin and doubt that they could not discern the light that flashed from the sacrificial offerings. Just as the moon reflecting the rays of the sun gives sufficient light to guide one safely through the night, so the light of the great antitypical Lamb of God, reflected from the Levitical laws and sacrificial offerings, was sufficient to lead the people safely unto the kingdom of God.

There are many people to-day who long for peace, and claim to feast upon God and His word day by day, and yet they stumble along in darkness; because, like the one in the type, who ate of the flesh the third day, thus signifying that he believed the Lord still dead, they go through life mourning as if the Lord of life and glory were still lying dead in Joseph's tomb instead of being alive in heaven at the right hand of the Father, ready to send light and help to every trusting follower here upon the earth. The message He sends to us from the heavenly sanctuary is, " I am He that *liveth,* and was dead; and, behold, I am alive forevermore." [5]

---

[1] John 11 : 39.   [2] Ps. 16 : 10.   [3] Acts 2 : 25-32.
[4] 1 Cor. 15 : 3, 4.   [5] Rev. 1 : 18.

TYPE   ANTITYPE

Christ is our peace. Eph. 2 : 14.

Lev. 3 : 1. The peace-offering   1 John 3 : 5. No sin in Christ.
must be without blemish.

Lev. 7 : 29, 30. Fat was sep-   2 Cor. 13 : 5. " Examine your-
arated from the offering. Fat   selves; . . . prove your
was a type of sin. Ps. 37 : 20.   own selves."

Lev. 7 : 31. The fat was burned.   Matt. 25 : 41. Sin and sinners to
                                    be burned.

Lev. 7 : 32, 33. The shoulder   Isa. 9 : 6; Luke 15 : 5. The gov-
was the priest's portion.   ernment s h a l l be upon
                                    Christ's shoulder.

Lev. 7 : 31. " The breast shall   Isa. 40 : 11. " He shall . . .
be Aaron's and his sons'."   carry them (the lambs) in
                                    His bosom."

Deut. 18 : 3. The two cheeks   Matt. 26 : 67; Isa. 50 : 6. They
were given to the priest.   spit in the Saviour's face.

Lev. 7 : 15, 16. Flesh could be   1 Cor. 15 : 3, 4. Christ lay in
eaten the first and second   the grave the first and second
days.   days.

Lev. 7 : 17, 18. None of t h e   Matt. 28 : 6; Luke 24 : 21. The
flesh was to be eaten the third   third day the angel over the
day.   empty tomb said, " He is not
                                    here : for He is risen."

CHAPTER XXIV

THE CLEANSING OF THE LEPER

F all the diseases to which mankind is heir, there is none more loathsome than leprosy. The individual lives for years with this dread disease slowly eating away portions of his body until he longs for death as a release.

From earliest times leprosy has been a type of sin; and a very fitting type it is of that loathsome spiritual disease which destroys the soul of the one who violates his conscience again and again until he has no power to resist, and becomes wholly surrendered to evil.

When Miriam became jealous of her sister-in-law, and she and Aaron murmured against Moses, "the anger of the Lord was kindled against them. . . And, behold, Miriam became leprous, white as snow." After God had taught the lesson that the sins

(162)

of jealousy, murmuring, and fault-finding are to the spiritual life what leprosy is to the physical being, then, in answer to Moses' prayer, she was healed. [1]

When Gehazi, the servant of Elisha, coveted the treasures of Naaman, and told a falsehood and dissembled to obtain them, the decree came to him from the Lord, "The leprosy therefore of Naaman shall cleave unto thee." [2] It is not strange that, with the record of the experiences of Miriam and Gehazi before them, the Jews should look upon leprosy as a judgment from the Lord.

The leper was not allowed to mingle with the people. There was no exception, from the king on the throne to the lowliest bondservant. The command of the Lord was, "The leper in whom the plague is, his clothes shall be rent, and his head bare, and he shall put a covering upon his upper lip, and shall cry, Unclean, unclean. . . He shall dwell alone; without the camp, shall his habitation be." [3]

As leprosy was a type of the worst sins, the ceremony for the cleansing of the leper embraced more than any other offering. The priest who had examined the leper and pronounced him unclean, was the only one that could pronounce him clean. The priest went outside the camp and examined the leper, and if the leprosy was healed, then the healed man was to bring "two birds alive and clean, and cedar wood, and scarlet, and hyssop," unto the priest. One of the birds was killed in an earthen vessel held over running water; then the living bird, the scarlet, and the cedar were all dipped in the blood. The priest sprinkled the blood seven times upon the one who was to be cleansed, and pronounced him clean. [4]

Leprosy is a very contageous disease; everything the leper touches is contaminated. Sin also is a dreadful disease, and the earth, air, and water are all cursed by the sins of humanity, and

[1] Num. 12:9-15.
[3] Lev. 13:45, 46.
[2] 2 Kings 5:20-27.
[4] Lev. 14:4-7.

must be cleansed by the same blood which cleanses man. Therefore, after the leper was pronounced clean, the live bird, its
feathers scarlet with the blood, was let loose to fly through the
air. The blood was not only sprinkled on the person who had
been unclean, but it was thus carried through the air that was
laden with germs of disease and sin,[1] in type of the blood of
Christ which will give a new heaven — a new atmosphere — to
this sin-cursed earth.

Before man sinned, there was no decaying vegetation; the
lovely trees were not destroyed by insect pests, but all was free
from the curse. Nothing but the blood of Christ can restore
vegetation to its Eden beauty. In type of this regenerating
power, a piece of cedar, the giant of the forest, and of hyssop,
the small plant " that springeth out of the wall,"[2] were dipped in
the blood. These were chosen to represent the two extremes
in vegetation, thus embracing all.

The animal life also is cursed by sin, but through the redeeming power of the blood of Christ the time will come when " the
wolf shall dwell with the lamb, and the leopard shall lie down
with the kid; and the calf, and the young lion, and the fatling
together; and a little child shall lead them."[3]

The scarlet wool dipped in the blood represented the animal
kingdom.[4] The blood of the bird was placed in an *earthen* dish
held over running water. Thus we see that in the cleansing of
the leper the blood came in direct contact not only with the
leper, but with all else cursed by sin; viz., earth, air, water, vegetation, and the animal kingdom.

These wonderful types were but compacted prophecies of the
far more wonderful Antitype. When Christ knelt in agony upon
the cold ground of the garden of Gethsemane, the great drops of
blood fell down from His face to the ground.[5] Four thousand

[1] Jer. 9: 21.   [2] I Kings 4: 33.   [3] Isa. 11: 6.
[4] Heb. 9: 19.   [5] Luke 22: 44.

years before, when Cain slew his brother, the earth had first felt
the touch of human blood, which fell as a withering curse, blight-
ing the fruitfulness of the land. [1]   Many times since has the bosom
of the earth not only been spotted with the blood of man, but
rivers of blood have deluged the ground as armed hosts of human
beings, led on by Satan, have slaughtered one another. Every
drop of this blood has added to the curse. [2]   But how different
the effect of the blood of the blessed Saviour! In it was healing,
cleansing power. [3]

The curse of sin rests heavily upon the atmosphere, which is
so laden with disease germs that " death is come up into our
windows, and is entered into our palaces, to cut off the children
from without, and the young men from the streets." In the
type the blood of the offering dripped from the bird as it flew
through the air. From the great antitypical Offering, as He hung
on Calvary, the precious, healing blood dripped from His wounded
hands and feet *through the air,* and fell upon the rocks beneath.
The types of the old Levitical service were not a meaningless
ceremony, but a prophecy of the great Antitype.

From the earliest times, the water has been affected by the
curse of sin. [4]   The bird killed over the running water was a
type of the death of Christ, which would remove the curse of
sin forever from the waters of the earth. The blood of Christ
came in direct contact with water; when the soldier thrust the
cruel spear into the side of the Saviour, " forthwith came there-
out blood and water;" [5] not a mixture of blood and water, but
blood *and* water, two copious streams.

" The wonderful symbol of the living bird dipped in the blood
of the slain bird, and then set free to its joyous life, is to us the
symbol of the atonement. There were death and life blended, presenting to the searcher of truth the hidden treasure, the union of

[1] Gen. 4 : 11, 12.   [2] Isa. 24 : 5, 6.   [3] Num. 35 : 33.
[4] Ex. 15 : 23.   [5] John 19 : 34.

the pardoning blood with the resurrection and life of our Redeemer.

The bird was slain over living water; that flowing stream was a symbol of the ever flowing, ever cleansing efficacy of the blood of Christ."

The cross upon which the Saviour hung, and which was stained with His precious blood, was made of the trees of the forest; while a small reed of hyssop supported the sponge that was dipped in vinegar and given Him to quench His thirst.

As the Saviour hung upon the cross, He listened for some word or token from humanity that would indicate that His sacrifice was appreciated; but only jeers, taunts, and curses were borne to His ears from the surging mass below. Even one of the thieves by His side joined in the railing; but the other thief reproved him, and turning to Jesus said, "Lord, remember me when Thou comest into Thy kingdom." The reply of Jesus, "Verily I say unto thee to-day, shalt thou be with me in paradise;" [1] contained an assurance of pardon. Even while the cleansing blood of Christ was flowing from His veins, the thief rejoiced in its power to cleanse from sin. He who was thought by His enemies to be conquered, died a mighty Conqueror, and the thief experienced the fulfilment of the promise, "Though your sins be as scarlet, they shall be as white as snow." [2]

There was a significance in the color of the wool dipped in the blood of the typical offering. It is almost impossible to re- move scarlet stains, but "though your sins *be as scarlet,*" the blood of Christ can make them "white as snow." You may be condemned and counted as an outcast by every one on earth; but if you look to the Saviour and claim His cleansing power, He will wash away your sins, and put joy and rejoicing in your heart.

In the typical service, notwithstanding the fact that when the

[1] Luke 23 : 39-43.   [2] Isa. 1 : 18.

one to be cleansed from leprosy was sprinkled with the blood, he was pronounced clean, yet there was something more for him to do. On the eighth day after he was pronounced clean, he was to appear before the priest with two lambs, a meat-offering, and a log of oil. The priest presented the man to be cleansed at the door of the tabernacle, and waved one of the lambs and the log of oil before the Lord. He then slew the lamb, and took some of the blood and put it upon "the tip of the right ear" of him that was to be cleansed, "and upon the thumb

of his right hand, and upon the great toe of his right foot," [1] thus consecrating his ears to hear only those things that would tend to keep him clean, his hands to the service of God, and his feet to travel only in the way of the Lord's commandments.

Then the priest took the log of oil, and after sprinkling a portion of it before the Lord, he put some of it "upon the tip of the right ear" of him that was to be cleansed, also "upon the thumb of his right hand, and upon the great toe of his right foot," and then anointed his head with the remainder of the oil. [2]

This service was not an empty form, but a type of a blessed antitype, which is fulfilled in every Christian who presents him-

[1] Lev. 14: 10-14.　　　　[2] Lev. 14: 15-18.

self for service before the Lord, after the Lord forgives his sins and pronounces him clean. Of Mary, Jesus said, " Her sins, which *are many,* are forgiven; for she loved much: but to whom little is forgiven, the same loveth little." [1]   The leper cleansed from that loathsome, living death, felt so thankful to God for freedom and cleansing that he consecrated his life to the Lord for service. Not only is the oil, an emblem of the Holy Spirit which prepares the Christian for service, touched to his ear, hand, and foot, but it is poured upon his head, thus betokening a full surrender of the entire being to the service of His Master who has redeemed him. The books of heaven record the names of many who have fulfilled this beautiful antitype by surrendering their entire being to the service of their Redeemer.

The Levitical law provided for the cleansing of houses and garments infected with leprosy. If an owner of a house saw any signs of leprosy, he was to report the matter to the priest, who at once proceeded to examine the house. First the house was to be emptied, and if the priest saw " greenish or reddish " streaks upon the walls, the house was to be shut up for seven days. If at the end of that time the walls were still covered with the mold, they were to be scraped and the stones taken out and the house thoroughly repaired. If the spots appeared again, this proved that the leprosy did not come from any leak or defect in the walls, but that the location was damp and unhealthful, and the house was to be torn down. [2]

If the health laws of the land to-day were as watchful over the homes of the people as were the old Levitical laws, there would be less of that dread disease, tuberculosis.

The laws in regard to garments infected with leprosy were very rigid. [3] If the plague of leprosy was so deep seated that it could not be removed by washing, then the garment was to be

[1] Luke 7:47.   [2] Lev. 14:34-45.   [3] Lev. 13:47-59.

burned in the fire. There is a deeply spiritual lesson in this instruction. God has given very definite directions in regard to the dress of His followers. [1] He never designed that His people should follow the foolish fashions of the world. [2] There should be a marked difference between the dress of the Christian and that of the worldling. [3] Individuals may argue that they have overcome pride, that when they wear fashionable apparel and dress like the worldling, it does not hurt them, for they have conquered pride. As well might a person who had just recovered from small-pox wear the garments infected by the disease. He reasons that as he has had the disease once and recovered, there is no danger of his taking it a second time, hence there is no danger in the garments; but he sows the germ of the disease wherever he goes. In like manner the Christian who fails to obey the Lord's instruction in regard to dress, misrepresents the Lord, and sows seeds of pride and vanity in the hearts of weaker members. It is better to follow the instruction given in the Levitical service, and even burn garments infected with pride and vanity, than to misrepresent our Lord and Master even in our dress.

TYPE   ANTITYPE

" The entire system of Judaism was the gospel veiled."

Lev. 14 : 6, 7. Blood was sprinkled on the one to be cleansed.   I Peter 1 : 2. The sprinkling of the blood of Jesus cleanses from sin.

[1] I Peter 3 : 3, 4; I Tim. 2 : 9.   [2] Isa. 3 : 16-26.   [3] Num. 15 : 38, 39

Lev. 14: 6. Cedar, scarlet, and hyssop were dipped in the blood. 1 Kings 4: 33. Cedar and hyssop are extremes in vegetation. Heb. 9: 19.

John 19: 29. The hyssop was brought in connection with the Saviour, while the cross was made from the trees of the forest.

Lev. 14: 5. The bird was killed and the blood caught in an earthen vessel.

Luke 22: .44. Jesus' blood came in contact with the earth.

Lev. 14: 6, 7. The bird that had been dipped in the blood was let loose to fly through the air. Jer. 9: 21. Air is unclean.

Rev. 21: 1. There will be a new heaven (atmospheric heaven), as the result of Christ's death. His blood dropped through the air from the cross.

Lev. 14: 14, 17. The tip of the ear was touched with the blood and oil.

Isa. 42: 18-20. God's servants are deaf to things they should not hear.

Lev. 14: 14, 17. The thumb of the right hand was touched with blood and oil.

Ps. 119: 48. "My hands also will I lift up unto Thy commandments, which I h a v e loved."

Lev. 14: 14, 17. The toe of the right foot was touched with the blood.

Gen. 17: 1. "I am the Almighty God: walk before Me, and be thou perfect."

SECTION VI

Services of the Sanctuary

Before the Throne My Saviour Stands

A RISE, my soul, arise,
   Shake off thy guilty fears;
The bleeding Sacrifice
   In my behalf appears;
Before the throne my Saviour stands;
My name is written on His hands.

He ever lives above,
   For me to intercede;
His all-redeeming love,
   His precious blood, to plead;
His blood was shed for all our race,
And sprinkles now the throne of grace.

Five bleeding wounds He bears,
   Received on Calvary;
They pour effectual prayers,
   They strongly speak for me:
Forgive him, O, forgive! they cry,
Nor let the contrite sinner die!

The Father hears Him pray,
   His dear, anointed One;
He cannot turn away
   The presence of His Son;
His spirit answers to the blood,
And tells me I'm a child of God.

—Charles Wesley.

CHAPTER XXV

THE COURT AND ITS SERVICES

HE tabernacle was surrounded by a court one hundred cubits long and fifty cubits wide. This court was enclosed by curtains of fine twined linen hung from pillars of brass. The pillars were trimmed with chapiters and fillets of silver, and the curtains were suspended from silver hooks. The court formed an oblong, and was placed with its longest sides toward the north and south and the ends toward the east and west. The door, or entrance, of twenty cubits width, was in the center of the east end of the court. The curtains forming the door of the court were of " blue, and purple, and scarlet, and fine twined linen wrought with needlework," and were suspended from four pillars of brass, trimmed with silver. [1]

The height of the court was only half that of the tabernacle, so that above the beautiful curtains of the court and the glitter of

[1] Ex. 27:9-18.

the silver and brass of the many pillars, could be seen the golden walls of the tabernacle, with its gorgeous curtains and coverings. As the one outside the court, in order to behold the glories of the tabernacle, had to look above the court; so the one who by faith beholds the beauties of the heavenly sanctuary, must lift his thoughts above the things of this earth, and center them upon heavenly things.

There were two principal articles of furniture in the court, the laver and the altar of burnt-offering. The altar was overlaid with brass; the laver and all the vessels of the court that were used in the services connected with the altar, were of brass. The great brazen altar was placed between the sanctuary and the gate, but nearer the gate than the sanctuary. [1]

No part of the sanctuary or of the court was made according to the plans of men; but every part was fashioned after the divine model. When the Lord had given Moses the directions in regard to making the brazen altar, He added, " As it was showed thee in the mount, so shall they make it." [2]

The altar was a hollow box, five cubits square and three cubits high, made of boards of acacia wood. There was a horn of the same wood on each corner. A network of brass in the center held the fire and gave draft for it, and allowed the ashes to fall beneath. The entire altar with the horns was all overlaid with brass. [3]

It was "an altar most holy: whatsoever toucheth the altar shall be holy," was the divine decree. [4] It was because of this, no doubt, that Adonijah and Joab fled and caught hold of the horns of the altar when they feared death at the hands of Solomon. [5]

All burnt-offerings of the sanctuary were burned upon the brazen altar. The fire was kindled by the Lord Himself, [6] and

[1] Ex. 40:6, 7.
[2] Ex. 27:8.
[3] Ex. 27:1-8.
[4] Ex. 29:37.
[5] 1 Kings 1:50; 2:28.
[6] Lev. 9:24.

was kept burning continually. It was never to go out. [1] The fire which destroys all sin from the earth, like the fire on the brazen altar, will come down from God out of heaven, and will not be quenched as long as there is any sin to be consumed. [2]

"Joab fled and caught hold of the horns of the altar."

The entire body of the whole burnt-offering and portions of various offerings were burned upon this brazen altar. It consumed that which typified sin; and as the fires were continually burning, it has been called "the altar of continual atonement." Sin separates man from God, [3] and all sin must be put away before the sinner can be at-one-ment with God. Therefore the work done upon this altar was a symbol of the final destruction of sin, which will be necessary before the redeemed can enjoy their eternal inheritance.

Paul referred to this altar as a type of Christ. [4] All the work connected with the altar of burnt-offering typified the work connected with the destruction of sin,— a work which Christ alone can do. The Father has delivered into the hands of His Son the final destruction of sin and sinners. [5]

[1] Lev. 6:13. [2] Rev. 20:9; Mark 9:43-48. [3] Isa. 59:2.
[4] Heb. 13:10. [5] Ps. 2:7-9.

The horns of the brazen altar were often touched with the blood of the different offerings, and the blood of *every* sin-offering was poured out at the base of this altar.

With only a few exceptions, all the sacrifices were slain in the court, at the door of the tabernacle of the congregation, as the entrance of the first apartment was often called; for the whole congregation of Israel could assemble in the court and at this door. None but priests could enter within the sacred precincts of the tabernacle itself, for it typified the heavenly sanctuary, where God and Christ abide, surrounded by shining cherubim and seraphim. All the work performed in the court was typical of work done in the earth, while the work performed in the first and second apartments of the sanctuary was typical of work done in heaven.

No sacrifice was ever slain within the sanctuary; but the offerings were slain in the court, and the blood and flesh were carried within the sanctuary by the priest. Christ, the great antitypical Sacrifice, was slain in the antitypical court, this earth, and then entered the antitypical sanctuary in the heavens with His own blood and the same body in which He bore our sins on Calvary. Sins are forgiven, and are blotted out from the books in the heavenly sanctuary; but they are not destroyed there. Just as in the type the fires of the brazen altar in the court consumed that which in type represented sin; so in the antitype, the wicked will be " on the breadth of the *earth* " when fire comes down from God out of heaven and devours them. [1] This earth is the great antitypical court, where all the work typified in the court of the earthly sanctuary will meet its fulfilment.

The constant burning upon the altar of that which typified sin, caused an accumulation of ashes. The priests in the earthly sanctuary served " unto the example and shadow of

[1] Rev. 20 : 9.

heavenly things," [1] and even the removal of the ashes was directed of the Lord to be done in a manner to typify a portion of the final work of Christ. The priest was to be clothed in the pure white linen garments, when he removed the ashes from the altar. The ashes were first taken up by the priest and placed "beside the altar" on the east side. [2] When the time came to remove them from beside the altar, the priest laid aside his priestly robes, and "put on other garments;" then h e carried t h e ashes forth without the camp, and poured them out in "a clean place." [3] Ashes are a l l that will re- main of sin, sinners, and the devil af- ter the fires of the l a s t d a y h a v e finished their work.[4] When t h e purify- ing fires of the L o r d h a v e re- moved t h e last trace of sin, t h e r e will appear a new earth, a

Ashes "beside the altar."

clean place, without one taint of sin upon it; and as the righteous walk over the face of the clean, pure earth, the ashes of sin and all that clung to sin in this earth will be under their feet. Truly the type will then have met its antitype, and the ashes of all sin will be in "a clean place."

When the priest placed the ashes beside the altar, he was clothed in his priestly robes. The ashes represented the confessed sins of the righteous. When Christ bears the confessed sins of His people, He wears His priestly robes; but the time comes when He will place the sins of the righteous on the head of Satan, lay aside His priestly garments, and come to this earth clad in kingly robes, to gather out of His kingdom all

[1] Heb. 8:5.
[2] Lev. 6:10; 1:16.
[3] Lev. 6:11.
[4] Mal. 4:1-3; Eze. 28:18, 19.

things that offend and do iniquity. [1] Then *all* sin and sinners will be burned in the fire. Not in priestly robes will Christ come out into the antitypical court, the earth, to complete the final destruction of sin; but as King of kings and Lord of lords.

Much of the typical service was directed by the Lord in a way to arouse a spirit of inquiry in the minds of the young, so that they themselves would ask for information. The Passover was planned so that the children would say, " What mean ye by this service?" [2] The twelve stones were piled up on the banks of Jordan as a " sign " to attract the attention of the children, so that in answer to their question, " What mean ye by these stones?" they might be taught of the time when God stayed the floods of Jordan before the hosts of Israel. [3] If the curiosity of the child is aroused and he himself makes the inquiry, the lesson is more forcibly impressed upon his mind.

It would seem that for this reason God had the ashes of the sacrifice at first placed on the east of the altar, where they would be so conspicuous that every child entering the court could not fail to see and ask, " What mean ye by these ashes?" and then he would be taught by the parent the wonderful truth that all sin would be finally burned to ashes in the fires of the last day.[4]

As the children went without the camp with their parents, their attention would be attracted by the unusual sight of ashes being placed in a perfectly clean place; and in reply to their questions the beautiful lesson of the new earth, which will come forth from the fires that destroy the last trace of sin, would be impressed upon their young minds. By the ashes and the blood at the base of the altar in the typical services of the court, the purifying of this earth from sin was kept before the minds of Israel.

While the congregation of Israel could gather in the court,

[1] Matt. 13:41.
[2] Ex. 12:26.
[3] Joshua 4:1-7.
[4] Mal. 4:1-3.

the priests alone were to perform the work at the altar.[1] The Levites were given charge of the sanctuary, but they could not perform the service of the altar, for that typified work which none but Christ could do. He alone can destroy sin.

The laver was between the brazen altar and the door of the sanctuary. The laver and its base were both of brass. Water was kept in them, for the priests to wash both their hands and their feet before they entered the sanctuary to perform any service. They were also required to wash both hands and feet before they went " near the altar to minister, to burn offering made by fire unto the Lord." Death was the penalty for performing service at the altar or within the tabernacle without first washing in the laver.[2] As the people in the court beheld the priests wash in the water before they performed the work of the holy office, may it not have taught them the truth that Christ gave to Nicodemus, " Except a man be born of water and of the Spirit, he cannot enter into the kingdom of God"?[3]

TYPE	ANTITYPE
Ex. 27: 9-18. There was a court surrounding the tabernacle, in which the offerings were slain. Lev. 4: 4, 14, 15, 24, 29.	John 12: 31-33. The great antitypical Offering was slain in the earth.
Lev. 6: 10, 11. The ashes from the altar were placed in a clean place.	Mal. 4: 1-3. The ashes of the wicked will be left on the clean earth.

[1] Num. 18: 2-7.   [2] Ex. 30: 17-21.   [3] John 3: 5; Titus 3: 5; Eph. 5: 26.

Lev. 6: 10. The priest was attired in priestly garments when he placed the ashes by the altar.

Heb. 2: 17. Christ is High Priest to make reconciliation for the sins of the people.

Lev. 6: 11. When the priest carried the ashes without the camp unto a clean place, he laid aside his priestly robes, and put on other garments.

Rev. 19: 14-16; Isa. 63: 1-4. When Christ comes to the earth to destroy sin and sinners, He will have changed His priestly garments for those of a king.

CHAPTER XXVI

THE WORK IN THE FIRST APARTMENT
OF THE SANCTUARY

HE work in the first apartment consisted principally of the morning and evening daily services, the individual sin-offerings, and services on feast days and on special occasions. God's visible presence was manifested in the first apartment, or tabernacle of the congregation. There at the first veil, or door, of the tabernacle of the congregation, [1] where the people presented their sin-offerings, God met and communed with the children of Israel. Sometimes the cloud of glory, representing the visible presence of the Most Holy, filled the first apartment so that no one was able to enter. [2]

God's presence manifested in the first apartment of the earthly sanctuary was a shadow of the glorious presence and throne of the Father in the first apartment of the heavenly sanctuary, where,

[1] Ex. 29:42, 43; 30:36; Num. 17:4.
[2] Ex. 40:34, 35; 1 Kings 8:10, 11; 2 Chron. 5:13, 14; 7:2.

(181)

after enduring " the cross, despising the shame," the Saviour sat down " at the right hand of the throne of God." [1]

The service each morning and evening was very important. Within the first apartment the high priest offered incense upon the golden altar, and trimmed and lighted the lamps. [2] None but the high priest could perform this sacred work, which typified the adding of the fragrant incense of Christ's righteousness to the prayers of God's people, to render them acceptable before God. [3] He also trimmed and lighted those lamps that were a shadow of the Holy Spirit emanating from God, which at some time in life shines into the heart of every one, [4] inviting him to accept the Lord and His service, and which shines continually in the life of the

First apartment of the sanctuary.

individual who walks in the light, and is faithful to God.

While the high priest within the sanctuary was performing the daily service morning and evening at the golden altar, the priests

[1] Heb. 12:2.
[2] Ex. 30:6-8.
[3] Rev. 8:3,4.
[4] John 1:9.

in the court were burning the whole burnt-offering, the meat-offering, and the drink-offering, upon the brazen altar, and the people were gathered without, praying. [1]

When the children of Israel were carried into captivity, the faithful ones prayed, like Daniel, with their windows open toward Jerusalem. [2] They turned toward the temple, where, from the altar of continual intercession, the incense was ascending. This type represented those who may be held captive in cruel bondage by Satan, the prince of this world. It matters not where they may be nor how strong the bands that hold them, if they will resolutely turn their faces from their surroundings toward the heavenly sanctuary, where Christ pleads His blood and presents His righteousness in the sinner's behalf, the prayer of faith will bring peace and joy to the soul, and will break asunder the bands with which Satan has bound them. Christ sets before such an " open door, and no man can shut it." [3] It makes no difference what the surroundings may be, the soul can be free in God, and no human being, not even the devil, can prevent it. " This is the victory that overcometh the world, even our faith." [4]

Day by day, as sinners presented their sin-offerings at the door of the first apartment, confessing their sins, either by the blood sprinkled before the Lord or a portion of the flesh eaten in the first apartment, the confessed sins were transferred in type to the first apartment of the sanctuary. The priest met the sinner at the first veil of the sanctuary, and carried within the veil either the blood or the flesh. The sinner could not look within the sanctuary, but by faith he knew that the priest was faithful to present his sin-offering before the Lord, and he left the sanctuary rejoicing in sins forgiven.

In the antitype of that service we confess our sins, and although we can not see the work in the heavenly sanctuary, we

[1] Luke 1 : 10.
[2] Dan. 6 : 10.
[3] Rev. 3 : 8.
[4] 1 John 5 : 4.

know that Christ pleads His blood and marred flesh,[1]— the prints of the nails,— before the Father in our behalf, and we rejoice in the forgiveness of sins. The sins are covered, hid from view. " Blessed is he whose transgression is forgiven, whose sin is covered." [2]

As day by day the sins of the people were thus in figure transferred to the sanctuary, the place became defiled, and must be purified or cleansed. Sins are forgiven and covered when confessed, and will never be uncovered if the one who confesses them re-

mains faithful; but if he forsakes the Lord and turns back into the world, that part of his past life which, while he was faithful, was covered with Christ's righteousness, appears open and uncovered on the books of heaven; for he himself has withdrawn from Christ, and must meet the record of his entire life in the judgment.

The Lord taketh pleasure in them that fear Him, in those that hope in His mercy. Ps. 147:11

This is very forcefully taught in the parable of the unmerciful servant, who, after he had been forgiven his entire debt, dealt harshly with his debtors, and the Lord then required him to pay all that had been once forgiven him. [3]

The time will come when the sins of the righteous will not

[1] Isa. 49 : 15, 16. [2] Ps. 32 : 1. [3] Matt. 18 : 23-35.

only be forgiven and covered by the blood of Christ, but all trace of them will be forever removed from the books of heaven, and even the Lord will never remember them again. This work was symbolized by the work in the second apartment on the day of atonement.

TYPE

ANTITYPE

Ex. 29 : 42, 43. The visible presence of God was manifested in the first apartment of the earthly sanctuary.

Rev. 4 : 2-5. The seven lamps were seen in heaven before the throne.

Ex. 30 : 7, 8. The high priest trimmed and lighted t h e lamps.

Rev. 1 : 13. Christ was seen among the golden candle-sticks in the heavenly sanctuary.

Ex. 40 : 24, 25. The lamps in the earthly sanctuary were burning before the Lord.

Rev. 4 : 2, 5. The seven lamps of fire were seen burning before the throne of God in heaven.

Heb. 9 : 6. "The priests went always into the first tabernacle, accomplishing the service of God."

Heb. 7 : 25. Christ ever liveth to make intercession for us.

Lev. 4 : 7; 10 : 16-18. By the blood and the flesh the sins were transferred to the earthly sanctuary.

1 Peter 2 : 24; 1 John 1 : 7. By the merits of the sacrifice of the body and blood of Christ, our sins are forgiven.

Lev. 4: 7. The marks of sin touched the horns of the altar.

Num. 18: 7. None but the priests could look within the veil. All that remained of the sin-offering without the veil was burned. All trace of the sin-offering was covered from sight.

Jer. 2: 22. The actual sin is marked before the Lord in heaven.

Ps. 32: 1. When we confess our sins, they are transferred to the heavenly sanctuary and covered, nevermore to appear, if we are faithful.

CHAPTER XXVII

A WONDERFUL PROPHECY

T HE daily round of service during the year typified the work of confessing sins and leaving them with Christ, our great Sin-bearer, in the heavenly sanctuary. But Christ will not always bear the sins of the world. There will come a time when He will blot out the last trace of sin from the books of heaven. Then the sins of the righteous will be laid upon Satan, the originator of sin, and he, with all sin and sinners, will be consumed in the lake of fire.

God is a God of justice, and before either the sins of the faithful or the names of the unfaithful are blotted from the books of heaven,[1] there will be an examination of the records,— an in-

[1] Rev. 3:5.

vestigative judgment. The service in the second apartment of the sanctuary was a type of this work. It was called the day of atonement, or the cleansing of the sanctuary. The record states: "On that day shall the priest make an atonement for you, to cleanse you, that ye may be clean from all your sins before the Lord."[1]

When men and angels were placed on probation, a time of judgment was appointed when they would be judged. The resurrection of Christ is a pledge, or assurance, of the judgment. God "hath *appointed* a day, in the which He will judge the world in righteousness, by that man whom He hath ordained; whereof He hath given assurance unto all men, in that He hath raised Him from the dead."[2]

The day of judgment is a definite time set apart in which to perform a specific work. It is a period of time. "God shall judge the righteous and the wicked: for there is a *time* there for every purpose, and for every work."[3] God did not leave the world in darkness in regard to the time of the day of judgment, of which the day of atonement, or the cleansing of the sanctuary, was a type; but through the prophet Daniel He foretold when that event would take place.

In the eighth chapter of the book of Daniel, we read that in the last days of the Babylonian kingdom, the prophet was given a prophetic view of the history of the world from that time until the end of all earthly kingdoms. He saw a ram having two horns; and a rough goat with a notable horn between his eyes, came from the west and overcame the ram and trampled him under foot. Then the goat grew very strong; and when he was strong, the great horn was broken, and in its place came up four notable horns. "Out of one of them came forth a little horn which waxed exceeding great," until "he magnified himself even

[1] Lev. 16:30.   [2] Acts 17:31.   [3] Eccl. 3:17.

to the Prince of the host;" that is, claimed to be equal to the Prince of the host.

While the prophet was watching this little horn persecuting the people of God on the earth, his attention was arrested by a conversation between two heavenly beings, which he records as follows: " Then I heard one saint speaking, and another saint said unto the Numberer of secrets, or the Wonderful Numberer, which

. . " *He saw a ram having two horns, and a rough goat with a notable horn between his eyes.*"

spake, How long shall be the vision concerning the daily sacrifice, and the transgression of desolation, to give both the sanctuary and the host to be trodden under foot? And He [the Wonderful Numberer, the Prince of hosts] said unto me, Unto two thousand and three hundred days; then shall the sanctuary be cleansed." [1] Daniel did not understand the vision, and One

[1] Dan. 8: 1-14, margin.

having authority over the heavenly forces commissioned the angel Gabriel to make him understand it. Gabriel then gave the following brief explanation:

"The ram which thou sawest having two horns are the kings of Media and Persia, and the rough goat is the king of Grecia: and the great horn that is between his eyes is the first king [Alexander the Great]."

He then said that the four kingdoms into which Grecia would be divided, represented by the four horns, would not be as strong as Grecia, but that the kingdom represented by the little horn; viz., the Roman kingdom, which grew out of one of the four horns, would destroy the people of God, and would even stand up against the Prince of princes Himself when He should come to the earth. This last view was more than Daniel could endure. When

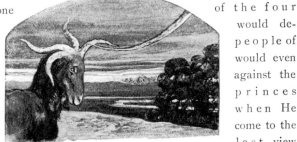

"Out of one of them came forth a little horn which waxed exceeding great."

he saw that this power would even take the life of the Prince of princes, he fainted; and when Gabriel said, "The vision of the evening and the morning which was told is true," he found it was useless to proceed, as Daniel was not able to comprehend. [1]

Daniel was sick for some days, but soon began to pray for a full explanation of the vision. We have his prayer recorded; it is not long. When he began to pray, God in heaven commissioned Gabriel to go and answer the prophet's prayer, and before he had finished praying the angel touched him. [2]   Heaven and

[1] Dan. 8:20-27.   [2] Dan. 9:1-23.

earth are brought very near together by the prayer of faith. The one who holds on by simple faith until an answer is sent from heaven, is beloved by the Lord. [1]

Gabriel assured Daniel that he was come to give him " skill and understanding," and told him to " consider the vision." All had been made plain except the question asked the " Wonderful Numberer," and His reply. All heaven is interested in the work of God on the earth, and it was not idle curiosity but intense interest which prompted the question, " How long shall be the vision concerning the daily *sacrifice,* and the transgression of desolation, to give both the sanctuary and the host to be trodden under foot?" The word " sacrifice " is given in italics in the authorized version of the Bible, showing that it " was supplied by man's wisdom, and does not belong to the text."

At the time the question was asked, the sanctuary, or temple built by Solomon, lay in ruins, and God's people were in captivity in a foreign land. The vision had revealed to the angels as well as to Daniel that far down in the future a power would arise that would bring a worse persecution upon the people of God than they had ever experienced, which was fulfilled in the twelve hundred sixty years of papal persecution, known in history as the Dark Ages. [2] This persecution could not affect the heavenly sanctuary, as no earthly power can reach heaven; but it trod underfoot the host who worshiped toward the heavenly sanctuary, and by depriving the people of the word of God, it obscured the correct knowledge in regard to the heavenly sanctuary for a long period of time.

When the Wonderful Numberer answered the question, He directed His words to Daniel instead of to the one who asked the question. None but the Father or the Son could reveal the time appointed for the great court of judgment to convene in the

[1] Dan. 9 : 23.   [2] Dan. 8 : 23-25.

heavenly sanctuary. It was Christ then, who numbered the years to intervene before. the opening of the great judgment. He is truly called the Numberer of Secrets, or the Wonderful Numberer. [1]

When Daniel was told to consider the vision, no doubt the words addressed directly to him would come into his mind: " Unto two thousand and three hundred days [evening, morning]; then shall the sanctuary be cleansed." [2] As Daniel's mind reviewed these words, Gabriel began the explanation of the portion of the vision he had been unable to explain during his previous visit.

The prophecy regarding the two thousand three hundred days of Dan. 8: 14 is one of the grandest prophecies in the entire Bible. There are other lines of prophecy that foretell the rise and fall of nations, but the two thousand three hundred days definitely locates two of the greatest events in the history of all mankind; viz., the time when Christ would come to the earth and offer Himself as a ransom for the lost race; and the opening of the great tribunal in heaven, when the Judge of all the earth will decide the eternal destiny of every soul that has ever lived upon the earth.

During Gabriel's first visit to Daniel, he explained the symbols of the ram, the rough goat, and the four horns, and gave an account of the work of the little horn; but Daniel fainted before he had explained the two thousand three hundred days; therefore when he returns to give the prophet skill and understanding and asks him to consider the vision, he immediately introduces the subject of time. His first words are, " Seventy weeks are determined upon thy people, and upon thy holy city." The word " determined " signifies *cut off* from some longer period of time. The only time period under consideration is the two thousand three hundred days. Therefore, seventy weeks were to be

[1] Dan. 8:13, margin.   [2] Dan. 8:14, margin.

cut off from that period, and allotted to the Jews and their holy city. [1]

A day in prophetic time represents a year of real time. [2] Seven years make a week of years. [3]   Seventy weeks would be 70 x 7 = 490 years. Four hundred and ninety years were determined upon the Jewish people to accomplish six things; viz.,

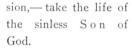

1. " To finish the transgression," to commit the crowning act of all transgression,— take the life of the sinless S o n of God.

2. "To make an end of sin." Christ partook of death, " that through d e a t h He might destroy him that had the power of death, that is, the devil," and thus forever end all sin. [4]

3. "To make reconciliation for iniquity." Christ " made peace through the blood of His cross," and reconciled " all things unto Himself." [5]

"**Heaven and earth are brought very near together by the prayer of faith.**"

4. " To bring in everlasting righteousness." The death of Christ opened the way by which every son and daughter of Adam could obtain everlasting righteousness if he desired it.

5. "To seal up the vision."   Events transpired within

[1] Dan. 9:24-27.   [2] Num. 14:34; Eze. 4:6.   [3] Gen. 29:27.
[4] Heb. 2:14.   [5] Col. 1:20.

those four hundred ninety years that sealed, or established, the entire vision of the two thousand three hundred years.

6. "To anoint the most holy." When the time came to begin the service in the earthly sanctuary, the entire sanctuary was anointed;[1] and when Christ entered the heavenly sanctuary to perform the work of which the earthly service was a type, the heavenly sanctuary was anointed, before He began His ministry in the first apartment. The heavenly sanctuary is spoken of as most holy to distinguish it from the earthly.

Wonderful changes were wrought in the history of the church during that four hundred ninety years. After the angel had enumerated the events to take place during that period, he told Daniel where to locate it in the history of the world, by announcing the date of the beginning of the period; "Know, therefore, and understand, that from the going forth of the commandment to restore and to build Jerusalem, unto the Messiah the Prince, shall be seven weeks and threescore and two weeks: the street shall be built again, and the wall, even in troublous times."[2]

The long period of two thousand three hundred days from which the seventy weeks, or four hundred ninety years, were cut off, began with the going forth of the great threefold commandment[3] to restore and build Jerusalem, which went forth 457 B. C. This decree did not go into effect until about the middle of the year,[4] which would make the exact date for the going forth of the decree 456½ B. C.

Gabriel divides the seventy weeks into three divisions; viz., seven weeks, sixty-two weeks, and one week.[5] The prophet Nehemiah gives an account of the rebuilding of the walls during troublous times.

The seven weeks and the sixty-two weeks, or sixty-nine weeks in all, were to extend to Messiah the Prince. Sixty-nine weeks

[1] Ex. 40 : 9.   [2] Dan. 9 : 24, 25.   [3] Ezra 6 : 14.
[4] Ezra 7 : 9.   [5] Dan. 9 : 25-27.

equals 69 x 7 = 483 years. This taken from 456½ B. C. brings us to 26½ A. D. In the spring of A. D. 27, or 26½ A. D., Jesus at His baptism was anointed with the Holy Ghost, and henceforth was the Christ, the Messiah, the anointed One. [1]

After the seven weeks and the threescore and two weeks passed, Messiah was to " be cut off, but not for Himself." He died to atone for the sins of the world. After stating that the Messiah would be cut off, Gabriel adds, " He shall confirm the covenant with many for one week: and in the midst of the week He shall cause the sacrifice and the oblation to cease." [2] Christ's ministry after His baptism continued three and one-half years, or half a prophetic week.

Christ was cut off in the midst of the seventieth week, but the entire seventy weeks had been " determined " upon the Jews. Christ directed His disciples to begin their work at Jerusalem, and it was not until the stoning of Stephen in A. D. 34, or three and one-half years after the crucifixion, that the gospel went to the Gentiles. The covenant was confirmed by the disciples, [3] for they confined their labors to the Jews until 34 A. D., the close of the period allotted to that people. [4]

The seventy weeks, or four hundred ninety years, ended in A. D. 34. Four hundred ninety years taken from the entire period of two thousand three hundred years, leaves eighteen hundred ten years of the period remaining in A. D. 34 [2300-490 = 1810]. This added to A. D. 34 brings us to eighteen hundred and forty-four A. D. [34 + 1810 = 1844].

" Unto two thousand and three hundred days [years]; then shall the sanctuary be cleansed." [5] The earthly sanctuary ceased to exist long before this date; but the time had come for the antitype of the cleansing of the sanctuary, the work performed on the day of atonement in the earthly sanctuary, to begin in the

[1] John 1:41; Luke 3:21, 22; Acts 10:38, margin.   [2] Dan. 9:27.
[3] Heb. 2:2, 3.   [4] Acts 8:1-4.   [5] Dan. 8:14.

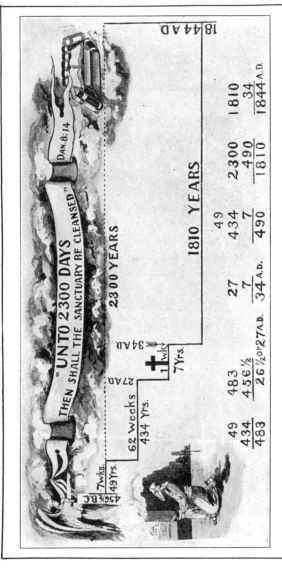

NOTE:— The twenty-three hundred days, or years, of Dan. 8:14 is the longest line of prophecy in the Bible with definite dates, marking the beginning and close. It locates four very important events: 1st, the baptism of Christ; 2nd, the crucifixion of Christ; 3rd, the gospel going to the Gentiles; 4th, the opening of the investigative judgment in heaven. The crucifixion of Christ in the midst of the seventieth week "sealed the vision," and established the other dates.

heavenly sanctuary. In 1844 the great Court from which there is no appeal convened in the most holy place of the heavenly sanctuary.

This wonderful prophecy of two thousand three hundred years began with the restoration of God's people to their earthly possessions, and the rebuilding of the holy city Jerusalem; but again the Jews proved unfaithful to their trust, and the land of promise with the holy city passed from their control into the hands of the heathen.

The coming of Christ and His death on Calvary, like a great seal, fixes definitely the entire prophecy, and insures the inheritance of the earth to the faithful; and the judgment which opened at the close of that wonderful period of prophetic time will give to the faithful a " court title " to the eternal inheritance and the city of God, the New Jerusalem.

**Events definitely located by the two thousand
three hundred years**

Baptism of Christ. Dan.9: 25 ; John 1 : 41, margin; Luke 3 : 21.
Death of Christ. Dan. 9 : 26, 27.
Anointing the heavenly sanctuary. Dan. 9 : 24.
Gospel going to the Gentiles. Dan. 9 : 27; Heb. 2 : 3 ; Acts 8 :4.
Opening of the investigative judgment. Dan. 8 : 14.

SECTION VII

The Autumnal Annual Feasts

The Sprinkled Blood

THE sprinkled blood is speaking
　　Before the Father's throne,
The Spirit's power is seeking
　　To make its virtues known;
The sprinkled blood is telling
　　Jehovah's love to man,
While heavenly harps are swelling
　　Sweet notes to mercy's plan.

The sprinkled blood is speaking
　　Forgiveness full and free,
Its wondrous power is breaking
　　Each bond of guilt for me;
The sprinkled blood's revealing
　　A Father's smiling face,
The Saviour's love is sealing
　　Each monument of grace.

The sprinkled blood is pleading
　　Its virtue as my own,
And there my soul is reading
　　Her title to Thy throne.
The sprinkled blood is owning
　　The weak one's feeblest plea;
'Mid sighs, and tears, and groaning,
　　It pleads, O Lord, with Thee.

— Anon.

CHAPTER XXVIII

THE FEAST OF TRUMPETS

HE trumpet was not only used as a musical instrument among the ancient Israelites, but it also filled an important place in their religious and civil ceremonies. It was associated with the entire life of the children of Israel. It was used on their joyful days and on their solemn days; and at the beginning of every month it was sounded over their burnt-offerings and their peace-offerings. It was to be a reminder to the Israelites of the Lord their God. [1]

In obedience to the command of God, Moses made two silver trumpets to be used in calling their assemblies and in regulating the journeyings of the children of Israel. [2] When the priests blew both the trumpets, all the people were to assemble at the

Num. 10:10.   [2] Num. 10:2.

door of the tabernacle; if one trumpet sounded, only the princes responded. [1]

The call for summoning to the religious assemblies was different from the sound of an alarm, which was blown to gather the army for war. God promised that when they blew the alarm for war, they should " be remembered before the Lord," and should be saved from their enemies. [2]

In the time of Solomon, great skill was shown in the blowing of trumpets, so that the notes from one hundred and twenty trumpets came forth as " one sound." [3]

When God wished to gather the hosts of Israel at the base of Mt. Sinai to listen to the proclamation of His holy law, from the midst of the glory of the Lord that covered the mountain, " the voice of the trumpet exceeding loud " was heard, and the people trembled; and as the " voice of the trumpet sounded long, and waxed louder and louder," even Moses, that holy man of God, said, " I exceedingly fear and quake." [4]

God designed that every blast of the trumpet blown by His people, whether for joy or for sorrow, for worship or for war, should be a memorial, or reminder, of the power of God to comfort, sustain, and protect His people; "that they may be to you," He said, " for a *memorial* before your God: I am the Lord your God." [5]

Every child of God having full faith in the promises, who went forward and blew the trumpets *in obedience to God's command,* beheld the deliverance of the Lord, whether confronted by obstacles as high as the walls of Jericho, [6] or by enemies as numerous as the hosts of Midian. [7]

While the sound of the trumpet was often heard by the children of Israel, yet there was one day in each year especially set aside for the purpose of blowing the trumpets. Of this day

[1] Num. 10: 2-8.   [2] Num. 10: 9.   [3] 2 Chron. 5: 12, 13.
[4] Ex. 19: 16, 19; Heb. 12: 21.   [5] Num. 10: 10.   [6] Joshua 6: 4, 5.   [7] Judges 7: 19-23.

the Lord said: " In the seventh month, on the first day of the
month, ye shall have a holy convocation; ye shall do no servile
work: *it is a day of blowing the trumpets unto you.*" [1]

Each month of the year was ushered in with the sound of the
trumpet, [2] and eleven sacrifices were offered; but on the first day
of the seventh month, in addition to the eleven offerings slain the

"The blast of the rams' horns before the walls of Jericho."

first of each month, ten other sacrifices were offered. [3]   The
day was kept as a ceremonial or annual sabbath, and was one of
the seven days of holy convocation connected with the annual
feasts. [4]

[1] Num. 29:1.   [2] Num. 10:10.
[3] Num. 28:11-15; 29:1-6.   [4] Lev. 23:24.

This Feast of Trumpets was "a memorial." Some have thought it to be a memorial of the creation of the world, as it was celebrated at "the year's end, or revolution of the year," [1] and might have been a memorial of the time when "all the sons of God shouted for joy" at the creation of the world. [2] Dr. William Smith says: "The Feast of Trumpets . . . came to be regarded as the anniversary of the birthday of the world."

It is quite evident that, like the Passover, the Feast of Trumpets was both commemorative and typical. It came ten days before the day of atonement, the type of the great investigative judgment which opened in 1844, at the end of the long prophetic period of the twenty-three hundred years of Dan. 8: 14.

In the type the trumpets were blown throughout Israel, warning all of the near approach of the solemn day of atonement. In the antitype we should expect some world-wide message to be given in trumpet tones, announcing the time near when the great antitypical day of atonement, the investigative judgment, would convene in the heavens. [3] Beginning with the years 1833-34 and extending down to 1844, such a message was given to the world in trumpet tones, announcing, "The hour of His judgment is come." [4]

William Miller and others, in their study of the declaration in Dan. 8: 14, "Unto two thousand and three hundred days; then shall the sanctuary be cleansed," found that this long prophetic period would end in 1844. They failed to connect this text with the ancient typical sanctuary, but applied the term "sanctuary" to this earth, and taught that in 1844 Christ would come to the earth to cleanse it and judge the people.

William Miller was joined by hundreds of other ministers in America, who proclaimed this message with great power. Edward Irving, with many other consecrated men, preached the

[1] Ex. 34: 22, margin.   [2] Job 38: 4-7.
[3] Dan. 7: 9, 10.   [4] Rev. 14: 6, 7.

same in England; while Joseph Wolff and others heralded it in Asia and other portions of the world.

During the ten years preceding the tenth day of the seventh month (Jewish time) in 1844, every civilized nation on the earth heard in trumpet tones the announcement of the message of Rev. 14: 6, 7, " The hour of His judgment is come." This message was due at this period of the world's history. Paul in his day

" Blessed be the king that cometh in the name of the Lord."

preached of a " judgment *to come*," [1] but the burden of the message given during these years was, " the hour of His judgment *is come*."

The fact that the men who proclaimed this message misunder-

[1] Acts 24 : 25.

stood the full import of it, did not prevent their fulfilling the antitype of the ancient type. When the followers of Christ cried before Him, " Blessed be the King that cometh in the name of the Lord," [1] and spread palm branches in the way, believing that Jesus was entering Jerusalem to take the earthly kingdom, they fulfilled the prophecy of Zech. 9 : 9. If they had known that in a few days their Lord would hang upon the accursed tree, [2] they could not have fulfilled the prophecy; for it would have been impossible for them to " rejoice greatly."

In like manner the message due to the world between 1834 and 1844 could never have been given with the power and joyfulness demanded to fulfil the antitype, if those giving it had understood that the Saviour, instead of coming to this earth, was to enter the most holy apartment of the heavenly sanctuary, and begin the work of the investigative judgment.

God hid from their eyes the fact that there were two other messages to be given to the world before the Lord should come to the earth in power and glory; [3] that He could not come until they had fulfilled the antitype. Then to comfort them in their disappointment, He allowed them by faith to look within the heavenly sanctuary, [4] and catch a glimpse of the work of their great High Priest officiating for them.

The prophet Joel evidently connected the closing work of the gospel on earth with the blowing of the trumpets, for he writes as follows: " *Blow ye the trumpet in Zion,* and sound an alarm in My holy mountain : let all the inhabitants of the land tremble : for *the day of the Lord cometh, for it is nigh at hand.*" [5]

The sound of trumpets was heard many times in the past, from the trumpet of the Lord's host upon Mt. Sinai, when the whole earth shook, [6] to the blast of the rams' horns before the walls of Jericho.

[1] Luke 19 : 35-40.	[2] Gal. 3 : 13.	[3] Rev. 14 : 6-14.
[4] Rev. 11 : 19.	[5] Joel 2 : 1.	[6] Heb. 12 : 26.

The time is coming when the trumpet of the Lord will again be heard by mortals, when its notes will "shake not the earth only, but also heaven."[1] The clear notes of that trumpet will penetrate the deepest recesses of the earth; and, just as anciently the trumpet summoned all Israel to appear before the Lord, so every child of God sleeping in the earth will answer the trumpet call, and come forth to meet his Lord. In old ocean's caverns the clarion tones will be heard, and the sea, obedient to the call, will give up the dead that are in it.[2] The whole earth will resound with the tread of the innumerable company of the redeemed, as the living and the resurrected saints gather to meet their Lord in answer to the welcome summons of the last trumpet call that will be given on

e that dwelleth in the secret place of the most High shall abide under the shadow of the Almighty.

PS. 91:1

this sin cursed earth.[3]

Then all the discordant notes will forever cease, and the redeemed will hear the Saviour say, " Come, ye blessed of My Father, inherit the kingdom prepared for you from the foundation of the world."[4]

In the ancient typical service, as the people of God met for worship at the beginning of each month and upon the Sabbath, in obedience to the clear notes of the silver trumpets; in like manner we can imagine that when the earth is made new, and " from one *new moon* to another and from *one Sabbath* to another "[5]

---

[1] Heb. 12 : 26. [2] Rev. 20 : 13.
[3] I Cor. 15 : 51, 52; I Thess. 4 : 16, 17. [4] Matt. 25 : 34. [5] Isa. 66 : 22, 23.

the redeemed assemble to worship before the Lord, it will be in response to the notes of the heavenly trumpets, of which those used in the ancient service were a type.

TYPE   ANTITYPE

Lev. 23 : 24-27. Trumpets blown, announcing that the day of atonement was drawing near.

Rev. 14 : 6, 7. The first angel's message announced that the real day of atonement, the judgment, was at hand.

Num. 28 : 11-15. Many sacrifices were made at the Feast of Trumpets.

Heb. 10 : 32-37. Those who proclaimed the first angel's message sacrificed much; they "took joyfully the spoiling" of their goods.

Num. 10 : 3-10. The sound of the trumpet assembled Israel to appear before the Lord.

1 Cor. 15 : 51-53. The trumpet of God will summon the saints to meet the Lord when He appears.

CHAPTER XXIX

THE DAY OF ATONEMENT,
OR
THE WORK IN THE SECOND APARTMENT

THE tenth day of the seventh month was the day of atonement. [1] It was regarded as more sacred than any other day in the yearly round of service. It was a ceremonial sabbath and a fast day. [2] The Israelite who did not afflict his soul upon that day was cut off from among the people. [3] So sacred is the day regarded, even at the present time, that although the Jews have rejected Christ and few have any regard for the Sabbath, yet when the tenth day of the seventh month comes, no Jew will do any business or work upon that day, however wicked he may be.

There were several sacrifices offered upon the day of atone-

[1] Lev. 23:27.   [2] Lev. 23:30.   [3] Lev. 23:28-30.

ment. Before he entered upon the regular work of the day, the high priest offered a bullock for himself and his house. [1]

The chief service of the day was the offering of the goats. Two goats were brought to the door of the sanctuary, where lots were cast upon them, one for the Lord, the other for the scape-goat, or Azazel. [2] The high priest killed the Lord's goat, and then, clad in his gorgeous robes, with the breastplate of judgment bearing the names of the twelve tribes of Israel over his heart, and the sacred onyx stones with the names of the tribes on his shoulders, he passed with the blood of the goat into the most holy place. Just as he entered within the second veil, carrying the golden censer filled with coals of fire from the altar before the Lord, and his hand full of incense, he placed the incense upon the coals in the censer, that the cloud of fragrant incense might cover him as he passed in before the visible presence of God, as manifested between the cherubim above the mercy-seat. With his fingers he sprinkled the blood upon the mercy-seat above the broken law of God. Then going out into the first apartment, he touched the horns of the golden altar with the blood. [3]

When he had " made an end of reconciling the holy place, and the tabernacle of the congregation, and the altar," he went out into the court. In type the high priest now bore in his person all the sins of the children of Israel which had been confessed and transferred to the sanctuary. He then laid his hands upon the head of the scapegoat, and confessed " over him all the iniquities of the children of Israel, and all their transgressions in all their sins, putting them upon the head of the goat," and the goat was sent away, " by the hand of a fit man into the wilderness." The goat bore upon him all the iniquities unto a land " not inhabited," a " land of separation." [4]

[1] Lev. 16:6-14.
[3] Lev. 16:15-19.
[2] Lev. 16:8, margin.
[4] Lev. 16:20-22, margin.

Going back into the tabernacle of the congregation, the high priest laid aside his gorgeous priestly robes, and put on his other garments;[1] then coming again into the court, he cleansed the court from its defilement of sin. The bodies of the animals whose blood had been taken within the sanctuary, were carried out of the camp and burned. When the sun set on the day of atonement, the sins were all gone into the "land of separation," and nothing

"The goat was sent away, by the hand of a fit man into the wilderness."

but ashes remained as a reminder of them.[2]

Thus was carried on the type of that heavenly work which is to decide the eternal destiny of every soul that has ever lived upon the earth. In type and shadow the confessed sins of Israel had been transferred to the sanctuary during all the year; the cleansing of the sanctuary was the removing of those sins. "It was therefore necessary that the patterns of things in the heavens should be purified with these [the blood of animals]; but the heavenly things themselves with better sacrifices than these."[3]

Every sin is marked before the Lord in heaven.[4] When sins are confessed and forgiven, they are covered.[5] This was typified by their being transferred to the sanctuary, where no human eyes except those of the priest ever beheld the stains of the blood of the

[1] Lev. 16:23. [2] Lev. 16:24-28.
[3] Heb. 9:23. [4] Jer. 2:22. [5] Ps. 32:1.

14

sin-offering upon the horns of the golden altar before the veil.

It could not be possible that the books of heaven will always hold the records of sin, or that Christ will always bear the sins of the world. As the typical work was performed at the close of the year, so the cleansing of the heavenly sanctuary will take place near the end of Christ's priestly work. The cleansing of the heavenly sanctuary necessitates an examination of the records— an investigative judgment.

The earthly sanctuary was cleansed on the tenth day of the seventh month of each year; the heavenly will be cleansed once for all. This work was begun in 1844 A. D., at the end of the prophetic period of the two thousand three hundred days.[1] In the typical service the Lord went into the holy of holies on the day of atonement, for He promised that His presence would be there.[2] The high priest made special preparation for entering upon the service of the day of atonement. [3]

The prophet Daniel was given a view of the antitypical work in the heavenly sanctuary. He describes it thus:

" I beheld till the thrones were cast down, and the Ancient of days did sit, whose garment was white as snow, and the hair of His head like the pure wool: His throne was like the fiery flame, and His wheels as burning fire. A fiery stream issued and came forth from before Him: thousand thousands ministered unto Him, and ten thousand times ten thousand stood before Him: the judgment was set, and the books were opened." [4]

The Bible was written in an oriental country, and the custom there is to " cast down " seats for guests. The Revised Version of the Bible renders it, " I beheld till the thrones were placed." The position of the Father's throne was changed. Daniel beheld the thrones cast down, or placed, their position being changed; then the Ancient of days, the Father, took His seat upon the

[1] Dan. 8 : 14.
[2] Lev. 16 : 2.
[3] Lev. 16 : 4-6.
[4] Dan. 7 : 9, 10.

throne. In other words, Daniel beheld t h e Father's throne changed from the first apartment of the heavenly sanctuary to the second. His attention was attracted by the great wheels which looked like burning fire as they moved beneath the glorious throne of the infinite God. [1] Myriads of the heavenly host were gathered to witness the grand scene. Thousand thousands ministered unto Jehovah as He took His seat upon the throne to judge the world.

No mirror ever portrayed the features of the face as accurately as the books of heaven have portrayed the life record of each individual. All are " judged out of those things which were written in the books, according to their works." [2]

Behold the scene. The Father is seated on the throne of judgment. The angels, who have been " ministering spirits " to those whose cases are to come in review before God, stand ready to obey commands. The books are opened. But there is something lacking yet. Daniel's attention is now attracted to the " clouds of heaven " — myriads of angels — bearing the Saviour in before the Father in triumph. [3] Earthly soldiers have often borne in triumph on their shoulders commanders who have led them to grand victories on fields of blood and carnage. Christ, the Archangel, the Commander of the hosts of heaven, has led the angels in many a battle. They fought under Him when the arch-enemy of all righteousness was cast out of heaven. They beheld their Commander 'die an ignominious death to redeem the lost race. They have sped quickly at His command to save many a soul from being overcome by Satan. The time has now come when Christ is to receive His kingdom, and claim His subjects; and the angels love to bear their mighty Commander in triumph before the judgment-seat, where, as the books reveal one life record after another, Christ confesses the name of every overcomer

[1] Eze. 10 : 1-22.   [2] Rev. 20 : 12.   [3] Dan. 7 : 13, 14.

before the Father and before the innumerable company of angels. [1]

God's throne is a movable structure. As in the type His visible presence was manifested in the outer apartment of the earthly sanctuary, so in heaven the throne of God was in the first apartment when Christ ascended and sat at the right hand of His Father. But Daniel saw not only the Father and Christ change their position, but the position of the thrones also was changed, when the "judgment was set, and the books were opened." Type had met antitype. The High Priest in the heavenly sanctuary entered the most holy place, and as in the type God promised to meet the high priest in the most holy, so the Father passed into the holy of holies before the High Priest, and was there when the angels bore Christ triumphantly in before Him.

The earthly high priest bore the names of Israel on his person as he entered the most holy place; [2] but lest some fainting soul might fear he would be forgotten, our High Priest sends down the words, " Can a woman forget her sucking child, that she should not have compassion on the son of her womb? yea, they may forget, *yet will I not forget thee."* And then as if to make assurance doubly sure, He lifts His hands bearing the print of the cruel nails, and says, " Behold [look], I have graven *thee* upon the palms of My hands; *thy walls are continually before Me."* [3]

The earthly high priest presented blood to atone for the sins of the people; our High Priest pleads His own blood. " Father, *My blood, My blood, My blood."* The earthly high priest carried the censer with the fragrant incense; Christ presents the fragrant righteousness of His own character, which He imputes to every one whose sins are all confessed and covered with His blood when their names come up in review before the great Judge.

[1] Rev. 3 : 5.   [2] Ex. 39 : 6-17.   [3] Isa. 49 : 15, 16.

In the earthly sanctuary the high priest paused in the first apartment to touch the horns of the golden altar and cleanse it from all sins that had been transferred to it;[1] for while the services of the day of atonement were going forward, if one remembered unconfessed sins, he could still bring his sin-offering and be forgiven.[2] So while our High Priest officiates before the Father in the investigative judgment, any one who realizes he is a sinner can come confessing his sins and be forgiven through the merits of Christ, the great Sin-bearer.

Our High Priest, when His work is finished in the inner apartment of the heavenly sanctuary, will tarry a moment in the outer apartment, that the sins which have been confessed while He was in the most holy place may be taken, together with the sins of the righteous of all ages, and carried forth without the sanctuary.

Behold I have graven thee upon the palms of My hands.
ISA. 49:16

While Jesus pleads as our High Priest, there is hope for every repentant sinner; but when He at last comes forth from the sanctuary, mercy's door will be forever closed. There will be no intercessor then.[3] In the type, when the high priest came out of the sanctuary, he had "made an end of reconciling." When our High Priest comes forth from the sanctuary, He will proclaim, "He that is unjust, let him be unjust still: and he which is filthy, let him be filthy still: and he that is righteous, let him be righteous still: and he that is holy, let him be holy still."[4] Every

[1] Lev. 16:18, 19.
[2] Num. 29:7-11.
[3] Isa. 59:16.
[4] Rev. 22:11.

"While Jesus pleads as our High Priest, there is hope for every repentant sinner."

case is decided for eternity. Probation is forever ended. All who wait until that time, hoping to be saved, will find no one to plead their case before the Father; they will be eternally lost.

In the type, after the high priest had finished the work within the sanctuary on the day of atonement, he came forth bearing the sins of all Israel, and placed them upon the head of the scapegoat. The scapegoat had no part in reconciling the people to God. The work of reconciling was all ended [1] when the scapegoat was brought forward to act his part in the service. The only work of the scapegoat is to act as a vehicle to carry the sins of the righteous into the "land of separation."

The term "scapegoat" has become a synonym of an evil one. Azazel, the Hebrew rendering of scapegoat, is a proper name,

[1] Lev. 16:20.

and is understood to represent the devil. When our High Priest has finished His work in the heavenly sanctuary, He will place all the sins of the righteous, which He has borne thus far, upon the head of Satan, [1] the instigator of sin. Satan will then be left upon the desolate earth, [2] a land not inhabited, for one thousand years, at the end of which time he will be burned to ashes in the fires of the last day. [3]

In the type, after the high priest had placed the sins of Israel upon the head of the scapegoat, he left the robes worn while officiating as high priest in the sanctuary, and put on other garments, and began a work in the court. He had the bodies of the animals whose blood had been carried into the sanctuary taken without the camp and burned. At the close of the day, ashes were the only thing to be seen of the sin-offerings.

Our High Priest lays aside His priestly garments, and clad as King of kings He rides forth a mighty Conqueror to " gather out of His kingdom all things that offend, and them which do iniquity; and shall cast them into a furnace of fire." [4] Christ comes to set in order the antitypical court — this earth; and when the great antitypical day of atonement ends, nothing will remain that will in any way be a reminder of sin, except the ashes under the feet of the righteous. [5]

The word " atonement " means at-one-ment; and when Christ pronounces the decree which determines the eternal destiny of every soul, He and the subjects of His kingdom are at-one-ment. Sin will never again separate Christ from His people.

But the territory of His kingdom is still cursed by sin, so the at-one-ment of Christ and His kingdom will not be complete in every sense of the term until from the fires of the last day there comes forth a new earth with every mark of the curse removed. Then not only the subjects of Christ's kingdom, but the entire

[1] Ps. 7 : 16.   [2] Jer. 4 : 23-27 ; Zech. 1 : 2, 3.
[3] Mal. 4 : 1-3 ; Rev. 20 : 9, 10 ; Eze. 28 : 18, 19.   [4] Matt. 13 : 41, 42.   [5] Mal. 4 : 3.

earth, will be at-one-ment with Christ and the Father. [1] Sin will never again arise to mar the earth; but it will be the home of the redeemed forever.

TYPE   ANTITYPE

Lev. 16 : 29, 30. On the tenth day of the seventh month the sanctuary was cleansed.

Dan. 8 : 14. " Unto two thousand and t h r e e hundred days; then shall the sanctuary be cleansed."

Lev. 16 : 15-19. The sanctuary was cleansed, and sins removed by the blood of the Lord's goat, at the end of the year's service.

Acts 3 : 19, 20. Sins will be blotted from the heavenly records near the end of Christ's work as high priest.

Lev. 16 : 2. God's presence was in the most holy place on the day of atonement.

Dan. 7 : 9, 10. The Father enters the most holy place of the heavenly sanctuary before the opening of the judgment.

Lev. 16 : 4-6. The high priest made special preparation to enter the most holy apartment.

Dan. 7 : 13, 14. Christ is borne into the most holy apartment by the angels of heaven.

Ex. 28 : 9-21. The high priest bore the names of Israel over his heart and on his shoulders when he entered the most holy place.

Rev. 3 : 5. Christ knows each name, and confesses the names of the overcomers before the Father and the angels.

[1] Isa. 62 : 4.

Lev. 16 : 20. When the high priest came out of the sanctuary, he had " made an end of reconciling."

Rev. 22 : 11, 12. When Christ comes out from the heavenly sanctuary, He announces the eternal destiny of every soul.

Lev. 16 : 21. The sins were all laid upon the scapegoat.

Ps. 7 : 16. Sin will return upon the head of the originator of sin.

Lev. 16 : 22. The goat shall bear the sins into a land not inhabited, a land of separation.

Rev. 20 : 1-3. Satan will be left on the desolate earth for one thousand years.

Lev. 16 : 23. The high priest left the robe he wore while officiating in the most holy place in the sanctuary, and put on other garments.

Rev. 19 : 11-16. Christ lays aside His priestly robes, and comes to the earth as King of kings and Lord of lords.

Lev. 16 : 27. The bodies of the sacrifices were taken without the camp and burned, and nothing but ashes remained as a reminder of sin.

Matt. 13 : 41-43; Mal. 4 : 1-3. Christ will " gather out of His kingdom all things that offend, and them which do iniquity," and they will be burned in the fires of the last day. Only ashes will remain.

CHAPTER XXX

DUTY OF THE CONGREGATION ON THE DAY OF ATONEMENT

 OD expected His ancient people to serve Him faithfully every day in the year, and He accepted their services; but when the day of atonement came, there were special requirements enjoined upon them *during that day,* which, if they failed to observe, they were cut off from the people of Israel.

God has accepted the service of His people down through the ages; but when the antitypical day of atonement arrived, and the investigative judgment opened in the heavenly sanctuary, God expects the antitypical congregation on earth to fulfil their part of the antitype just as faithfully as Christ, our High Priest, fulfills His part in the heavens.

Anciently the congregation was not accepted as a whole; but it was an individual work. [1] So to-day each one answers for himself before God. We must not content ourselves by doing just as our fathers did, who passed away before the judgment opened in the courts of heaven. God requires special service of His people *now*. They are to live while their cases are being decided in heaven, and Satan brings to bear upon the last generation, which are weaker physically than any previous generation, all the wisdom he has gained in a six thousand years' warfare. Those who, in the investigative judgment, are accounted worthy, will live for a time without a Mediator. Their experience will be different from that of any other company that has ever lived upon the earth. There are many reasons why God in His infinite mercy has enjoined special duties upon the last generation, that they might be more strongly fortified against the attacks of the enemy, and not be overthrown by his devices.

In the ancient service, if an individual failed to keep the day of atonement as God directed, his sins were not confessed over the scapegoat by the high priest; but he was cut off from among the people of God. [2] The individual who, during the antitypical day of atonement, or the investigative judgment, thinks that Christ will plead his case while he himself ignores the work God has enjoined upon the antitypical congregation, will find at last that his name is blotted out from the book of life. We are saved by faith in our High Priest, but faith without works is dead. [3] If we have a living faith, we shall gladly do as the Lord directs.

Four things were required of each individual member of ancient Israel on the day of atonement — the twenty-four-

[1] Lev. 23 : 29, 30.   [2] Lev. 23 : 28-30.   [3] James 2 : 17.

hour period in which the typical work of atonement was performed, and which was "an example and shadow" of the real work.

1. "The day of atonement . . . shall be a holy convocation unto you." 2. "Ye shall afflict your souls." 3. "Offer an offering made by fire unto the Lord." 4. "Ye shall do no work in that same day." [1]

That day was to be a holy convocation. The people were to assemble for religious worship. Paul speaks thus of individuals who, in the days when the High Priest should soon come forth from the heavenly sanctuary, would forsake the religious assembly: "Having a High Priest over the house of God; let us draw near with a true heart, in full assurance of faith, having our hearts sprinkled from an evil conscience. . . . Not forsaking the assembling of ourselves together, *as the manner of some is;* but exhorting one another: and so much the more *as ye see the day approaching.*" [2]

The one that takes no pleasure in meeting with those of like faith to worship God, has an "evil conscience," and has lost faith in the near coming of our High Priest from the heavenly sanctuary. There is a special blessing in worshiping with others. God promises that where even two or three are gathered in His name, He will meet with them. [3] This first requirement is a spiritual thermometer by which every Christian can test his spiritual condition. If he absents himself from the worship of God because he takes no pleasure in it, his spirituality is very low.

Each individual was to "afflict" his soul — search his heart, and put away every sin, spend much time in prayer. With this was connected abstinence from food. This was so forcibly impressed upon the minds of ancient Israel that even at the

[1] Lev. 23 : 27, 28.   [2] Heb. 10 : 21-25.   [3] Matt. 18 : 20.

present day, the Jews fast upon the tenth day of the seventh month.

The individual who realizes that the judgment is going on in the heavenly sanctuary, and that his name will surely be presented before that great tribunal, will search his heart and pray earnestly that God will accept him. We need often to meditate upon the work of our High Priest in the heavenly sanctuary, lest

The blood of Christ alone can atone for sin.

by having the mind filled with earthly thoughts, we, like the foolish virgins, will find when too late that the bridegroom has come, the door is shut; that the work is finished, and we have no part in it.

In the typical service the congregation in the court listened for the tinkling of the golden bells on the robes of the high priest, and in that way followed him in his work. Our High Priest has given signs in the heavens, in the earth, and among the nations to mark the progress of His work; and he said that when we see these signs fulfilled we are to know that He is near, even at the door. [1]

The antitypical day of atonement covers a period of years. In the type there was a fast of twenty-four hours required. During this one day there was to be *complete* control of the appetite; and it was a type of the self-control to be exercised during

[1] Luke 21 : 25-33 ; Matt. 24 : 29-35, margin.

the antitypical period of years. God designs that His people shall be masters of their appetites, and keep under the body.[1] Satan would give loose rein to the appetite, and let it control the person.

In spite of the fact that an army of faithful workers are doing all in their power to withstand the flood of intemperance, Satan is working with such power that drunkenness and crime are increasing in the earth at an alarming rate. Back in 1844, when the investigative judgment opened in heaven, only men and a few women were slaves to tobacco; but now thousands of children are being destroyed by it, and many women are addicted to the filthy habit. Wineries and breweries are increasing in the land, and intoxicating beverages are served in thousands of homes.

God calls upon His people to be *masters* of their appetites instead of *slaves* to it, that they may have clearer minds to comprehend divine truth and follow the work of their High Priest in the heavenly sanctuary.

How few are willing to deny themselves the things their appetite craves, even when they know the claims of God! The prophet Isaiah, looking down through the ages, describes the state of things as follows: " In that day did the Lord God of hosts call to weeping, and to mourning, and to baldness, and to girding with sackcloth: and behold, joy and gladness, slaying oxen, and killing sheep, eating flesh and drinking wine." [2] What a vivid picture of the present condition of the world! God calls upon His people to afflict their souls, to control their appetite, to partake of food that will give good blood and a clear mind to discern spiritual truths; but instead of obeying, they engage in " eating flesh and drinking wine." The prophet records the final result of this course: " It was revealed in mine ears by the Lord

[1] 1 Cor. 9:27.   [2] Isa. 22:12, 13.

of hosts, Surely this iniquity shall not be purged from you till ye die." [1]

The Saviour gave special warning against the evil of giving loose rein to the appetite during the time when the records of human lives are being examined and individuals are being *accounted* worthy or unworthy of eternal life: "Take heed to yourselves, lest at any time your hearts be overcharged with *surfeiting,* and *drunkenness,* and cares of this life, and so *that day come upon you unawares.* . . . Watch ye therefore, and pray always that ye may be *accounted worthy* to escape all these things that shall

"How few are willing to deny themselves the things their appetite craves, even when they know the claims of God!"

come to pass, and to stand before the Son of man." [2] The warning is against "surfeiting"— overeating, and "drunkenness"— eating injurious food. In other words, the Saviour designs that His people, during the antitypical day of atonement, shall take heed to both the *quantity* and the *quality* of their food. One can becloud the mind and ruin the health by overeating of the best of food. The glutton and the drunkard are classed together: "Be

[1] Isa. 22:14.   [2] Luke 21:34-36.

not among winebibbers; among riotous eaters of flesh; for the drunkard and the glutton shall come to poverty." [1]

Our first parents failed on the test of appetite; [2] but where they failed, Christ triumphed. [3] And it is possible for a Christian, with the indwelling Christ in the heart, to be complete master of his appetite,— to abstain from all food that is injurious, however much the natural appetite may crave it, and not to overeat of good food.

As He entered upon His earthly ministry, the Saviour was not only tested upon the point of appetite, but from childhood He was taught to control His desires. In speaking of His childhood, Isaiah says, " Butter and honey shall He eat, *that He may know to refuse the evil, and choose the good.*" [4] His manner of eating developed in Him spiritual power to discern between good and evil. Many who have gone into drunkards' graves have eaten " butter and honey," but Jesus ate it in a way to develop spiritual strength. He ate it according to the Bible rule. There are three texts which, taken together, contain a rule for eating honey, and the same rule will apply to all food that is good. They read as follows: " My son, eat thou honey, *because it is good.*" [5] " Hast thou found honey? *eat so much as is sufficient for thee.*" [6] " *It is not good to eat much honey.*" [7] The one who follows the above instruction, and eats none but *good* food and only *" so much as is sufficient,"* will enjoy good health and a clear mind. God wishes His people to have good health, with souls free from condemnation. [8] Satan delights in beclouding the brain and destroying the health. All who will fulfil the antitype will be masters of their appetites, that they may prepare to meet the Saviour when He comes to the earth as King of kings and Lord of lords.

The third requirement enjoined upon the typical congregation on the day of atonement was to " offer an offering made by

[1] Prov. 23:20, 21. [2] Gen. 3:1-6. [3] Matt. 4:3, 4.
[4] Isa. 7:14, 15. [5] Prov. 24:13. [6] Prov. 25:16.
[7] Prov. 25:27. [8] 3 John 2.

fire unto the Lord." The offerings made by fire were consumed upon the altar. In the antitype we do not offer burnt-offerings of bullocks and rams; but God expects us to fulfil the antitype of the offering consumed upon the altar. He desires that the "whole spirit and soul and body be preserved blameless unto the coming of our Lord Jesus Christ;"[1] that the entire life of the

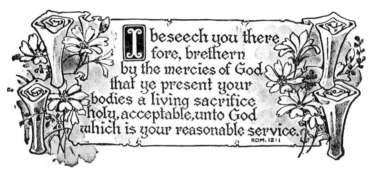

I beseech you therefore, brethren by the mercies of God, that ye present your bodies a living sacrifice holy, acceptable, unto God which is your reasonable service. ROM. 12:1

Christian be laid upon the altar, ready to be used as the Lord directs. None can do this who do not daily accept Christ as their sin-offering, and know what it is to be "accepted in the Beloved."

The day of atonement was kept as a ceremonial sabbath by the ancient congregation.[2] All work was laid aside, and the entire thought was given to seeking God and serving Him. God's work was given the *first* thought during the entire day. Such was the type; but it does not follow that on the antitypical day of atonement no one should attend to personal business, for God never intended His people to be "slothful in business."[3] He promises to bless them in temporal things if they fulfil the antitype by looking after His work and service first, and their temporal interests second.[4] This was beautifully taught by the Saviour's words: "Take heed to yourselves, lest at any time your

[1] 1 Thess. 5 : 23.
[2] Lev. 23 : 31.
[3] Rom. 12 : 11.
[4] Matt. 6 : 31-33.

15

hearts be overcharged with . . . *cares of this life,* and so that day come upon you unawares." [1]

Satan is liable to entrap more well-meaning people in this snare than in any other of his many deceptions. He often persuades good people that the daily cares of the household are so important that they have no time to study God's word and pray, until, for lack of spiritual food and communion with God, they become so weak spiritually that they accept the doubts and unbelief the enemy is constantly presenting. When the time comes that they think they do have time to study their Bibles, they find they have lost all relish for God's word.

God is testing the great antitypical congregation. Who will fulfil the antitype, and not forsake the assembly of God's people? Who will keep a clear mind by controlling the appetite, and a pure heart by prayer and deep heart-searching? Who will lay all their interests upon God's altar, to be used for His glory, and never let the " cares of this life " crowd out God's work or a study of His word? Over such as these our High Priest will say, " He that is righteous, let him be righteous still: and he that is holy, let him be holy still." [2]

TYPE	ANTITYPE
Lev. 23 : 27. " It shall be a holy convocation unto you." All were to assemble for worship.	Heb. 10 : 25. God's p e o p l e should not forsake assembling together as the end draws near.

[1] Luke 21 : 34.   [2] Rev. 22 : 11.

Lev. 23: 27, 29. In the type, all were to afflict the soul, spend the day in " prayer, fasting, and deep searching of heart."

Luke 21 : 34-36; Isa. 22 : 12-14. The admonition is, " Watch, . . . and pray always," and avoid surfeiting and drunkenness.

Lev. 23 : 27. " Offer an offering made by fire," an entire consecration.

1 Thess. 5 : 23; Rom. 12 : 1. The whole spirit, and soul, and body are to be fully consecrated to God.

Lev. 23 : 30. All personal work was to be laid aside on the day of atonement.

Luke 21 : 34-36; Matt. 6: 32, 33. The cares of this life are not to come in and crowd out God's work.

Blessed be the Lord who daily loadeth us with benefits, even the God of our salvation. Selah. Ps. 68:19

CHAPTER XXXI

THE NATURE OF THE JUDGMENT

HE judgment is spoken of by every Bible writer. It is mentioned over a thousand times in the Sacred Writings. It is more solemn than death; for death separates friends only until the resurrection, but the judgment separates them forever. No one can escape it. To ignore the thought of the judgment and live without preparing for it, will not evade it. Solomon recognized this fact when he wrote, " Rejoice, O young man, in thy youth, and let thy heart cheer thee in the days of thy youth, and walk in the ways of thine heart, and in the sight of thine eyes: but *know thou, that for all these things God will bring thee into judgment.*" [1]

The decisions of earthly courts may often be changed by money and friends, and the guilty may be released; but not so in

[1] Eccl. 11:9.

(230)

the heavenly court. There every one must meet the record of his own life. " Every one . . . shall give account of himself to God." [1] Earthly parents have been known to sacrifice everything they possessed to save ONE child from the condemnation of earthly courts. Think you our heavenly Father would let Satan destroy all His earthly children without an effort to save them? He risked all heaven for their sakes. " God so loved the world, that He gave His only begotten Son, that whosoever believeth in

Rejoice, O young man, in thy youth; and let thy heart cheer thee in the days of thy youth, and walk in the ways of thine heart, and in the sight of thine eyes, but know thou that for all these things God will bring thee into judgment.
Eccl. 11:9

Him should not perish, but have everlasting life." [2]   No human being can face his life record in the books of heaven, and escape condemnation, unless belief in Christ and a love for His service is a part of that record.

Christ, the heavenly Advocate, will plead the cases of all who have given Him their sins. He says, " I, even I, am He that blotteth out thy transgressions for *My own sake,* and will

[1] Rom. 14:12.   [2] John 3:16.

not remember thy sins." [1] The life record, scarlet with sins and wretchedness, the Saviour covers with the spotless robe of His righteousness; and the Judge, looking upon it, sees only the sacrifice of His Son, and the record is, "Accepted in the Beloved." Who can reject such infinite love?

The judgment involves, first, the investigation of every case, the testimony of witnesses, and the plea of the advocate, if there is an advocate. Then comes the decision of the court; after that follows the execution of the sentence rendered by the court. A just sentence can not be rendered in any court until the witnesses have borne their testimony; for that reason a just sentence could not be executed upon an individual at death.

Through their writings, Payne and Voltaire h a v e made more infidels since their death than while living. A just sentence could not be passed upon them until the record of the lives of those who had been lost through their influence, appeared as witnesses in their case. On the other hand, the influence of the righteous is like the waves on the surface of a lake, which continue to widen until they reach the shore. Abel, "being dead, yet speaketh." [2] Wycliffe, that fearless man of God, could not have been judged at the close of his life, for thousands have been enlightened by the influence of his life since his voice was hushed in death.

If the Bible record were silent upon this point, it would still be apparent at a glance that the judgment could not be held before the last generation had lived their life; but the Bible is not silent. The date of the opening of this great tribunal was revealed by the Lord thousands of years before it took place. Peter taught the same truth. "Repent ye therefore, and be converted, that your sins may be blotted out, when the *times of re-*

[1] Isa. 43:25.   [2] Heb. 11:4.

freshing shall come from the presence of the Lord; and He s h a l l send Jesus Christ, which before was preached unto you." [1] The sins will be blotted out just before the coming of the Lord.

The investigative judgment is an examination of the life record kept in heaven. Daniel says that when the judgment was set, " the books were opened." [2] There are several books mentioned in connection with the records of heaven. The book of remembrance records even the thoughts of the heart. [3] How just and merciful is our God that He takes cognizance of it when we only think upon His name! Often when pressed by temptation, our souls cry out after the living God, and a faithful record is kept of it all. Many deeds are done in darkness, hidden from even the most intimate associates; but when the books of heaven are opened, God " will bring to light the hidden things of darkness, and will make manifest the counsels of the heart." [4] " For God shall bring every work into judgment, with *every secret thing,* whether it be good, or whether it be evil." [5] Not only the deeds are recorded, but the motives or counsels of the heart that prompted the deed; and of the bitter tears of repentance shed in secret the Lord says, Are they not all in My book?

Our daily conversation, the words spoken without thought, we may count of little worth, but " every idle word that men shall speak, they shall give account thereof in the day of judgment: for by thy words thou shalt be justified, and by thy words thou shalt be condemned." [6] Words are the index of the heart, " for out of the abundance of the heart the mouth speaketh." [7] The

[1] Acts 3: 19, 20.   [2] Dan. 7: 9, 10.   [3] Mal. 3: 16.   [4] 1 Cor. 4: 5.
[5] Eccl. 12: 14.   [6] Matt. 12: 36, 37.   [7] Matt. 12: 34.

place of birth and the environment, everything that can in any way influence the life record, is all recorded in the books of heaven. [1]

The most wonderful book of all the heavenly records that pertain to humanity, is the book of life. This book contains the names of all who have professed the name of Christ. [2] To have one's name recorded in that book is the highest honor given to mortals. [3]

It is a source of great rejoicing to know that our names are written in heaven, [4] but the life must be in harmony with heavenly things if our names are to remain with the righteous. The names of the wicked do not remain in the book of life; [5] they are written in the earth; [6] for all their hopes and affections have clung to earthly things. When the cases of all whose hearts are the dwelling-place of the Most High and whose lives show forth His character, come up in the heavenly court, Jesus Christ the righteous will be their Advocate. [7] He will confess their names before the Father and before the · angels. Their sins will be blotted out, and their names retained in the book of life; and they will be clothed with the white raiment of Christ's righteousness. [8]

"The witness of the angels who have kept the record . . . condemns them."

On the day of atonement in the typical service only those sins which had been confessed and transferred to the sanctuary through the sin-offering, were carried out and laid upon the

---

[1] Ps. 87:4-6. [2] Phil. 4:3. [3] Luke 10:19, 20.
[4] Luke 10:20. [5] Ex. 32:33; Rev. 13:8; 17:8. [6] Jer. 17:13.
[7] 1 John 2:1. [8] Rev. 3:5.

head of the scapegoat. In the investigative judgment, only the cases of those who have confessed their sins will be investigated. Their names will be in the book of life, and Peter states, " Judgment must begin at the house of God; and if it first begins at us what shall the end be of them that obey not the gospel of God? " [1] The cases of those who have not served God will go by default. There will be no one to present them. They have no advocate in the heavenly court.

Sad indeed will be the state of those who have started on the heavenly way, but after experiencing the joy of sins forgiven and the peace of God in the heart, have returned to the world and its follies. Their names have been written in the book of life, and their cases will be presented, but only to have the sentence, " Unfaithful," passed upon them, and their names blotted forever from the book of life.

When the Saviour comes in the clouds of heaven, He will give reward to the righteous; but final judgment upon the wicked can not yet be executed, for all are to be judged " out of those things which were written in the books, according to their works." [2]

During the thousand years following the second advent of Christ to the earth, the righteous will join with Christ in judging the wicked. [3] Then the justice of God in condemning the wicked will be demonstrated before all. The fact that they had no part in the first, or investigative judgment, that their names were not in the book of life, and no one represented them in the court of heaven, is sufficient to condemn them. The books of heaven, containing a faithful record of their lives, condemn them. The witness of the angels who have kept the record also condemns them; but with all that evidence, God has each name considered by the saints from the earth.

[1] 1 Peter 4 : 17.   [2] Rev. 20 : 12.   [3] Rev. 20 : 4; 1 Cor. 6 : 2, 3.

There will be many among the lost who have been accounted righteous; and if they should be destroyed without an examination of the records by the saints, there might be occasion to question the justice of God; but when the records reveal how some have worked from selfish motives, and others have been guilty of cherished sins covered from the view of their fellow-men, the awfulness of sin and the longsuffering of God will be appreciated.

The Saviour said that those who had followed Him while here on earth would judge the twelve tribes of Israel. [1] Then when the records revealing the fact that the chief priests cried, " Crucify Him! crucify Him!" are opened in heaven, John, who followed his Lord through that cruel trial, will be able to say, " I heard them speak the awful words."

As the long list of names is brought in review, the saints can appear as witnesses. When the tyrant Nero's name comes up, and the record states how he tortured the saints of God, witnesses will be there who can say, " We are the ones who were burned to light his garden." Redeemed ones gathered out of every age will sit in judgment on the cases of the wicked, and the punishment will be meted out to each one according to his works.

In the day of judgment, God will call to the heavens above. He will call for the records that have been preserved by angels,— records of men's lives, of the words they have spoken, of the deeds they have done; even the most secret acts will then be called upon to bear testimony, for " our God shall come, and shall not keep silence; a fire shall devour before Him, and it shall be very tempestuous round about Him. He shall call to the heavens from above, and to the earth, that He may judge His people." There is one class of people who will then be gathered. He says, " Gather My saints together unto Me; those that have

[1] Matt. 19 : 27, 28.

made a covenant with Me by sacrifice. And the heavens shall declare His righteousness: for God is judge Himself." [1]

This day of God's investigative judgment we h a v e now entered, and the executive part of it will take place at the close of probation, after the witnesses have borne their testimony.

When the judgment of the wicked closes, the saints, the angels, and all the universe will be in harmony with the decisions rendered. At the end of the thousand years, when fire from heaven devours the wicked as " stubble fully dry," [2] all the universe will say, " Even so, Lord God Almighty, true and righteous are Thy judgments." [3]

THE THREE BOOKS OF JUDGMENT

1. Book of Life

Luke 10 : 20. Names written in heaven.

Luke 10 : 19, 20. To be enrolled in the book of life is the highest honor given mortals.

Phil. 4 : 3. Names of faithful workers recorded.

Ex. 32 : 33. The names of those that cling to sin will be removed.

Rev. 3 : 5. Names of the faithful retained.

Rev. 13 : 8; 17 : 8. Wicked are not recorded.

Rev. 20 : 15. None will be saved whose names are not recorded in the book of life.

Isa. 4 : 3, margin.

Ps. 69 : 28; Eze. 13 : 9.

Heb. 12 : 23; Dan. 12 : 1.

[1] Ps. 50 : 3-6.   [2] Nahum 1 : 9, 10.   [3] Rev. 16 : 7.

2. Book of Remembrance

Mal. 3 : 16.   Records every word.

Matt. 12 : 36, 37.   Idle words.

Ps. 56 : 8.   Tears of repentance.

Ps. 87 : 4-6.   Birthplace and environments.

Eccl. 12 : 13, 14.   Every secret act.

1 Cor. 4 : 5.   Counsels of the heart.

3. Book of Death

Jer. 17 : 13.   Those that forsake God are written in the earth.

Jer. 2 : 22.   Sins all recorded.

Job 14 : 17.   Sins sealed up.

Deut. 32 : 32-36.   The sins of the wicked are all " laid up in store " until the day of judgment.

Hos. 13 : 12.   **Sin bound up.**

CHAPTER XXXII

THE FEAST OF TABERNACLES

THE Feast of Tabernacles was the last feast in the yearly round of service, and typified the final consummation of the entire plan of redemption. It began on the fifteenth day of the seventh month, when the harvests were all gathered from field, vineyard, and olive groves. As the time approached, from all parts of Palestine, groups of devout Jews might be seen wending their way to Jerusalem. And not only from the Holy Land, but believing Jews from all the surrounding countries went up to Jerusalem to attend the Feast of Tabernacles. The Lord required all the men to attend this feast, but many of the women and children went also. [1]

[1] Ex. 23: 16, 17.

It was a time of great rejoicing. All were expected to bring a thank-offering to the Lord. Burnt-offerings, meat-offerings, and drink-offerings were presented at this time. [1] The Feast of Tabernacles began five days after the day of atonement, and all Israel were rejoicing in their acceptance with God, and also for the bounties of the harvest which had been gathered.

The feast continued seven days, the first and the eighth days being observed as ceremonial sabbaths. [2]

This feast was commemorative as well as typical. It commemorated their desert wanderings; and in remembrance of their tent homes, all Israel dwelt in booths during the seven days. In the streets, on the housetops, in their courts, and in the courts of the house of God, booths were made of "boughs of goodly trees, branches of palm-trees, and the boughs of thick trees, and willows of the brook." [3] It was a period of rejoicing, and all were to share the feast with the Levites, the poor, and the stranger. [4]

Every seventh year "the solemnity of the year of release" came during the Feast of Tabernacles, when debtors were released from their obligations. [5] At this time the entire Levitical law was read in the hearing of all; men, women, and children; and even the strangers within their gates, were required to listen to the reading of the law. [6]

The first new year began in the autumn, for at creation, time began with fruit-trees laden with fruit all ready to furnish food for man. [7] The Feast of Tabernacles, or Feast of Ingathering, as it was also called, was held in the "year's end," or the "revolution of the year." [8] The civil year of the Jewish calendar always ended in the autumn, but the sacred year began in the springtime; hence the Feast of Tabernacles was held in the seventh month of the sacred year.

[1] Lev. 23:37. [2] Lev. 23:36, 39. [3] Lev. 23:40-43; Neh. 8:15, 16.
[4] Deut. 16:13-17. [5] Deut. 31:10; 15:1-4. [6] Deut. 31:11-13.
[7] Gen. 1:29; 2:5. [8] Ex. 34:22, margin.

Some very interesting Bible scenes are connected with this feast. Solomon's temple was dedicated at the Feast of Tabernacles. [1] When Israel returned from the Babylonian captivity, this was the first feast celebrated after the wall of Jerusalem was restored, and was a time of great rejoicing. [2]

At this time the children of Israel not only commemorated their tent life by living in booths, but the temple was especially illuminated in remembrance of

"The last day, that great day of the feast."

the pillar of fire that guided them in their wanderings; and on the last day of the feast a beautiful service, the crowning service of "the last day, that great day of the feast," commemorated the miraculous supply of water in the desert. [3] The priest dipped a flagon of water from the Kedron, and bear-

[1] I Kings 8:2, 65.   [2] Neh. 7:73; 8:17, 18.   [3] John 7:37.

ing it aloft, meanwhile marching to the sound of music and chanting portions of the one hundred twenty-second psalm, he entered the temple court. By the altar were two silver basins, and as the priest poured the water into one basin, another priest poured a flagon of wine into the other basin; and the wine and water, mingling together, flowed through a pipe back to the Kedron.

Many incidents in Christ's life cluster around the last Feast of Tabernacles which He attended. It was on the day of this service that He stood in the temple court and cried, " If any man thirst, let him come unto Me, and drink." [1] It was Christ who led them by the pillar of cloud; He it was who supplied the water from the rock. " They drank of that spiritual Rock that went with them: and that Rock was Christ." [2] He, the great Lifegiver, was in their midst; yet even while celebrating His power to quench their thirst, they were ready to kill Him.

While this feast commemorated the journeying of Israel in the wilderness, it also commemorated their deliverance f r o m Egyptian bondage. It would be well if every one who has been delivered from the darkness of sin would occasionally celebrate his deliverance by recognizing the leadings of the Lord in the journey of his life, and thank Him for the many blessings received.

The Feast of Tabernacles followed the day of atonement, which meets its antitype in the judgment; hence must typify an event which comes after the close of the judgment. When Christ leaves the heavenly sanctuary, it will be but a short time until He comes to the earth to gather His people. Then He will take them to heaven, where they will behold the glory He had with the Father before the world was. [3]

For one thousand years the saints will reign with Christ in

[1] John 7 : 37-39.   [2] 1 Cor. 10 : 4, margin.   [3] John 17 : 5, 24.

heaven [1] before they return to their eternal home,— this earth, freed from every curse. The New Jerusalem with its gates of pearl and streets of gold, will be the metropolis of the glorious abode of the redeemed. The beauties of the new earth are such that the redeemed in heaven, surrounded by the glories of the throne of the Eternal, will look forward with joyful anticipation to the time when they shall " reign on the earth." [2]

As we journey through this wilderness of sin and sorrow, it is our blessed privilege by faith to watch the movements of our High Priest, and be ready to greet with joy His appearance when He comes to take His faithful ones to sojourn with Him for a time in the heavenly courts, before they share in the eternal bliss of the earth made new. Every feast, as well as every offering and service, in the Levitical ceremonies, pointed to the beautiful home of the redeemed. Each one is a guideboard on the great pathway of life, pointing toward the heavenly home.

The Jews failed to read these guideboards aright, and to-day are wandering over the earth without the light from the blessed Messiah and the cross of Calvary shining upon their pathway. Let us take warning by their failure, and not make the same fatal mistake by failing to discern the light still reflected from types and symbols, for they are all illuminated by the light of the cross. Each one reveals some special trait in the wonderful character of our Redeemer.

The entire system of Judaism was the gospel. True, it was veiled in types and symbols, but the light from Calvary illuminates the entire Jewish economy; and the one who will study it in the light of the cross, will gain such an intimate acquaintance with Him who is the Antitype of every service, that by beholding they will become changed into His image, from glory to glory. [3]

[1] Rev. 20:4. [2] Rev. 5:9, 10. [3] 2 Cor. 3:18.
16

The typical service shines the brightest when placed by the side of the Antitype. A study of any part of the Levitical system points to some characteristic in the life of Christ; while a study of the entire system of Judaism more nearly reveals the fulness of His character than any other portions of the Scriptures. The entire Bible is full of it. Every Bible writer refers to the Levitical service to illustrate divine truth; and the person who is familiar with the entire sanctuary service, not only receives a blessing from the study, but also understands more fully other portions of the Sacred Book, for the different feasts and sacrifices are referred to frequently all through the Bible.

TYPE   ANTITYPE

Lev. 23 : 27, 34. The Feast of Tabernacles came only a few days after the day of atonement.

Rev. 22 : 11, 12. Quickly after the decree that closes the judgment Christ comes for His people.

Lev. 23 : 40-42. The people dwelt in booths, they lived in camp life.

Rev. 20 : 9. The dwelling place of the redeemed before the earth is made new is called the " camp of the saints."

Lev. 23 : 42. All that were born Israelites could participate in the Feast of Tabernacles.

John 3 : 5. It is the " new birth " that entitles a person to share in the " camp of the saints."

SECTION VIII

Levitical Laws and Ceremonies

The Year of Jubilee

OH, glory to God! it is coming again,
    'Tis the glad jubilee of the children of men;
Then blow ye the trumpet, shout glory, and sing,
    And join in the praises of Jesus the King.

'Tis the glad antitype of that day long ago
    When the hosts of the Lord might not gather or sow;
When the minions of Israel from labor were free,
    And the land was to rest in the glad jubilee.

Yes, gladder by far is that rest by and by,
    When on wings like the eagle we mount to the sky;
We shall dwell evermore in that land of the blest,
    In that grand jubilee, in that sabbath of rest.

                    —*Mrs. L. D. Avery-Stuttle.*

CHAPTER XXXIII

THE JUBILEE

HE Jubilee was the climax of a series of sabbatical in-stitutions. The weekly Sabbath was the first religious institution given to man. [1] The seventh day of the week was hallowed, and set apart to be kept as the rest-day of Jehovah. [2]

After the children of Israel entered the promised land, God commanded that every seventh year should be " a sabbath of rest unto the land, a sabbath for the Lord. " The people were not allowed to sow their fields nor prune their vineyards during the seventh year; neither could they gather into their storehouses that which grew of its own accord. The owner of the land could take all he wished for immediate use; but his servants and the strangers

[1] Gen. 2 : 2, 3.   [2] Isa. 58 : 13, 14; Ex. 20 : 8-11.

and even the beasts, had equal rights with the owner in enjoying the fruits of his fields during the sabbatic year. [1]

The seventh month of the sacred [2] year, the month Tisri, was called by some writers the sabbatical month, as more of the annual sabbaths and feasts came in that month than in any other one month in the year. The first day of this month was the Feast of Blowing of Trumpets; the Day of Atonement came on the tenth day, and the Feast of Tabernacles began on the fifteenth day; and in every fiftieth year, the tenth day of Tisri ushered in the Jubilee. [3]

The keeping of the weekly Sabbath was a token that the people belonged to God; and in allowing their land to rest during the seventh-year sabbath, they acknowledged that not only they themselves, but their land, their time, and all they possessed, belonged to God. [4]

The Lord took special delight in the seventh-year sabbath, and the disregard of His command to keep it was offensive in His sight. The children of Israel were carried into Babylonian captivity because they had not allowed " the land to enjoy her sabbaths." [5] In their love of greed and gain, they had worked the land *every* year, and God took them away and let the land lie desolate, that it might keep the sabbath during the seventy years.

If God's command had always been obeyed and the land had had its rest every seventh year, the earth would not have " waxed old like a garment," [6] but would have remained productive.

God's commands will all be honored, and as the land lay desolate seventy years, keeping the sabbath during the Babylonian captivity, to atone for the disobedience of ancient Israel; so, after the second coming of Christ, the land will lie desolate one thou-

[1] Lev. 25 : 1-7. [2] The Jewish sacred year began in the spring, and the civil year in the autumn. [3] Lev. 25 : 8-11. [4] Eze. 20 : 12, 20. [5] 2 Chron. 36 : 18-21. [6] Isa. 51 : 6.

sand years, keeping sabbath to atone for the many Sabbaths that have been disregarded since that time. [1]

The weekly Sabbath was a stepping-stone leading up to the other sabbatic institutions; and besides being a memorial of creation, it pointed forward to the final rest of the Jubilee. When the people of God for the sake of worldly interests,

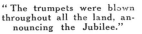

" The trumpets were blown throughout all the land, announcing the Jubilee."

disregarded it, they placed themselves where they could not appreciate God's original design in giving them the Sabbath of rest. [2]

The Jubilee was the fiftieth year following seven weeks of years, and would occur *once* at least in the lifetime of every individual who lived out his natural life. [3]

The Day of Atonement was the most solemn of all the feasts, and the Jubilee the most joyful. At the close of the Day of Atonement, when the sins of Israel had all been forgiven and borne by the scapegoat into the wilderness, then the people who realized what God had done for them, were prepared to for-

[1] Rev. 20 : 1-4; Zeph. 1 : 1-3; Jer. 4 : 23, 27.　　[2] Jer. 17 : 21-27.　　[3] Lev. 25 : 10, 11.

give the debts of their fellow-men, to release them from servitude, and to restore all to their own land as willingly as they expected God to give them their eternal inheritance in the antitypical jubilee.

At the close of the Day of Atonement, on the tenth day of the seventh month, in the sabbatical year which closed the last of the seven weeks of years (49 years), the trumpets were blown throughout all the land, announcing the Jubilee.

Jewish tradition states that every Israelite was supplied with a trumpet of some kind at this time, and when the hour arrived which closed the Day of Atonement, *every one* blew nine blasts with his trumpet. God had said, the trumpets were to sound throughout *all* the land. [1]

How like the final trumpet of the Lord [2] was the blast of the Jubilee trumpets in ancient Israel! The toiling slave arose and threw off his shackles. To the avaricious and covetous man, who had oppressed the hireling and the widow to gain his possessions, it came as a death knell to all his hopes. [3] Every person in bondage was freed, and all returned to their own land. [4]

There is no account of any religious services, or offerings, being required during the Jubilee, different from the ordinary services of other years. It was a time when all, rich and poor, high and low, shared alike of that which grew of itself in the fields and vineyards.

The Jubilee followed the seventh-year sabbath, thus bringing two sabbath years in succession. But God made ample provision for His people by commanding His blessing upon the forty-eighth year, when the earth yielded enough to keep the people for three years. [5]

There is no mention in the Bible of the Jubilee's ever being observed, and for this reason some writers think it may not have

[1] Lev. 25 : 9.   [2] 1 Cor. 15 : 51-53.   [3] Isa. 2 : 20, 21.
[4] Lev. 25 : 12, 13.   [5] Isa. 37 : 30; Lev. 25 : 11, 12.

been kept; but all the other Mosaic festivals were observed, and it would be strange if one that is so organically connected with the other feasts, and is really the climax of all other festivals, should have been omitted.

The Jubilee must have been observed, for the law of the inalienability of landed property, which was based upon the Jubilee, existed among the Jews. [1] Josephus speaks of it as being permanently observed.

Instances are recorded where the work of the Jubilee year was performed by the Israelites. Nehemiah, in his great reformatory work, required the Jews to give freedom to their servants, and to restore the lands and vineyards to the original owners. [2]

On the eve of the Babylonian captivity, Zedekiah proclaimed liberty to every one. He evidently designed to celebrate the Jubilee. If he had done so, it would have given him liberty, but he was too vacillating to carry out the requirements. The Lord sent a message, saying that he had done right in proclaiming liberty, " every man to his neighbor," but that in failing to grant it, he had polluted the name of the Lord. [3]

All the commercial interests of the ancient Israelite taught the gospel. While he was allowed to dwell in the promised land and enjoy its privileges, yet he was only the steward, not the owner. The divine decree was: " The land shall not be sold forever: for the land is Mine; for ye are strangers and sojourners with Me." [4] Notwithstanding the fact that the Lord owns the world, yet He counts Himself a stranger and sojourner with His people upon the earth, until the antitypical Jubilee, when Satan, the present prince of this world, will meet his doom.

If a man became involved and was obliged to sell his home, it was sold with the understanding that it should return to its

[1] Num. 36:4, 6, 7; Ruth 4:1-4.   [2] Neh. 5:1-19.
[3] Jer. 34:8-17.   [4] Lev. 25:23.

original owner when the Jubilee trumpets were blown in the land. If the unfortunate man had one near of kin able to redeem his land, the purchaser could not hold it, even until the Jubilee. [1]

A poor widow has misfortune after misfortune, until her wealthy neighbor, who has long coveted her land, has gained possession, and she in sorrow is obliged to leave the home of her childhood and labor for a mere pittance, that fails to supply the needs of her household. The wealthy neighbor continues to advance money, until finally she herself is sold to him as a servant. Her case seems hopeless.

But in a far country she has an elder brother. He hears of her misfortune and comes to the rescue. Her brother reckons with the man who has purchased the woman, and pays the redemption money, and she is free. Then the brother begins to reckon what is due on the land; but the man objects, for the same spirit rules him that disputed with Michael, the archangel, when He came from a far country to redeem the body of Moses from the prison-house of the grave, [2] and he says, "No! I will not release the land. It joins my farm, I will not part with it. What right have you to interfere?" Then the brother produces evidence of his kinship, that he is "one that hath right to redeem." [3] He offers the redemption money, and the home is redeemed to the rightful owner. A stranger might have wished to help the poor widow, but his money could never have released her; the price must be paid by "one that hath right to redeem" — one near of kin.

How forcefully was the power of Christ thus taught in the every-day commercial life of the Israelite!

An angel could not redeem mankind, nor the world. His life would have been powerless, for he was not "nigh of kin"

[1] Lev. 25:25-28.   [2] Jude 9.   [3] Ruth 2:20, margin.

unto humanity. [1] Christ left the heavenly courts, partook of flesh and blood, " that through death He might destroy him that had the power of death, that is, the devil; and deliver them who through fear of death *were all their lifetime subject to bondage.* For verily He took not on Him the nature of angels; but He took on Him the seed of Abraham." [2] He became the

"He is not ashamed to call them brethren."

" first-born among many breth-ren," [3] the one *nigh of kin,* that He might have right to redeem every son and daughter of Adam; and down through the ages, comes the cheering assurance that " He is not ashamed to call them brethren." [4]

" Thus saith the Lord, Ye have sold yourselves for nought; and ye shall be redeemed without money, [5] even " with the precious blood of Christ, as of a lamb without blemish and without spot." [6]

[1] Lev. 25:47-49. [2] Heb. 2:14-16. [3] Rom. 8:29.
[4] Heb. 2:11. [5] Isa. 52:3. [6] 1 Peter 1:18, 19.

Have you yielded to temptation until you are bound in abject slavery to Satan? Remember, you have an Elder Brother who is able and willing to redeem you from the slavery of sin, and make you a free man in Christ Jesus. In order to be free, you must acknowledge Him as "one nigh of kin" to you. If the poor widow had disowned her brother when he came to redeem her from servitude, he would have been powerless to help her.

Satan may bind the soul until he thinks it is his forever; but when the soul cries out for help, and claims Christ as the "one near of kin," "one who has power to redeem," and Christ presents the redemption price,— "His precious blood,"— Satan is powerless to hold the soul.

The study of the Levitical laws in regard to land and servants gives new beauty to the name *Redeemer*. Job knew the power of the "one who had right to redeem." Hear him in confidence saying, "I *know* that *my Redeemer* liveth." His faith grasped a power that not only redeemed from sin, but will bring forth the patriarch's body even after the worms have consumed it. [1]

While at any time one could be given freedom and re-instated in his former home by "one nigh of kin" who had right to redeem, yet the Jubilee was looked forward to as the great day of release for all Israel. It was then that every wrong was righted and every Israelite re-instated in his own possession. [2]

If one sold a dwelling-house in a walled city, during the first year after the sale it might be redeemed; but if not redeemed the first year, it remained in the hand of the purchaser. It did not revert to its original owner in the Jubilee, for houses were the work of man, and had no part in the Jubilee, which released only the *land* and *persons*. [3]

The cities of the Levites were under different regulations;

[1] Job 19 : 23-27.   [2] Lev. 25 : 28, 33, 40, 41.   [3] Lev. 25 : 29, 30.

they were the only walled cities that had a part in the Jubilee.
If a man purchased a house of a Levite, the house that was sold
" and the city of his possession " went out free in the year of
Jubilee. [1]

The priests were a type of Christ. Our great antitypical
Priest has prepared a walled city for His people, [2] and in the
antitypical Jubilee, they will receive the city. The regulations
in regard to the cities of the Levites were a constant reminder
of the New Jerusalem to be given to God's people in the great
final Jubilee.

God designed that His people should remember Him in all
their business transactions, in every detail of life. The value
of property depended upon the length of time intervening between the date of purchase and the Jubilee. [3]

In the type, the Jubilee was ushered in at the close of the
Day of Atonement. In like manner we understand that the
antitypical Jubilee will follow the antitypical Day of Atonement.

" The Lord shall cause His glorious voice to be heard." [4]
Then the pious slave will rise and shake off the chains that
bind him. The trumpet of the Lord's jubilee will resound through
the length and breadth of the land. Saints sleeping in Satan's
prison-house — the grave — will hear the glad sound, and he
" that made the world as a wilderness, and destroyed the cities
thereof; that opened not the house of his prisoners," " did not
let his prisoners loose homeward," [5] will be powerless to hold
his prey; for our Redeemer has said, " The prey of the terrible
shall be delivered,"— yea, delivered forever from the power of
sin and Satan. [6]

God's original plan was, that man should possess the earth.
" The heaven, even the heavens, are the Lord's: *but the earth
hath He given to the children of men.*" [7]

[1] Lev. 25 : 32, 33.   [2] Heb. 11 : 10, 16.   [3] Lev. 25 : 15, 16.
[4] Isa. 30 : 30.   [5] Isa. 14 : 17, margin.   [6] Isa. 49 : 25.   [7] Ps. 115 : 16.

Adam was given dominion over the earth and everything upon it. [1] But God's plans were thwarted, and Satan became prince of this world. In the antitypical Jubilee the redeemed of the Lord will be re-instated in the original home of man. The earth restored to its primeval beauty will be given to the children of men for their eternal home. [2] The seventh-day weekly Sabbaths, which the Lord sanctified and gave to mankind before the curse of sin rested upon the earth, will then be kept according to God's original design; and throughout eternity, " from one Sabbath to another, shall all flesh come to worship " before the Lord. [3]

" The Lord shall comfort Zion; He will comfort all her waste places; and He will make her wilderness like Eden, and her desert like the garden of the Lord; joy and gladness shall be found therein, thanksgiving, and the voice of melody." [4]

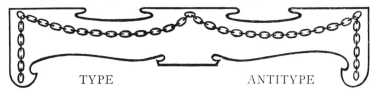

TYPE   ANTITYPE

Lev. 25 : 10. The Jubilee gave liberty to every one.

I Thess. 4 : 16, 17. The living and the dead will all be given freedom.

Lev. 25 : 9. The blast of the trumpet announced the Jubilee.

I Cor. 15 : 51-53. The blast of the trumpet of the Lord, gives freedom to all.

Lev. 25 : 9. The Jubilee began on the Day of Atonement, the type of the judgment.

Rev. 22 : 11, 12. Immediately after the decree is issued which closes the judgment, Christ comes.

[1] Gen. 1 : 26.
[3] Isa. 66 : 22, 23.

[2] Matt. 5 : 5; Ps. 37 : 11, 34.
[4] Isa. 51 : 3.

Lev. 25 : 13. In the year of the Jubilee every man returned to his own possessions.

Lev. 25 : 23. The Lord always owned the land. Man was only a steward.

Lev. 25 : 48, 49; Ruth 2 : 20, margin. Only one nigh of kin had the right to redeem.

Lev. 25 : 47-51. The persons of those sold in bondage were redeemed and set free.

Lev. 25 : 25-28. The land could be redeemed by one nigh of kin.

Lev. 25 : 29, 30. D w e l l i n g - houses in walled cities did not revert to the original owners in the Jubilee.

Lev. 25 : 32, 33. D w e l l i n g- houses in the cities of the Levites could be redeemed. They all reverted to the original owners in the Jubilee. The priests were a type of Christ.

Gen. 2 : 2, 3. The weekly Sabbath was a stepping-stone toward the Jubilee.

Isa. 35 : 1-10. The ransomed of the Lord will enjoy the redeemed earth forever.

Ps. 24 : 1; 1 Cor. 10 : 26, 28. The Lord owns all the earth. He has never relinquished His title to the land.

Heb. 2 : 14-16. Jesus was born of the seed of Abraham, that He might be nigh of kin.

Rom. 8 : 23; Hosea 13 : 14. He that is nigh of kin, says, " I will ransom them from the power of the grave.

Eph. 1 : 14. Christ has purchased the possession of His people.

Rev. 16 : 19; Jer. 4 : 26. All earthly cities will be destroyed at Christ's second coming.

Heb. 11 : 10, 16; Rev. 21 : 1-27. Christ, the antitypical priest, has a city which will be given to His people in the antitypical Jubilee.

Isa. 66 : 22, 23. The Sabbath will be observed on the new earth forever.

CHAPTER XXXIV

CITIES OF REFUGE

N the early history of the world, provision was made for the punishment of the murderer. "Whoso sheddeth man's blood, by man shall his blood be shed," was the decree of Jehovah. [1]

The one nearest of kin to the murdered man, usually executed the murderer; but lest in the excitement of the occasion undue haste should be exercised and individuals be slain who did not deserve death, God made provision that the murderer might flee and lay hold upon His altar. None could be taken from the altar without an examination, and if it was found that the murderer had presumptuously planned to kill the man, then he was taken from the altar and slain; otherwise his life was spared. [2]

After the children of Israel entered the promised land, six

[1] Gen. 9:6.   [2] Ex. 21:13, 14.

cities were set apart as cities of refuge. These were conveniently located, three on each side of the river Jordan. [1] The roads leading to these cities were always to be kept in good repair, that the one fleeing before the avenger of blood might not be hindered in his flight. [2] The cities were on elevated ground, and could be seen at a distance.

When the murderer reached the gate of the city of refuge, he declared " his cause in the ears of the elders of that city," before he was given a place within. [3] His case was also tried by the judges of the city near where the murder was committed, and if it was not a premeditated murder, but the deed had been done accidentally or unintentionally, then the guilty man was restored again to the city of refuge whither he had fled. [4]

The Saviour refers to this judgment in Matt. 5 : 21. If at any time the slayer passed outside of the limit of his city of refuge, his life could be taken by the avenger of blood, " because he should have remained in the city of his refuge." [5] The decree was, " He shall dwell in that city, . . . until the death of the high priest that shall be in those days : then shall the slayer return . . . unto his own house, unto the city from whence he fled." [6]

Cities of refuge in Israel were far different from the *asyla* of the Greeks and Romans, which often served as a protection for the most profligate characters. The cities of refuge served as a protection for *only* those who had slain a person without enmity. The cities of refuge were cities belonging to the Levites, thus those confined within were under the best influence. They were associated with the religious teachers of Israel, and had every opportunity to reform their lives and establish righteous characters.

The instruction in regard to the cities of refuge was but a part of the great system of Levitical laws and ceremonies which

[1] Joshua 20 : 2, 7, 8.   [2] Deut. 19 : 3.   [3] Joshua 20 : 3-5.
[4] Num. 35 : 12, 24, 25.   [5] Num. 35 : 26-28.   [6] Joshua 20 : 6.

17

taught the simple truths of the gospel of Christ. Tyndale says that " while there is a *'starlight of Christ'* in all the Levitical ceremonies, there is in some so truly the *'light of the broad day,'* that he can not but believe that God had showed Moses the secrets of Christ and the very manner of His death beforehand." Dr. Adam Clarke says the whole gospel could be preached from the particulars given of the cities of refuge.

Every time an Israelite looked upon one of the cities of refuge, God designed he should be reminded of Christ, the " tower of the flock, the stronghold of the daughter of Zion," [1] to whom every sin-burdened soul could flee for shelter.

Satan, the accuser, is upon the track of every one; he as " a roaring lion, walketh about, seeking whom he may devour." [2] But the person who forsakes sin and seeks righteousness stands securely sheltered by the atoning blood of Christ. [3]

Solomon, who was beset by temptations and sin, understood this when he wrote, " The name of the Lord is a strong tower: the righteous *runneth* into it and is safe." [4] David knew what it was to dwell in the antitypical city of refuge when he said: " I will say of the Lord, He is *my refuge* and my fortress; my God; in Him will I trust." [5]

There could be no delay in seeking a city of refuge. As soon as the murder was committed, the murderer must flee at once; no family ties could hold him; his life depended upon his speedy flight to the city. O that all might learn the lesson, and instead of delaying and trying to quiet our accusing conscience, when we know we have sinned, flee at once to Christ, confess our sins, and . dwell in the refuge Christ has prepared. He has made ample provision that all may " have a strong consolation, who have fled for refuge to lay hold upon the hope set before us." [6]

[1] Micah 4:8.
[4] Prov. 18:10.
[2] 1 Peter 5:8.
[5] Ps. 91:2.
[3] Ex. 12:13; 1 John 1:7, 9.
[6] Heb. 6:18.

Anciently the one who had fled to the city, found life within its walls, but death awaited him if he passed beyond its boundary. The beloved disciple was familiar with this truth when he wrote, " This is the record, that God hath given to us eternal life, and this life *is in* His Son. *He that hath the Son hath life;* and *he that hath not the Son of God hath not life."* [1] It is not sufficient simply to *believe* in Christ; we must *abide* in Him if we ever hope to obtain life. God has promised to " hold thy right hand." The one who abides within the refuge will feel and know His sheltering care, and when assailed by the enemy, may hear the Saviour saying, "Fear not, I will help thee." [2]

In ancient Israel the one who had fled for refuge could not spend part of his time outside the city, and the remainder within its sheltering walls. There was no safety at *any time*

" Fear not, I will help thee."

outside the city. Likewise, our only safety is to *dwell* " in the secret place of the Most High," and *" abide* under the shadow of the Almighty." [3] No man can serve two masters. [4] We can not give the world and its pleasures the best of our time and thought, and hope to be sheltered from the final consequences of sin. We will receive our " wages," or final reward, from the master we serve. If the best of our life is spent in the service of the world,

[1] I John 5 : 11, 12.
[2] Isa. 41 : 13.
[3] Ps. 91 : 1.
[4] Matt. 6 : 24.

"No Cross, no crown."

we place ourselves outside the antitypical city of refuge, and will finally receive the " wages," — death, which will be given every one who takes the world as his master. [1]

When the high priest died, those who had fled to the cities of refuge during his term of office could return to their homes. They were free forever from the avenger of blood, and he could no longer harm them lawfully. [2]

Every high priest was a type of Christ, our High Priest. The earthly priest ceased to be high priest when he died. Our High Priest never dies; but the time will come when He will lay aside His priestly robes, and clothe Himself in a vesture upon which will be written the name, *" King of kings, and Lord of lords."* [3]

No longer will He plead the cause of His people before the throne of God, for each case will have been decided for eternity. To those who have confessed every sin and remained cleansed by the blood of Christ, He will say, " Come, ye blessed of My Father, inherit the kingdom prepared for you from the foundation of the world." They will then go to their own inheritance with no fear of the avenger of blood, for the righteous will be forever beyond the power of Satan. [4]

Satan has usurped authority over this world. He haunts the steps of every son and daughter of Adam. But God always has

[1] Rom. 6 : 23.
[2] Num. 35 : 25.
[2] Rev. 19 : 16.
[4] Jer. 31 : 16, 17.

had a refuge in the earth. Abel dwelt securely within its sacred precincts, [1] and Job realized its sheltering power when Satan assailed him with his fiercest temptations. [2]

The weakest child of God, who lives continually within this refuge, can never be overthrown by the enemy of souls; for the angels of God encamp around such a one to deliver him. [3]

This refuge is illustrated by many symbols throughout the Bible, each one revealing some special feature of God's pro-

"How often would I have gathered thy children together, as a hen doth gather her brood under her wings, and ye would not!"

tecting care. Jesus, as He wept over those who had refused His love said: "How often would I have gathered thy children together, as a hen doth gather her brood under her wings, and ye would not!" [4]

Happy is the soul who can say in every time of temptation,

[1] Heb. 11:4.   [2] Job 1:10.
[3] Ps. 34:7; John 10:29.   [4] Luke 13:34.

" Our soul is escaped as a bird out of the snare of the fowlers: the snare is broken, and we are escaped. *Our help is in the name of the Lord,* who made heaven and earth." [1]

TYPE	ANTITYPE
Joshua 20: 2, 3; Deut. 19: 4, 5. The cities were to be a shelter for all who slew any one unaware or unwittingly.	Rev. 22: 16, 17; John 7: 37; 1 John 1: 7. Christ is the only refuge in this world from sin and destruction.
Deut. 19: 2-4. The roads were to be kept open, in good condition, that none be hindered in fleeing to the city.	1 Cor. 11: 1; Mal. 2: 8. God designs that His p e o p l e should be examples for the world to copy; but when they sin, they become stumbling-blocks in the way of others.
Joshua 20: 3, 4. The one who fled for refuge confessed his sin at the gate of the city, and if he had not premeditated the murder, he was received.	1 John 1: 9. " If we confess our sins, He is faithful and just to forgive us our sins, and to cleanse us from all unrighteousness."
Deut. 19: 11-13. If the murderer hated the one he had slain and planned the murder, then he was not received into the city, but was given over to the avenger of blood.	Matt. 7: 21-23; Heb. 10: 26-29; 12: 16, 17. Some may through fear of punishment come with only lip service, while in their hearts they are cherishing sin; such will not be accepted.

[1] Ps. 124: 7, 8.

Num. 35 : 24, 25. Being received into the city did not forever settle the fate of the murderer. He must stand in judgment before the congregation, and there his destiny was decided.

Num. 35 : 26, 27. Within the city was life, outside the city was death.

Joshua 20 : 6; Num. 35 : 28. After " the death of the high priest that shall be in those days," the slayer might return to " the land of his possession."

Acts 17 : 31; Rev. 3 : 5. Every one will be judged before the judgment bar of God for the deeds done in the body.

1 John 5 : 11, 12. " He that hath the Son hath life; and he that hath not the Son of God hath not life."

Matt. 25 : 34. When Christ lays aside His priestly robes and reigns as king, then all, who abide in Him, will receive their inheritance in the earth made new.

CHAPTER XXXV

THE ROCK

ROCK has always been used as a synonym for strength and solidity. The parable of the house built upon a rock, is an example. [1]

The word "rock" is used many times in the Bible to illustrate the protecting care of God for His people.

The psalmist says, "The Lord is my rock." [2] "Thou art my rock and my fortress." [3]

"Selah," which occurs over seventy times in the Psalms, and is defined by most commentators, "a pause or musical note," is also defined in the marginal reference to be "the rock." [4]

It is quite appropriate that in singing of the mighty power

[1] Matt. 7 : 24, 25.
[2] Ps. 18 : 2.
[3] Ps. 71 : 3.
[4] 2 Kings 14 : 7, margin.

of God in leading His people, the psalmist should pause at times and meditate upon Selah,— " the Rock;" the " spiritual Rock that followed them: and that Rock was Christ." [1]

Victories would often take the place of defeat in our daily lives if in our songs we inserted the same pauses used by the sweet singer of Israel. If in the rush of our daily lives we paused to meditate upon " the Rock," we could say with David, " In the secret of His tabernacle shall He hide me; He shall set me upon a rock." [2]

The forty years' wandering of the children of Israel was in Arabia Petra, or Rocky Arabia, as it was sometimes called. Rocks confronted them at every turn in their journey; but from these very rocks God caused water to flow to quench their thirst. Even so in our daily journeys, the rocks of difficulties that seem impenetrable to us, will, if we hide in Christ, prove but stepping-stones to greater victories.

God said, " I will stand before thee there upon the rock in Horeb; and thou shalt smite the rock, and there shall come water out of it, that the people may drink. And Moses did so in the sight of the elders." [3]

The thirsty multitude saw the pure, refreshing water gush out from the flinty rock. They drank, and were refreshed for their journey. " They thirsted not when He led them through the deserts: He caused the waters to flow out of the rock for them." [4]

It was not a meager supply of water, for it " ran in the dry places like a river." [5] During all their journey, they were miraculously supplied with water. The stream did not continue to flow from the first place where the rock was smitten, but wherever they needed water, from the rocks beside their encampment the water gushed out. Well might the psalmist bid the earth tremble

[1] 1 Cor. 10:4.   [2] Ps. 27:5.   [3] Ex. 17:6.
[4] Isa. 48:21.   [5] Ps. 105:41.

before the God who could turn
" the rock into a standing water,
the flint into a fountain of
waters." [1]

When the Israelites came in
sight of the promised land,
the water ceased to flow.
God told them they were
to draw water from
the wells as t h e y
passed through Edom. [2]
Strange as it may

" I will stand
before thee there
upon the rock in
Horeb; and thou shalt
smite the rock."

seem, after drinking
of t h e miraculous

[1] Ps. 114:8.
[2] Deut. 2:3-6.

streams in the desert for so many years, they now began to murmur and complain, because the water no longer gushed out of the rocks by their encampment.

Then it was that, on the very border of Canaan, Moses, the servant of the Lord, committed the sin which prevented him from entering the goodly land. The rock had once been smitten, and the Lord told Moses to gather the assembly of people, and to *speak* unto the rock before their eyes, and it would give forth water. Moses, who had borne patiently with their murmurings so long, now became impatient, and said, " Hear now, ye rebels; must we fetch you water out of this rock?"[1] He then smote the rock twice, and water gushed forth.

God is no respecter of persons, and although He had highly honored Moses, yet He punished him for his sin. When Moses smote the rock the second time, he ignored the great event of which the smitten rock was a type. Christ died *once* for the sins of the world,[2] and all who *speak* to Him, confessing their sins and claiming pardon, will receive the healing waters of salvation. Thus not only did Moses disobey God, but he marred the beautiful symbol which had been placed before the Israelites during all their desert wanderings.

The Bible writers often refer to the experiences connected with the smitten rock, to teach God's tender care for His people. Isaiah says, " A man shall be as a hiding-place from the wind, and a covert from the tempest; as rivers of water in a dry place, as the shadow of a great rock in a weary land."[3]

Paul tells us that this Man who was as " a hiding-place," " a covert," and as " rivers of water," was Christ, the Rock.[4] He is the " shadow of a great rock in a weary land." What He was to the Israelites, He will be to every one who puts his trust in Him. He says to-day, " If any man *thirst,* let him come unto

[1] Num. 20 : 10.   [2] Heb. 9 : 28.
[3] Isa. 32 : 2.   [4] 1 Cor. 10 : 4.

Me, and drink." [1] The one who heeds the call will "drink of the brook in the way: therefore shall he lift up the head." [2]

The refreshing water flows by every encampment. All can freely drink of the life-giving stream, flowing from the Rock smitten once upon Calvary's cross. "*Whosoever will,* let him take of the water of life freely." [3] Do you long to drink? Remember the Rock has been *smitten* for you. Do not make the mistake of Moses, and think you must smite it again. "*Speak* ye unto the Rock, . . . and it shall give forth His water." [4] Tell Him you are weary of sin, that you long to accept of His righteous-ness. Give Him your sins, and He will clothe you with His righteousness. [5]

The Amazon River pours into the Atlantic Ocean such an immense volume of water that for miles out at sea the water remains fresh. It is said that a ship sailing in the ocean near the mouth of the Amazon, had exhausted its supply of fresh water, and sig-naled to another vessel at a distance, asking for fresh water. The answer was signaled back, "Dip and drink." The captain thought they could not have understood, and signaled again. The same reply came back across the water. In indignation he said, "They say, 'Dip, and drink.' Throw the bucket over and try the water." To their surprise the bucket brought up fresh water, and their thirst was quenched.

Often we think we are in the enemy's land, and the Lord is afar

[1] John 7:37. [2] Ps. 110:7. [3] Rev. 22:17.
[4] Num. 20:8. [5] Gal. 1:4; Isa. 61:10.

off; but the stream of the river of life flows by every door. We have only to " dip and drink," if we wish to be led into the sunlight of God's presence and feel His sheltering care.

Like David we need often to cry, " Lead me to *the Rock that is higher than I.* For Thou hast been a shelter for me, and a strong tower from the enemy. I will abide in thy tabernacle forever:

I will trust in the covert of thy wings. Selah." [1]

While the foundation of the Christian church is the teaching of the apostles and prophets, Jesus Christ is the chief corner-stone. [2] Christ is " a living s t o n e, disallowed indeed of men, but chosen of God, and precious." [3]

Every soul on earth will sometime come in touch with this Stone. He will either fall on it and be broken, that he may be a new creature in Christ Jesus; or he will reject the Stone, and at last it will fall upon him and destroy him. [4]

Blessed is the one that makes Christ the chief corner-stone in all his daily work. Jesus to-day asks us, as He did Peter of old,

[1] Ps. 61:2-4.   [2] Eph. 2:20.
[3] 1 Peter 2:3, 4.   [4] Matt. 21:42, 44.

" Whom say ye that I am?" Our lives give the answer. Peter's answer was, " Thou art the Christ, the Son of the living God." This answer was given him from the Father.

Christ responded, *" Thou art Peter."* In these words He acknowledged Peter as His disciple, for He had given him the name of Peter when he called him to follow Him. [1]

The word " Peter " meant a stone, or a fragment of rock. Christ's manner of teaching was to use earthly things to illustrate heavenly lessons; and He took the name Peter, meaning a fragment of rock, to direct the mind to the solidity of the confession and the stability of the cause which was founded upon " the Rock," Christ Jesus, of which Peter, when he accepted Christ as His Master, became a portion, or fragment. Every true follower of Christ becomes one of the " living stones " in the great spiritual building of God. [2]

Christ did not say, *On thee, Peter,* will I build My church, but immediately changes the expression and says, " Upon *this Rock* I will build My church." [3]

Centuries before, Isaiah had written, " Behold, I lay in Zion for a foundation a stone, a *tried* stone, a precious corner-stone, a sure foundation." [4]   Peter and every other son of Adam has failed when tested.   Christ is the only one ever born of woman that has withstood every temptation, and is a *" tried stone,"* fit to be the chief corner-stone in the great church of God.

Christ has not placed any mortal man as the foundation of His church. Sad would have been the condition of the church if it had been built upon Peter; for only a short time after he made the above confession, his heart was so full of evil and wrong conclusions that, as the record states, Christ said to him, " Get thee behind Me, Satan: thou art an offense unto Me: for thou savorest not the things that be of God, but those that be of men." [5]

[1] John 1:42.   [2] 1 Peter 2:5.   [3] Matt. 16:13-20.
[4] Isa. 28:16.   [5] Matt. 16:23.

When the Saviour comes in the clouds of heaven, those who have rejected the Rock, Christ Jesus, will call for the mountains and rocks of earth to hide them from the wrath of the Lamb. [1] Our enemies then will witness to the fact that "their rock is not as our Rock." [2]

"Ascribe ye greatness unto our God. He is *the Rock,* His work is perfect: for all His ways are judgment: a God of truth and without iniquity, just and right is He." [3]

TYPE   ANTITYPE

"They drank of that spiritual Rock that followed them: and that Rock was Christ."   1 Cor. 10 : 4.

Ex. 17 : 6. The rock was smitten to save the people from thirst.

Heb. 9 : 28. "Christ was *once* offered to bear the sins of many."

Ps. 78 : 15, 16. "He brought streams also out of the rock, and caused waters to run down like rivers."

John 7 : 38. Christ said, "He that believeth on Me, . . . out of his belly shall flow rivers of living water."

Num. 20 : 8. "Speak ye unto the rock, . . . and it shall give forth his water."

Luke 11 : 9, 10. "Ask, and it shall be given you, . . . for every one that asketh receiveth."

---

[1] Rev. 6 : 15, 16.   [2] Deut. 32 : 31.   [3] Deut. 32 : 3, 4.

CHAPTER XXXVI

VARIOUS LEVITICAL LAWS AND CEREMONIES

THE Christian can have no life apart from Christ.[1] Every detail of his life is directed by the great Master. This was made very clear by the old Levitical rites and ceremonies.

The details of the every-day life of the ancient Israelite were under the direction of God. His food, his dress, his planting and building, his buying and selling, were all regulated by the laws of Moses. To the careless reader these requirements may seem but a collection of meaningless forms and ceremonies; but to the student of Scripture, who is watching for the steps of his Master, each Levitical law is a reflector, giving him precious rays of light from the Sun of Righteousness.

We read: " Thou shalt not wear a garment of divers sorts, as of

[1] John 15 : 4. 5.

woolen and linen together." [1] The question is often asked, Why was this requirement given? One of the first things God did for Adam and Eve after they had sinned, was to make clothes for them. [2]

Garments are a type of Christ's righteousness, with which He clothes every one whose sins are forgiven. [3] Before man sinned, he was clothed with a garment of light and glory, and God designs that our garments should remind us of the heavenly dress with which He will finally clothe the redeemed. [4]

God says, " I am the *first,* and I am the *last;* and beside Me there is no God." " My glory will I not give to another, neither My praise to graven images." [5]

Part of our life can not be clothed with the " filthy rags " of our own righteousness, [6] and the remainder with the pure, spotless robe of Christ's righteousness. We can not serve God in our home and church life, and serve mammon in our daily business life. The one who continues doing it will never enter the kingdom of heaven. " Ye can not serve God and mammon."

The Saviour taught the lesson that we can not patch our own filthy robes of self-righteousness with the righteousness of Christ. " No man putteth a piece of a new garment upon an old; if otherwise, then both the new maketh a rent, and the piece that was taken out of the new *agreeth not with the old."* [7]

The Israelite who conscientiously refused to mingle woolen and linen in his daily garments, and saw in it the lesson God designed to teach, would also refrain from sin. His entire dress, made of but one kind of cloth, would constantly remind him of the perfect robe of Christ's righteousness, given to the faithful.

As the Israelite started out each morning to assume his daily tasks, another command constrained him: " Thou shalt not plow with an ox and an ass together." [8] The ox was a clean animal;

[1] Deut. 22 : 11.   [2] Gen. 3 : 21.   [3] Isa. 61 : 10.
[4] Rev. 3 : 5; 19 : 8.   [5] Isa. 44 : 6; 42 : 8.   [6] Isa. 64 : 6.
[7] Luke 5 : 36.   [8] Deut. 22 : 10.

18

the ass, or donkey, was unclean. [1] While each was useful, yet
they were not to be yoked up together.

The Saviour prayed, not that we should be taken out of
the world, but that we might be *kept from the evil in the world.* [2]
While we may use the world as the Israelites used the unclean ass,
yet we are not to yoke ourselves up with any of the evil of the
world.

"Be ye unequally yoked together with unbelievers: for
what fellowship hath righteousness with unrighteousness? and what

2 Cor. 6:14

communion hath light with darkness? and what concord hath Christ
with Belial? or what part hath he that believeth with an infidel?" [3]

This command includes the marriage relation and every business
connection. Ungodly business men often use methods in conduct-
ing their business that a Christian could not use without compromi-
sing his Christian integrity.

The Christian is to bear Christ's yoke, and engage in no business
in which Christ can not help him carry the burden of cares and
perplexities connected therewith. The Saviour says to all, "Take
My yoke upon you, and learn of Me; for I am meek and lowly
in heart: and ye shall find rest unto your souls." [4]

[1] Lev. 11 : 3, 4.   [2] John 17 : 15.
[3] 2 Cor. 6 : 14-17.   [4] Matt. 11 : 29.

All the precepts of the Old Testament are irradiated with the glory of the Son of God. Especially is this true of the command, " Thou shalt not sow thy vineyard with divers seeds; lest the fruit of thy seed which thou hast sown, and the fruit of thy vineyard, be defiled." [1]

Horticulturists know the value of this command. Sowing together wheat and oats ruins the oats and injures the wheat. This, like the other Levitical laws, referred to more than the temporal prosperity of the Israelites. It taught them that if they would remain true to God, they must not associate with evil companions. " Be not deceived: evil communications corrupt good manners." [2]

The Revised Version of the New Testament reads, " Evil company doth corrupt good manners." The Twentieth Century New Testament makes it stronger, showing that the contamination of evil association affects more than the outward manners. It says, " Do not be deceived; good *character* is marred by evil company."

The Syriac New Testament gives us a side-light on what is included in the term " evil company " or " evil communication," as follows: " Be not deceived. Evil stories corrupt well-disposed minds." It matters not how they may be received, whether orally, or through the fashionable novels, or in the columns of the daily paper, the truth remains the same,— well-disposed minds are corrupted by them.

Just as truly as wheat, which furnishes us our daily bread, is injured by being mixed with other seed in the field; so the most spiritual-minded may be led astray by associating with evil persons, for " their word will eat as doth a canker." [3] " Did not Solomon king of Israel sin by these things? yet among many nations was there no king like him, who was beloved of his God, and God made

[1] Deut. 22:9.   [2] 1 Cor. 15:33.   [3] 2 Tim. 2:17.

him king over all Israel: nevertheless even him did outlandish women cause to sin." [1]

" By beholding we become changed," is a law of our being. If we behold with open face the glory of the Lord, we are changed into His image. [2] If we let our minds dwell upon evil things, we become evil. Like David, we need to pray, " Turn away mine eyes from beholding vanity; and quicken Thou me in Thy way." [3]

To the individual building a house the command was given, " When thou buildest a new house, then thou shalt make a battlement for thy roof, that thou bring not blood upon thine house, if any man fall from thence." [4] The houses in Palestine generally have flat roofs, and on them men walk to enjoy the fresh air, converse together, sleep, etc. The need of the battlement is quite evident.

But there is also a deep spiritual lesson taught in the command. Every man builds his own character. Paul says, " Ye are God's *building*," and every building will be tested by the Lord. [5]

It is possible to build a character that will pass the test of the judgment, and in this world stand as a beacon light in the moral darkness of sin, guiding others safely into the haven of rest. On the other hand, like the housetop without any battlement, we may be the cause of ruin to many souls. In our character-building, we need to make straight paths for our feet, " lest that which is lame be turned out of the way." [6]

It is said that the rigid features of a marble statue may be made to vary their expression, so as even to smile, when skilful hands move a bright light before it; in like manner the plain command, " Thou shalt not muzzle the ox when he treadeth out the corn," [7] when viewed in the light of the New Testament, contains spiritual lessons for the Christian church.

In writing of the support of the Christian laborer, Paul says:

[1] Neh. 13 : 23-26. [2] 2 Cor. 3 : 18. [3] Ps. 119 : 37.
[4] Deut. 22 : 8. [5] 1 Cor. 3 : 9-17. [6] Heb. 12 : 13.
[7] Deut. 25 : 4.

"It is written in the law of Moses, Thou shalt not muzzle the mouth of the ox that treadeth out the corn. Doth God take care for oxen? or saith He it altogether for our sakes? *For our sakes, no doubt, this is written.*" [1]

Then he proceeds to explain that if we receive spiritual help from the Christian workers, we are in turn under obligation to give them of our "carnal" or temporal things. We have no more right to enjoy the spiritual aid derived from Christian workers without giving financial aid to support the work, than the ancient Israelites had to muzzle the ox that was patiently treading out his grain.

Paul closes his argument by showing that the same system of tithing given by God to sustain His work anciently, is still binding in the Christian church. "Do ye not know that they which minister about

"Thou shalt not muzzle the ox when he treadeth out the corn."

holy things live of the things of the temple? and they which wait at the altar are partakers with the altar? *Even so hath the Lord ordained that they which preach the gospel should live of the gospel.*" [2]

"Thou shalt not muzzle the ox when he treadeth out the corn,"

[1] 1 Cor. 9:9, 10.　　　　[2] 1 Cor. 9:13, 14.

contains a lesson for the Christian worker as well as for those for whom he labors. The muzzle is not put on the ox " *when* he treadeth out the grain," but if the ox stands idly by and does not tread out any grain, then it would be all right to muzzle him. The command is far reaching, and requires of the laborer in God's cause, faithful service; at the same time it lays upon others the obligation of faithfully supporting the gospel laborers.

Surely the following words of Tyndale apply to this text, " Similitudes have more virtue and power with them than bare words, and lead a man's understanding further into the pith and marrow and spiritual understanding of the thing, than all the words that can be imagined."

During the forty years' wandering in the wilderness, the children of Israel passed through varied experiences. Like humanity of the present day, they failed to be thankful for the protecting care of God. They did not see that God had shielded them from the poisonous reptiles that had infested their pathway through the desert. God removed His protecting care, and allowed the fiery serpents to come among the people, " and they bit the people; and much people of Israel died." [1]

The people confessed that they had sinned and spoken against God, and pleaded with Moses to pray for them. God told Moses to make a serpent of brass and set it up on a pole, and every one that would look upon it should live.

Hope sprang up in many hearts, as they lifted the heads of their dear ones and directed their eyes toward the serpent. As soon as the gaze of those who were bitten rested upon it, life and health came back to them.

The remedy was so simple — only " to look " — that some scoffed at it; but in refusing to look, they refused life.

The introduction to the wonderful words of John 3 : 16 are,

[1] Num. 21 : 5, 6.

" As Moses lifted up the serpent in the wilderness, even so must the Son of man be lifted up: that whosoever believeth in Him should not perish, but have eternal life." [1]

As the serpent was lifted up on the pole, *so* Jesus Christ was lifted up on the cross. *As* the Israelites were to look at the brazen serpent, *so* sinners must look to Christ for salvation. *As* God provided no other remedy than this *looking* for the wounded Israelite, *so* He has provided no other way of salvation than *faith* in the blood of His Son. *As* he who looked at the brazen serpent was *cured* and *did live; so,* he that believeth on the Lord Jesus Christ shall *not perish,* but shall have *eternal life.*

The fatal effects of sin can be removed in no other way than by the means God has provided. The old serpent, which is the devil, is wounding men and women on every side by his deadly bite; but Christ has shed His blood upon Calvary's cross, and every one who will look to Christ, *believing* that His *blood* will cleanse from all sin, will be free from the poison of the serpent's bite. [2]

Of the command, " Whether it be cow or ewe, ye shall not kill it and her young both in one day," [3] Andrew A. Bonar gives the following comment: " Some say this was meant simply to discourage cruelty. No doubt it had this effect. But a typical reason lies hid, and is very precious. The *Father* was to *give up* His Son; and the Son was to be, as it were, torn from t h e Father's care by the hands of wicked men. How could this be represented if *both* the ewe and her young were offered together? This part of the truth must never be obscured, that *'God so loved the world, that He gave His Son.'* And the bleatings of the tender lamb in its parent's ears, as it was taken from the fold, filling the air with sadness, represented the bleatings of 'the Lamb led to the slaughter,' who so sadly wailed, ' Eli! Eli! lama

[1] John 3: 14, 15.   [2] 1 John 1: 7, 9.   [3] Lev. 22: 28.

sabachthani?' . . . We see thus a picture hung up in every house of Israel of that great truth, ' God *spared not His own Son,* but delivered Him up for us all.' "

TYPE

ANTITYPE

Deut. 22 : 11. " Thou shalt not wear a garment of divers sorts, as of woolen and linen together."

Isa. 64 : 6; 61 : 10. We can not mingle the filthy rags of our righteousness with the robes of Christ's righteousness.

Deut. 22 : 10. " Thou shalt not plow with an ox and an ass together."

2 Cor. 6 : 14-17. " Be ye not unequally yoked together with unbelievers."

Deut. 22 : 9. " Thou shalt not sow thy vineyard with divers seeds; lest the fruit of thy seed which thou hast sown, and the fruit of thy vineyard, be defiled."

1 Cor. 15 : 33. Twentieth Century translation: "Good character is marred by evil company." Syriac Translation: " Evil stories corrupt well-disposed minds."

Deut. 22 : 8. " Thou shalt make a battlement for thy roof, that thou bring not blood upon thine house."

Heb. 12 : 13. " Make straight paths for your feet, lest that which is lame be turned out of the way."

Deut. 25 : 4. " Thou shalt not muzzle the ox when he treadeth out the corn."

1 Cor. 9 : 11 ; 1 Tim. 5 : 18. " If we have sown unto you spiritual things, is it a great thing, if we shall reap your carnal things?"

Num. 21 : 8, 9. Moses lifted up the serpent in the wilderness, and all that looked upon it, lived.

John 3 : 14, 15. "Even so must the Son of man be lifted up; that whosoever believeth in Him should not perish, but have eternal life."

SECTION IX

The Tribes of Israel

When the King Shall Claim His Own

IN THE glad time of the harvest,
  In the grand millennial year,
When the King shall take His scepter,
  And to judge the world appear,
Earth and sea shall yield their treasure,
  All shall stand before the throne;
Just awards will then be given,
  When the King shall claim His own.

O the rapture of His people!
  Long they've dwelt on earth's low sod,
With their hearts e'er turning homeward,
  Rich in faith and love to God.
They will share the life immortal,
  They will know as they are known,
They will pass the pearly portal,
  When the King shall claim His own.

Long they've toiled within the harvest,
  Sown the precious seed with tears;
Soon they'll drop their heavy burdens
  In the glad millenial years;
They will share the bliss of heaven,
  Nevermore to sigh or moan;
Starry crowns will then be given,
  When the King shall claim His own.

We shall greet the loved and loving,
  Who have left us lonely here;
Every heart-ache will be banished
  When the Saviour shall appear;
Never grieved with sin or sorrow,
  Never weary or alone;
O, we long for that glad morrow
  When the King shall claim His own.

—*L. D. Santee.*

CHAPTER XXXVII

REUBEN

THE Lord names individuals according to their character, and since He has chosen the names of the twelve sons of Jacob,— whence came the twelve tribes of Israel,— as names of the twelve divisions of the one hundred and forty-four thousand, there must be something in the character of Jacob's sons and of the twelve tribes of Israel worthy of careful study.

There is a significance in the meaning of names given to persons by the Lord. Jacob's name was not changed to Israel until, after long and weary wrestling, he had prevailed with God and men. [1] It was after Joses had given all his possessions to supply the needs of the cause of God, that he was called Barnabas, or "the son of consolation." [2]

[1] Gen. 32 : 24-28. [2] Acts 4 : 36, 37.

The company of one hundred and forty-four thousand, who will be redeemed from among men when the Saviour comes, and who throughout eternity will "follow the Lamb whithersoever He goeth," will enter the city of God marshaled in twelve companies, each bearing the name of one of the twelve tribes of Israel. [1] From these instances we conclude that there was a special significance to the names given to the twelve sons of Jacob.

In every ancient Israelitish family the eldest son inherited, as his birthright, a double portion of his father's estate, and the honor of officiating as priest in his father's house; and what was of more value to every true son of Abraham than wealth or earthly position, he inherited the spiritual birthright, which gave him the honor of being the progenitor of the promised Messiah.

But Reuben, the eldest of the twelve sons of Jacob, like his Uncle Esau, [2] lightly esteemed the birthright, and in an unguarded hour committed a sin that forever debarred him from all the spiritual and temporal rights of the first-born. He committed adultery with his father's wife, a sin which Paul said was not even "so much as named among the Gentiles," or heathen. [3]

Because of this sin,— the temporal birthright — the double portion of Jacob's earthly inheritance — was given to Joseph; [4] the priesthood to Levi; [5] and upon Judah, the fourth son of Jacob, was conferred the honor of becoming the progenitor of Christ. [6]

Jacob on his deathbed portrayed the character which Reuben as the first-born might have possessed. "Reuben, thou art my first-born, my might, and the beginning of my strength, the excellency of dignity, and the excellency of power." We can imagine the pathetic tone of the old patriarch's voice as he portrayed the real character of his first-born, the one who might have had the respect of all,— "Unstable as water, thou shalt not excel." [7]

[1] Rev. 14:1-4; 7:4-8.   [2] Gen. 25:34; Heb. 12:16.   [3] 1 Cor. 5:1; Gen. 49:4.
[4] 1 Chron. 5:1.   [5] Deut. 33:8-11.   [6] 1 Chron. 5:1, 2.   [7] Gen. 49:3, 4.

There are traces in the history of Reuben of the "excellency of dignity" which originally was bestowed upon him, as shown by his kindness in bringing home the mandrakes to his mother, [1] and trying to save the life of Joseph, when his brethren determined to kill him. [2]

Reuben was a vacillating character, "unstable as water." His

"Jacob on his deathbed portrayed the character which Reuben . . . might have possessed."

father had little confidence in his word; for when his brethren wished to take Benjamin down to Egypt, Jacob did not regard Reuben's pledge to return Benjamin safely to his father; but when Judah promised to stand as security for the lad, Jacob accepted the offer. [3]

The unstable nature of Reuben seems to have been transmitted to his descendants. The same selfish character was shown by

[1] Gen. 30:14.   [2] Gen. 37:21, 22, 29; 42:22.   [3] Gen. 42:37, 38; 43:8, 9.

19

the tribe of Reuben wishing to take possession of the first land conquered when they came out of Egypt. Moses evidently read their motive in the request, yet he granted them their possessions on "the other side of Jordan." As the result of this request they were among the first to be carried captive into Assyria by Tiglath-pileser, king of Assyria, about B. C. 740. [1]

The prophetic words of the patriarch, "Thou shalt not excel," were fulfilled in the history of the tribe of Reuben. That tribe furnished no judge, no prophet, no hero, unless it be Adina and the thirty men with him, who were reckoned among the valiant men of David's army. [2] These men were no doubt among the one hundred and twenty thousand of the tribes of Reuben, Gad, and Manasseh who went up to Hebron to make David king over Israel. [3]

Dathan and Abiram, of the tribe of Reuben, with Korah the Levite, were noted for the rebellion they instigated in the camp of Israel; and their destruction was an object-lesson of the fate of all who pursue a similar course. [4]

The territory chosen by the Reubenites placed them in close proximity to Moab. The towns in the inheritance of Reuben — Heshbon, Elealeh, Kirjathaim, Nebo, Baalmeon, Shibmah,— are familiar to us as Moabitish and not Israelitish towns.

It is not strange that Reuben, thus remote from the central seat of the national government and of the national religion, relinquished the faith of Jehovah. "They went after the gods of the people of the land whom God destroyed before them," and we hear little more of the tribe of Reuben until Hazael, king of Syria, held possession of their territory for a time. [5]

When as a tribe they had completely failed to do the work God intended they should do in their own land, the Lord permitted Pul and Tiglath-pileser to carry them into the upper part

[1] Num. 32 : 1-33; I Chron. 5 : 26.   [2] I Chron. 11 : 42.   [3] I Chron. 12 : 37, 38.
[4] Num. 16 : 1; Deut. 11 : 6.   [5] 2 Kings 10 : 32, 33.

of Mesopotamia, where they remained until, at the end of the seventy years' captivity, representatives of the twelve tribes were again gathered into the land of promise. [1]

The history of the tribe is a record of failures in carrying out the purposes of God. As Reuben, the first-born, had the opportunity to stand as a leader, so the tribe of Reuben, situated on the borders of Moab, might have proved true to God, and been a beacon light to lead the heathen to the true God; but they, like their father Reuben, were " unstable as water."

Although the patriarch and his descendants failed to carry out the purposes of God, yet the name of Reuben will be immortalized, for throughout eternity, the countless millions of the redeemed will read that name on one of the pearly gates of the New Jerusalem. Twelve thousand of the one hundred and forty-four thousand will be of this class, and will enter the kingdom of God under the name of Reuben.

How can one be thus honored who apparently made a failure of life? That is the great mystery of godliness. How can the thief, who made a complete shipwreck of his life, be with the Saviour in Paradise? It is through the power of the blood of Christ, the sin-pardoning Redeemer.

When Moses pronounced his parting blessing on the tribes of Israel, of Reuben he said: " Let Reuben live, and not die; and let not his men be few." [2] We might wonder how a character " unstable as water " could " live, and not die;" but the course pursued by Reuben at the time of a great crisis in Israel, explains how such a one can be an overcomer.

At the time of the battle of Megiddo, which is in many respects a type of the final battle of Armageddon, it is stated that " in the divisions of Reuben there were great searchings of heart." [3] Here is the secret of the whole matter.

[1] Ezra 6 : 17; 8 : 35; Neh. 7 : 73.   [2] Deut. 33 : 6.   [3] Judges 5 : 16, margin.

There are multitudes of men and women in the world to-day with characters like Reuben. They are "unstable as water," with no power in themselves to do any good thing; but if they will begin earnestly to search their hearts, they will discover their own weakness; and if they turn to God, He will come to their rescue, and pronounce over them, as He did over Reuben of old, "Let such a one live and not die."

SUMMARY

The birthright embraced,—

A double portion of property,

The priesthood of the family,

The progenitor of Christ.

Reuben had four sons, whose descendants formed the tribe which bore his name. 1 Chron. 5 : 3.

The tribe numbered 43,730, when they entered the promised land. Num. 26 : 7.

The Reubenites were carried captive into Assyria. 1 Chron. 5 : 26.

CHAPTER XXXVIII

SIMEON

 IMEON was the second son of Jacob's unloved wife, Leah. He was a man of strong passions. His life and that of the tribe which bears his name contain some of the darkest stains in the history of ancient Israel.

The crowning sin of Simeon's life was the murder of the men of Shechem. [1] Levi was connected with Simeon in this wicked work, but Simeon seems to have been the leading spirit; for the divine record always mentions his name first when speaking of the sin.

There is something pathetic in the whole affair. The prince of Shechem had ruined Dinah, the only daughter of Jacob. It is easy to imagine how an only sister would be loved and cherished by her brothers, and especially by the sons of Leah who

[1] Genesis 34.

(293)

was also the mother of Dinah. When Jacob reproved Simeon and Levi for the murder, their only reply was, " Should he deal with our sister as with a harlot?" [1]

Love for their sister evidently prompted the act of revenge. They also wished to rescue her; for Dinah had been enticed to the house of the prince of Shechem, and after the murder, Simeon and Levi brought her home with them. [2]

The words addressed to Simeon by Jacob, show that God does not overlook sin in any one. The fact that their only sister was ruined, was no excuse for committing that terrible act of vengeance.

When the sons of Jacob gathered around their father's couch to receive his parting blessing, the sight of Simeon and Levi brought vividly to the mind of the dying patriarch the details of this murder committed some forty years before, and he exclaimed, " Simeon and Levi are brethren; instruments of cruelty are in their habitations. O my soul, come not thou into their secret." And as if he shrank from the very thought of his name being tarnished by their wicked course, he continues, " Unto their assembly, *mine* honor, be not thou united; for in their anger they slew a man, and in their selfwill they digged down a wall. Cursed be their anger, for it was fierce; and their wrath, for it was cruel: I will divide them in Jacob, and scatter them in Israel." [3]

Both tribes were " divided " and " scattered." But how differently! The Levites held positions of honor, and were scattered over the country as religious educators and priests. The dispersion of the tribe of Simeon arose from corrupting elements in the tribe itself, which reduced their numbers and finally resulted in driving them from their inheritance.

When the land was divided among the different tribes, Simeon

[1] Gen. 34:31.   [2] Gen. 34:26.   [3] Gen. 49:5-7.

had no part given him; but as the allotment of Judah was too large for that tribe, Simeon was allowed to occupy a portion of the inheritance of Judah. Afterward some of the Simeonites were obliged to seek new territory, and were thus separated from the rest of their brethren. [1]

In the writings of the ancient Jewish doctors it is stated that the tribe of Simeon became so straitened in their habitations that a very great number of them were forced to seek subsistence among the other tribes by teaching their children. Truly they were divided in Jacob and scattered in Israel.

When Israel was numbered at Sinai, Simeon had 59,300 fighting men. Only two tribes surpassed it in strength. But when Israel was again numbered at Shittim, Simeon was the weakest of all the tribes, numbering only 22,200. Why this great change? The strong men of Simeon did not sacrifice their lives on the battle-field, fighting for the honor of God; they were slain because of the licentiousness of their own hearts. The twenty-fifth chapter of Numbers relates the sad story of the ruin of Simeon. It seems from the record that the chief men of Simeon were the leaders in that great apostasy. They became a prey to the harlots of Midian. Truly " she hath cast down many wounded; yea, many strong men have been slain by her." [2]

Solomon, the wisest of men, who was thrice called the beloved of God, became a slave to his passion, and thus sacrificed his integrity to the same bewitching power. [3]

The shores of the stream of time are strewn with the wrecks of characters that have been stranded upon the rock of sensual indulgence. Israel became a prey to licentiousness before they were led into idolatry. When licentious desires rule the heart, other sins quickly follow.

" Blessed are the pure in heart." [4]   He that ruleth his spirit

[1] 1 Chron. 4 : 27, 39, 42.   [2] Prov. 7 : 26.
[3] Neh. 13 : 26.   [4] Matt. 5 : 8.

is greater than he that taketh a city;[1] but " he that hath no rule over his own spirit is like a city that is broken down, and without walls." [2]

Some suppose that the omission of Simeon's name in the blessing of Moses was due to Moses' displeasure at the behavior of the tribe at Shittim.

Little is said of the position taken by this tribe when the

" He that hath no rule over his own spirit is like a city that is broken down, and without walls."

kingdom was divided; but there are two references that would seem to indicate that their sympathy was with the kingdom of Israel. [3]

The same fearless, warlike disposition manifested in the outbreaking sins committed by Simeon, was in the life of Judith used for the protection of God's people.

It is uncertain whether the book in the Apocrypha that bears her name is a history or a historic romance, but from the record there given, Judith will always remain one of the prominent figures among the deliverers of her nation. She, like Jael, slew

[1] Prov. 16 : 32.   [2] Prov. 25 : 28.   [3] 2 Chron. 15 : 9; 34 : 6.

the leader of the enemies' army. [1] She nerved herself for her tremendous exploit by a prayer to the " Lord God of my father Simeon;" also in her prayer she alluded to the massacre at Shechem. [2]

The history of Judith, who, like Esther, risked her life for the deliverance of her people, is in pleasing contrast to the record of the wicked course pursued by Simeon and his descendants.

In the Targum Pseudo-Jonathan, it is Simeon and Levi who plot to destroy young Joseph; and Simeon bound Joseph before he was lowered into the well at Dothan. This was only about two years after the same men had planned and executed the murder of the men of Shechem. Memory must have brought all these events very vividly to the mind of Joseph as he stood before his brethren and commanded that Simeon be bound as a hostage before the eyes of the very men who had once seen him bind Joseph with intent to murder him. [3]

It may be thought strange by some that the name of a man who was famous only for murder and sin, should be inscribed on one of the gates of the Holy City of God, and that one twelfth of the one hundred and forty-four thousand will enter the city of God bearing the name of that man. But the fact that one has committed sin will never exclude him from the kingdom of God. All have sinned. It is *unconfessed* sin that debars any one from receiving eternal life.

Jesus is the only one born of woman that is sinless. He alone of all the family of Adam will throughout eternity have an uncovered life record. No part of His record will be covered. But our life record, marred by sin, will be covered by Christ's righteousness. The blood of Christ can cleanse from sin of the deepest dye, and even murderers can enter heaven; not as murderers, but as pardoned sinners; for *" though your sins be as*

[1] Judges 4:21; Judith 13:6-9.   [2] Judith 9:2.   [3] Gen. 42:19-24.

scarlet, they shall be as white as snow; though they be red like crimson, they shall be as wool." [1]

Gathered out of the sin and wickedness of the last generation, there will be twelve thousand redeemed ones, who through the virtue of the blood of Christ, will be grafted into the tribe of Simeon, and throughout eternity will represent that tribe on the earth made new.

SUMMARY

Simeon had six sons, whose descendants formed the tribe which bore his name. Gen. 46: 10.

The tribe numbered 22,200, when they entered the promised land. Num. 26: 12-14.

Judith, the only noted character in the tribe, slew the leader of the enemies' army. Judith 13: 6-14.

[1] Isa. 1 : 18.

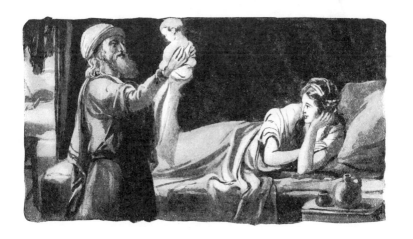

CHAPTER XXXIX

LEVI

HEN Leah gave birth to her third son, she said, " Now this time will my husband be joined unto me, because I have borne him three sons: therefore was his name called Levi," or " *joined*." [1]   Little did Leah, in the longing for the love of her husband, realize that the little babe would fulfil its name in a far broader sense than she anticipated, and help to join the children of Israel to their great Husband, the Creator of all things. [2]

The name of Levi seemed a prophecy of the life-work of the whole tribe. As Satan, through envy and jealousy, separated Leah from her husband's regard, so he sought to ruin Levi by persuading him to unite with Simeon in avenging the wrong done their only sister. [3]

[1] Gen. 29:34.   [2] Isa. 54:5.   [3] Genesis 34.

(299)

The words of Jacob on his deathbed reveal the magnitude of
the crime, and how the Lord regarded it. The old father's
heart was stirred at the remembrance, and he exclaimed, " O my
soul, come not thou into their secret; unto their assembly, *mine*
honor, be not thou united. . . . Cursed be their anger, for
it was fierce; and their wrath, for it was cruel." And then,
as if he could not bear to think of their ever growing into a
strong tribe to perpetuate such crimes, he exclaimed, " I will
divide them in Jacob, and scatter them in Israel." [1]   It was
more like a curse than a blessing; but when a sinner repents and
turns from his sins, our God turns even curses into blessings,
and thus it was in the case of Levi. [2]

There is nothing to indicate that the tribe of Levi had any
special pre-eminence over the other tribes during the Egyptian
bondage. It is quite evident that the original plan of having
the first-born officiate as priest of the household, continued until
the encampment at Sinai. The " young men of the children of
Israel " offered the sacrifices at that time. [3]   In the Targum
Pseudo-Jonathan, it is expressly stated, " He sent the first-born of
the children of Israel, for even to that time the worship was by
the first-born because the tabernacle was not yet made, nor the
priesthood given to Aaron."

Character is *formed* by the way individuals meet the common
events of every-day life; but it is *tested* by the way they meet the
crises of life. At Sinai the people of God passed through one of
the greatest crises in the history of the church, when the whole
multitude of Israel worshiped the golden calf. It was at this
time, when even God Himself was ready to destroy Israel, [4] that
the tribe of Levi came forward, and by their faithfulness helped
to save the cause of God.

When Moses came down from the mount and found the

[1] Gen. 49 : 5-7.   [2] Neh. 13 : 2.
[3] Ex. 24 : 5.   [4] Ex. 32 : 10.

children of Israel worshiping the golden calf, he stood in the gate of the camp, and said, " Who is on the Lord's side? let him come unto me. And all the sons of Levi gathered themselves together unto him. And he said unto them, Thus saith the Lord God of Israel, put every man his sword by his side, and go in and out from gate to gate throughout the camp, and slay every man his brother, and every man his companion, and every man his neighbor. And the children of Levi did according to the word of Moses." [1]

At the time of this crisis the honor of God and His cause was dearer to the Levites than all worldly connections; neither brothers, companions, or friends, stood between them and their duty to God. As a reward for their faithfulness, the priesthood,— a portion of the birthright,— was given to the sons of Levi. What Reuben lost by unfaithfulness in his father's home, Levi gained by being true to God before all Israel.

Jacob on his deathbed denounced Levi's sins; but Moses in his parting blessing, extolled him above all others. Of Levi he said, " Let thy Thummim and thy Urim be with thy holy one, whom thou didst prove at Massah, and with whom thou didst strive at the waters of Meribah; who said unto his father and to his mother, I have not seen him; neither did he acknowledge his brethren, nor knew his own children: for they have observed Thy word, and kept Thy covenant. They shall teach Jacob Thy judgments, and Israel Thy law: they shall put incense before Thee, and whole burnt sacrifice upon Thine altar. Bless, Lord, his substance, and accept the work of his hands." [2]

From the fall of man, each household had celebrated its worship with a priest of its own. When the time came to change this method of worship, God did it in a way that gave all Israel a thorough understanding of the matter.

[1] Ex. 32 : 26-28.   [2] Deut. 33 : 8-11.

The first-born males of all Israel were numbered, and found to be 22,000. Then the tribe of Levi was numbered, and there were 22,273. Thus the Levites outnumbered the first-born; so the redemption price for the first-born,— " five shekels apiece by the poll," was paid for the 273 Levites,— the number by which they outnumbered the first-born. [1] Then all the Levites were set apart for their life-work.

The sum of the numbers given in the third chapter of Numbers for each of the three branches of the tribe of Levi is 22,300. It is understood that these extra 300 were the first-born of Levi, and as such were already consecrated, and could not take the place of others.

The tabernacle was a sign to the children of Israel of their unseen King, and the Levites were as a royal guard that waited exclusively upon Him. When the people were encamped, the Levites were the guardians of the sacred tent. When they traveled, the Levites alone carried all that pertained to the sanctuary.

When Israel entered the promised land, the tribe of Levi was given no inheritance. It was not expected that they would spend their time and strength in cultivating the soil and rearing cattle. The spiritual welfare of *all* Israel was to be their burden; and, that they might the more easily perform this work, the Levites were given forty-eight cities, scattered throughout all the twelve tribes, and the tithe was used for their support. [2] Thus Jacob's prophecy was fulfilled; they were " divided in Jacob, and scattered in Israel."

The history of the temple and its service is a history of the Levites. When God was honored by His people, the Levites were given their appointed work; but when apostasy came in, the Levites were obliged to seek other employment for their support. [3]

[1] Num. 3 : 46-49.   [2] Num. 18 : 20, 21.   [3] Neh. 13 : 10, 11.

Levi, like the other tribes, had a checkered history; not all were true to God, but the tribe continued to exist in Israel to the time of Christ, and had a worthy representative among the early apostles in the person of Barnabas. [1]

It was in the time of a crisis that the Levites gained their great victory. In a crisis decisions are made quickly. Many fail at such times, because they do not have independent Christian characters. They are in the habit of following the leadings of those in whom they have confidence, and they have no strength in themselves. He who would always prove true in the crises of life, must have a clear connection with the God of heaven, and must fear God more than man.

Moses and Aaron are two of the most noted characters in the tribe of Levi. There was a marked contrast in the two men. Moses stood like a great rock, against which the waves beat continually. Aaron was gentler, and at times he seemed almost vacillating; but Aaron was a strong character, although different from his brother.

"Moses stood like a great rock."

"Aaron was gentler."

Aaron's crowning test came when his two sons were smitten

[1] Acts 4: 36.

down in the tabernacle, because, under the influence of strong drink, they offered strange fire before the Lord. Aaron was not allowed to show any signs of grief; thus teaching the people that God was just in punishing evildoers, even if they were his own sons.

This was no small test, and after studying Lev. 10: 1-11 we can better understand how, notwithstanding the murders committed in Levi's early life, the Lord could speak of Aaron as "the saint of the Lord." [1]

One twelfth of the one hundred forty-four thousand will be marshaled under the name of Levi. They will be persons who, on account of sin, merited only curses, but who forsook sin; and while men all around them were wavering and falling, they stood true to God and His cause, and will receive a rich blessing from the hands of a merciful God.

SUMMARY

Levi had three sons, whose descendants formed the tribe which bore his name. Gen. 46: 11.

Aaron and his sons officiated as priests.

The remainder of the tribe assisted in the work of the temple.

Noted Characters

Moses and Aaron were the most noted Levites in the Old Testament.

Barnabas and Mark are prominent characters in the New Testament.

[1] Ps. 106: 16.

CHAPTER XL

JUDAH

AME or pedigree, separate from character, has no weight in the records of heaven. Because Reuben failed to cultivate a character worthy of the first-born,—the one entitled to both the temporal and the spiritual birthright, — its blessings were taken from him, and given to others who had developed characters worthy of them.

Joseph, who had become a noted business manager, was given the double portion of his father's inheritance, — the temporai birthright; but it required more than ability to control great wealth to be entitled to the spiritual birthright, and to become the progenitor of the Messiah.

The records state that Judah, the fourth son, " prevailed above

(305)

his brethren, and of him came the Chief Ruler." [1]   Jacob, upon his deathbed, pronounced the prophetic words: " The scepter shall not depart from Judah, nor a lawgiver from between his feet, until Shiloh come; and unto Him shall the gathering of the people be " [2]

How did Judah prevail above his brethren, and thus inherit the spiritual birthright? This is a subject worthy of careful study by every one who desires a part in the great spiritual birth-

right by which we to-day may become heirs of the eternal inheritance. We have no record of Judah's ever prevailing over his brethren by force of arms. But a careful s t u d y of the lives of the twelve sons of Jacob, r e - veals the fact that Judah was a leader. When he offered to stand as surety for Benjamin, Jacob consented to let Benjamin go into Egypt, although Reuben's offer had been refused. [3]

When Jacob and his family arrived in Egypt, Jacob " sent Judah before him unto Joseph, to direct his face unto Goshen." [4]

When the sons of Jacob were in great perplexity because the ruler of Egypt demanded Benjamin as a hostage, it was Judah who pleaded their cause so earnestly that Joseph threw off

[1] 1 Chron. 5: 2.   [2] Gen. 49: 10.
[3] Gen. 43: 8-13; 42: 37, 38.   [4] Gen. 46: 28.

his disguise, and made himself known unto his brethren. [1]

By strict integrity to principle, Judah had won the confidence of his father and his brethren. The whole story is told in the blessing pronounced over Judah by his aged father, just before his death: "Judah, thou art he whom thy brethren shall praise: thy hand shall be in the neck of thine enemies; thy father's children shall bow down before thee." [2]

His brethren bowed down before Joseph, but the circumstances were different. Joseph's wealth and position, acquired in a foreign land, gave him the pre-eminence; but Judah won the respect of his brethren in the every-day contact of the home life. This confidence was not born in a moment; but day by day his strict integrity won their respect, until of their own free will, not from force of circumstances, they praised him and bowed down before him. A life of conflict and victory over the selfish tendencies of his own heart, is bound up in the words, "Judah, thou art he whom thy brethren shall praise."

It is worthy of note that Judah prevailed under the same circumstances in which Reuben failed. It was not sins committed against the public that debarred Reuben from the privileges of the first-born; he proved himself untrue in the home life. [3] He had no regard for the honor of his own family. His father and his brethren could not trust him in their private life. In the same home, surrounded by the same temptations and environments, "Judah prevailed above his brethren, and of him came the Chief Ruler." [4]

Twelve thousand of the one hundred and forty-four thousand will enter the holy city under the name of Judah, [5] — persons who, in times of perplexity, have been recognized by their brethren as trusted leaders.

"Judah is a lion's whelp: from the prey, my son, thou art gone

[1] Gen. 44: 14-34; 45: 1-3.   [2] Gen. 49: 8.   [3] 1 Chron. 5: 1.
[4] 1 Chron. 5: 2.   [5] Rev. 7: 5.

up: he stooped down, he couched as a lion, and as an old lion; who shall rouse him up?" [1] In these words Jacob gives the impression that it would be as easy to conquer a lion as to overcome one with the character of Judah; that it would be as safe to rouse an old lion as to contend with one who stood fast in his integrity to God.

Judah's is a character we may well covet,—that firmness that will not surrender our Christian integrity, but will know of a surety that the Lord is with us when we are assailed by Satan and all his hosts. [2]

Judah is mentioned oftener in the Scriptures than any other of the twelve patriarchs, except Joseph. Of the five sons of Judah, two died childless; but from the three remaining sons came the strongest tribe in all Israel.

At Sinai the children of Judah numbered 74,600. They evidently had a very small part, if any, in the apostasy at Shittim, where Simeon's numbers were greatly reduced; for Judah numbered 76,500 as they left Shittim to enter the promised land.

The tribe of Judah occupied a position among the other tribes similar to that which their progenitor held in his father's family. They were entrusted with the care of the priesthood. The nine cities occupied by the family of Aaron, the priests, were all within the territory of Judah and Simeon. [3] The remainder of the forty-eight cities occupied by the Levites were scattered throughout the other tribes.

Judah was an independent tribe. After the death of Saul, they did not wait for others to acknowledge David as king, but crowned him king of Judah, and David reigned over them seven and one-half years before he was crowned king over all Israel. [4]

After the death of Solomon, Judah and Benjamin remained true to the seed of David, and formed the kingdom of Judah.

[1] Gen. 49:9.
[3] Joshua 21:9-16.
[2] Matt. 7:24, 25.
[4] 2 Sam. 2:4, 11.

This kingdom retained their own land about 142 years after the kingdom of Israel was carried captive into Assyria. [1]

Zedekiah, king of Judah, was given the last opportunity of saving the holy city from falling into the hands of the heathen, [2] but he failed, and Judah, the kingly tribe, was carried captive into Babylon.

The scepter never fully departed from Judah until Shiloh came. Herod, the last king who reigned over the Jews, died a few years after the birth of Christ. In his first will Herod appointed Antipas as his successor; but his last will named Archelaus as the one to reign in his stead. The people were ready to receive Archelaus, but afterward revolted. Archelaus and Antipas both went to Rome to present their claims before Cæsar. Cæsar confirmed neither, but sent Archelaus back to Judea as ethnarch, [3] with the promise of the crown if he proved worthy of it; but he never received it. Thus the land

" Archelaus and Antipas . . . before Cæsar."

was " forsaken of both her kings " during the childhood of Christ, as prophesied by Isaiah. [4]

The tribe of Judah furnished a galaxy of names noted in sacred history. No other tribe furnished the world so many mighty

[1] 2 Kings 17:6; 2 Chron. 36:17-20. [2] Jer. 38:17-20.
[3] Matt. 2:19-22. [4] Isa. 7:14-16.

The fining pot is for silver, and the furnace for gold but the Lord trieth the hearts.

PROV.17:3

men of God. At the head of the list is the one incomparable name,— Jesus of Nazareth, the Lion of the tribe of Judah.

Caleb's great faith and dauntless courage has been an inspiration to men of all ages. In the prime of life his faith was strong. When other men saw only the giants of difficulties in the way of entering the land, he said, "We are well able to overcome it." [1] At the age of eighty-five, in the strength of God, he drove the enemies from the stronghold of Hebron. [2]

David has been honored above all earthly kings in being taken as a type of Christ, and inspiration calls the Saviour "the son of David." [3] Judah furnished a number of other kings who, surrounded by all the temptations of the court life, stood true to God.

After the captivity, when for a time it seemed as if the Israel of God were almost obliterated from the earth, four young men of Judah, true to the lion-like character of their tribe, risked their lives rather than defile themselves with the royal dainties [4] from the table of the king of Babylon. [5]

A few years later three of these men stood fearlessly before

[1] Num. 13:30.   [2] Joshua 14:6-15; 15:13-15.   [3] Matt. 21:9.
[4] Prov. 23:1-3.   [5] Dan. 1:8.

the king of Babylon, saying, " Be it known unto thee, O king, that we will not serve thy gods." [1] In fulfilment of the promise made over one hundred years before, [2] the Lord walked with those three sons of Judah through the fiery furnace, and they came forth unhurt. [3] And Daniel, true to the integrity of his tribe, faced hungry lions rather than have any interruption in his communion with God. [4]

SUMMARY

Judah was the progenitor of Christ. I Chron. 5 : 2; Gen. 49 : 10.

The tribe of Judah were the descendants of the three youngest sons of Judah.

The tribe numbered 76,500, when they entered the promised land. Num. 26:19-22.

The scepter did not depart from Judah until Shiloh came. Isa. 7 : 14, 16.

Noted Characters

Caleb, the son of Jephunneh. Num. 13 : 6.

Othniel, a nephew of Caleb, judged Israel forty years. Judges 3 : 9-11.

Ibzan of Bethlehem, of the land of Judah, judged Israel seven years. Judges 12 : 8-10.

Judah furnished many kings; prominent among them were David, Solomon, Jehoshaphat, Hezekiah, and Josiah.

The greatest character of all is Jesus, the Lion of the tribe of Judah. Rev. 5 : 5.

[1] Dan. 3 : 18.
[3] Dan. 3 : 24-27.
[2] Isa. 43 : 2.
[4] Dan. 6 : 7-10, 16-22.

CHAPTER XLI

NAPHTALI

APHTALI, the sixth son of Jacob, was the second son of Bilhah, Rachel's maid. The Bible is silent in regard to his personal history, except the statement that he had four sons from whom sprang the tribe of Naphtali; but Jewish tradition states that Naphtali was noted as a swift runner, and that he was chosen by Joseph as one of five to represent the family before Pharaoh.

In Jacob's dying blessing, Judah was compared to a lion, Dan to a serpent, Issachar to a strong ass, Benjamin to a wolf, but " Naphtali is a hind let loose: he giveth goodly words." [1] A hind, or female deer, is a timid animal, ready to flee at the first approach of danger. No one would attempt to bind a burden on a deer.

Naphtali indicates a character quite different from Issachar, couching down between two burdens, or Judah with his kingly

[1] Gen. 49 : 21.

power; yet Naphtali has a precious gift that every one may covet: "He giveth goodly words." Unencumbered by many of the heavy burdens and responsibilities borne by some of his brethren, he has time to find those who are downcast and discouraged, and by his "goodly words" to encourage the despondent and comfort the sorrowful.

Naphtali does not represent the unruly tongue that "is set on fire of hell;"[1] far from it, for he "giveth *goodly words,*" and "pleasant words are as a honeycomb, sweet to the soul, and *health* to the bones."[2]

Let no one think because Naphtali spoke "goodly words" that he represented a light, unstable character; for in the great typical battle of Megiddo, "Naphtali were a people that jeoparded their lives unto the death in the high places of the field."[3] The literal translation of the original is very emphatic, *"they desolated their lives to death;"* they were determined to conquer or die, and therefore plunged into the thickest of the battle. The cause of God was more precious to them than life, and they did not shrink from fighting in the high places of the field, exposed to the fiery darts of the enemy, if the success of the battle demanded it.

There will be twelve thousand of the tribe of Naphtali that throughout all eternity will "follow the Lamb whithersoever He goeth;" twelve thousand that during their probationary life on this earth spoke "goodly words," and in difficult places, fearlessly stood firm at their post of duty, ready to sacrifice their lives rather than compromise the cause of God.

In Moses' last blessing, of Naphtali he said, "O Naphtali, satisfied with favor, and full with the blessing of the Lord."[4] Surely, this is a condition to be coveted by every child of God,— "satisfied with favor." The Lord greatly favors every one whose

---

[1] James 3:5-8.   [2] Prov. 16:24.
[3] Judges 5:18.   [4] Deut. 33:23.

sins are forgiven; but how often we are dissatisfied and impatient, and go through life with downcast faces.

Because we are *not* "*satisfied*" with favor," we are *not* "*full* with the blessing of the Lord." The child of God who fully realizes what it is to be cleansed from sin and clothed with Christ's righteousness, will be "satisfied with favor:" and if he appreciates the many blessings he receives at the hand of the Lord, and counts them over day by day, he will find that his life "is full with the blessing of the Lord."

Naphtali joined with the rest of Israel in crowning David king at Hebron, and the record states that with other northern tribes they brought large quantities of provisions to Hebron at that time. [1]

Barak, of Kadesh-Naphtali, is the only great hero of this tribe, mentioned in the Bible. The battle fought by him under the direction of Deborah the prophetess was in many respects the greatest battle fought by the ancient people of God, and is a type, or object-lesson, of the great battle of Armageddon. [2]

The territory bordering on the west shore of the Sea of Galilee and extending northward, was given to Naphtali. It was a fertile country, and during the reign of Solomon was one of his commissariat districts, in charge of Ahimaaz, a son-in-law of the king. [3]

The territory of Naphtali lay in the path of the Syrian and Assyrian invaders. It was from the goodly land of Naphtali that Ben-hadad and Tiglath-pileser had their first taste of the plunder of the Israelites. In 730 B. C., Tiglath-pileser overran the whole of the north of Israel, and the tribe of Naphtali was carried captive into Assyria.

In the time of Christ, Naphtali no longer possessed the shore of the Sea of Galilee, but it was to be far more renowned than when

[1] 1 Chron. 12:40.   [2] Judges 4:6-24.   [3] 1 Kings 4:7, 15.

"The 'Light of the world' had His home in Galilee."

held by him. Isaiah, more than seven hundred years before Christ, had prophesied that the land of Zebulun and of Naphtali would see a great light,[1] and in fulfilment of it, Jesus, the " Light of the world," had His home in Galilee.　It was the cradle of the Christian faith, and from the shores of the Sea of

[1] Isa. 9 : 1, 2 ; Matt. 4 : 15, 16.

Galilee the leading disciples were called to their life-work.

O Galilee, sweet Galilee,
What memories rise at thought of thee!
In mortal guise upon thy shore
The Saviour trod whom we adore.

The waves which once His vessel bore
Will sound His praise forevermore;
And from thy depths, beloved sea,
We hear the call, " Come follow Me."

Through ages yet to come, thy name
Will sound His praise forevermore;
'Tis hallowed ground where once He trod,
The Prince of Peace, the Son of God.

O Galilee, sweet Galilee,
Thy blessed name will sacred be
In every clime, on every shore,
Till suns shall set to rise no more.

—*Mrs. C. L. Schacklock.*

SUMMARY

The tribe of Naphtali sprang from four sons of Naphtali. Gen. 46 : 24.

The tribe numbered 45,400, when they entered the promised land.   Num. 26 : 50.

Barak, of Kadesh-Naphtali, is the only great hero of this tribe.

Christ's work in the borders of what had been the land of Naphtali, was a subject of prophecy.   Isa. 9: 1, 2.

CHAPTER XLII

GAD

F THE childhood and personal life of Gad, the seventh son of Jacob, nothing definite is preserved. He was the first son of Zilpah, Leah's maid; but from the record given it seems that Gad and the other sons born to Jacob by Bilhah and Zilpah, were far from being exemplary characters in their early lives. [1]

The prophetic words of his dying father open up a volume in the life and character of this son: " Gad, a troop shall overcome him: but he shall overcome at the last." [2] Gad may be taken as a type of the backslider, who is overcome by a troop of temptations, but awakens to his danger; and in the strength given him from God, overcomes at last, and enters the pearly gates of the New Jerusalem, rejoicing in the Lord.

[1] Gen. 37:2.   [2] Gen. 49:19.

The secret of the Gadites' being victorious over their enemies, is given in the account of one of their great battles: *"They cried to God in the battle,* and He was entreated of them; because they put their trust in Him."[1]

When Peter found that he was actually sinking beneath the waves that he had been walking upon, he cried, "Lord, save me. And immediately Jesus stretched forth His hand, and caught him."[2] In like manner, the one who finds himself overcome by temptations over which in the past he has been victorious, has the privilege, like Gad and Peter, of crying out for help, and he will immediately receive it, if he puts his trust in God.

To every backslider the Lord sends this message: "Turn, O backsliding children, saith the Lord; for *I am married unto you*: and I will take you one of a city, and two of a family, and I will bring you to Zion."[3] The Lord uses the symbol of marriage to illustrate the close union between Himself and His people; and when they backslide and dishonor Him,— wonderful thought! — He still says, "Go and proclaim these words, . . . I am married unto you," — the backslider.

Again the Lord asks: "Where is the bill of your mother's divorcement, whom I have put away? or which of My creditors is it to whom I have sold you?" He answers the question Himself: "Behold, for your iniquities have ye sold yourselves."[4]

The Lord requires but one thing of the backslider: *"Only acknowledge thine iniquity,* that thou hast transgressed against the Lord thy God."[5] "If we confess our sins, He is faithful and just to forgive us our sins, and to cleanse us from all unrighteousness."[6]

To every backslider the Lord says, "Come now, and let us reason together: . . . though your sins be as scarlet, they shall

[1] 1 Chron. 5 : 20.   [2] Matt. 14 : 30, 31.   [3] Jer. 3 : 12-14.
[4] Isa. 50 : 1.   [5] Jer. 3 : 13.   [6] 1 John 1 : 9.

be as white as snow; though they be red like crimson, they shall be as wool." [1]

Hear the Lord pleading with the backslider: "Return, ye backsliding children, and *I will heal your backslidings.*" [2] That is a wonderful promise; but listen again to His pleading voice: "I will heal their backsliding, *I will love them freely*: for Mine anger is turned away." [3] It is no stinted portion that the backslider receives; the Lord *heals* his backslidings and loves him *freely.*

Who, that has ever once tasted the peace and joy of sins

The Gadites were Shepherds.

forgiven, can refuse such offers of pardon and love?

On one of the gates of the city of God, the name of Gad will be written, — Gad, the one who was overcome by a troop, but at the last became the victor.

Twelve thousand of the one hundred forty-four thousand will also be marshaled under the name of Gad, [4] — twelve thousand, who arise from backslidings and defeat, acknowledge their

[1] Isa. 1: 18.   [2] Jer. 3: 22.
[3] Hosea 14: 4.   [4] Rev. 7: 4, 5.

transgressions, claim the promises of God, wash their robes in the blood of the Lamb, and enter as victors the city of God. [1]

It is very difficult for the human heart to re-instate one who has betrayed his confidence and has spurned love and friendship; but the infinite God will not only heal our backslidings and love us freely, but He also says, " I, even I, am He that blotteth out thy transgressions for Mine own sake, and *will not remember thy sins.*" [2]

Because they were shepherds, the Gadites requested that their portion be given them out of the land first conquered " on the other side of Jordan." They took part in the conquest of the land on the west side of Jordan, and did not return to their families until they were given an honorable discharge by Joshua, at the door of the tabernacle in Shiloh. [3] Moses evidently refers to their choice of land and faithfulness in the parting blessing. [4]

Their inheritance lay between the territory of Reuben on the south and the half tribe of Manasseh on the north. At first the inheritance of Gad embraced half of Gilead; later they possessed all of it. [5] They became so closely identified with Gilead, that in some cases the name Gilead is used synonymously with Gad.

The character of the tribe was throughout fierce and warlike,— " men of might, and men of war fit for the battle, that could handle shield and buckler, whose faces were like the faces of lions, and were as swift as the roes upon the mountains." Such is the graphic description given of those eleven heroes of Gad, the least of them more than equal to a hundred, and the greatest to a thousand; that, undaunted by the swollen floods of Jordan, joined the forces of David at the time of his greatest discredit and embarrassment. [6]

Gad, although separated from the rest of Israel west of the

[1] Rev. 7 : 14. [2] Isa. 43 : 25. [3] Joshua 22 : 1-4.
[4] Deut. 33 : 20, 21. [5] 1 Chron. 5 : 11, 16. [6] 1 Chron. 12 : 8, 12, 13, margin.

"Men of might, and men of war fit for the battle."

Jordan, still retained some connection with them. From the following words of Ahab we should infer that Gad was considered a part of the northern kingdom: " Know ye that Ramoth in Gilead is ours, and we be still, and take it not out of the hand of the king of Syria?" [1]

Tiglath-pileser carried Gad captive into Assyria, [2] and the Ammonites inhabited their cities in the days of Jeremiah. The prophet bewails the condition in the following words: " Hath Israel no sons? hath he no heir? Why then doth Melcom (Moloch) inherit Gad, and his people dwell in his cities?" [3]

Of all the tribes of Israel, Gad and Reuben alone returned to the land their forefathers had left five hundred years before, with their occupations unchanged. The civilization and persecution in Egypt changed the occupation of most of the tribes.

Barzillai, the friend of David, was a Gileadite; [4] and so was Jephthah, that " mighty man of valor." Among the worthy characters of Gilead, or Gad, was " Elijah the Tishbite," who by his word locked heaven for three years and a half; and in answer to his prayer, the clouds emptied themselves again upon the earth.

Elijah was honored by God as only one other person was

[1] 1 Kings 22 : 3.   [2] 1 Chron. 5 : 26.
[3] Jer. 49 : 1, margin.   [4] 2 Sam. 19 : 32-39.

ever honored; [1] and when the time for his translation drew near, he crossed over Jordan into the land of his childhood, where, by the grace of God, he had gained that strength of character which enabled him fearlessly to rebuke Ahab and Jezebel his wife. It was from his own native land of Gilead that the chariots of God bore him in triumph into heaven. [2] Once he has returned to earth, when he with Moses " appeared in glory," on the mount of transfiguration, and talked with Jesus of the great sacrifice soon to be offered at Jerusalem. [3]

SUMMARY

The tribe of Gad were the descendants of the seven sons of Gad. Gen. 46: 16.

The tribe numbered 40,500, when they entered the promised land. Num. 26: 18.

Tiglath-pileser carried Gad captive into Assyria. I Chron. 5: 26.

Noted Characters

Barzillai, the friend of David. 2 Sam. 19: 32-39.

Jephthah, that " mighty man of valor." Judges 11: 1.

" Elijah the Tishbite " was from Gilead, or Gad. I Kings 17: 1.

---

[1] Heb. 11: 5.   [2] 2 Kings 2: 7-14.   [3] Luke 9: 28-31.

CHAPTER XLIII

ASHER

IKE several of the patriarchs, there is little personal history recorded of Asher, the eighth son of Jacob by Zilpah, Leah's maid. Leah greatly rejoiced at his birth, and named him Asher, which means, in the Hebrew, " happy." [1]

Of his childhood and early manhood we know nothing, only that he grew up with his brethren, and went into Egypt with the rest of the family. Asher had four sons and a daughter named Sarah, from whom sprang the tribe which bore his name. [2]

[1] Gen. 30 : 13, margin.   [2] I Chron. 7 : 30.

When the books of the Chronicles were written, the men of the tribe of Asher were spoken of as " choice and mighty men of valor;" and there were twenty-six thousand of them " that were apt to the war." [1]

When all Israel gathered at Hebron to make David king over Israel, Asher gathered forty thousand that were " expert in war." [2]

Since the name Asher (Aser, the Greek form of the word) is given to one division of the one hundred and forty-four thou- and, [3] the character of Asher is the most important thing for us to consider; and as little or nothing is recorded of his life, we shall have to take the prophetic words of Jacob and Moses as a guide in the study.

The patriarch Jacob's dying blessing on Asher was, " Out of Asher his bread shall be fat, and he shall yield royal dain- ties." [4] These words indicate prosperity.

When Moses pronounced his parting blessing upon the tribes of Israel, he said, " Let Asher be blessed with children; let him be acceptable to his brethren, and let him dip his foot in oil. Thy shoes shall be iron and brass; and as thy days, so shall thy strength be." [5]

Asher seems to have had an amiable disposition; for he was acceptable to his brethren. " Let him dip his foot in oil." Some people have the happy faculty of always getting out of difficulty as if everything was oiled; they apparently step over difficulties that others would fall under. They dip their feet in oil, and pass smoothly over the rough places in life.

The precious promise, " As thy days, so shall thy strength be," was given to Asher, the one Jacob said " should yield royal dainties," and of whom Moses said, " Let him dip his foot in oil." In ordinary life the one who dips his foot in oil, and ap-

[1] I Chron. 7 : 40. [2] I Chron. 12 : 36. [3] Rev. 7 : 6.
[4] Gen. 49 : 20. [5] Deut. 33 : 24, 25.

As thy days, so shall thy strength be.

Deut. 33:25

parently passes smoothly through life, receives little sympathy. Sympathy is usually extended to the one who does not have his feet oiled, and experiences all the roughness by the way; but God knows that the person who holds up his head and goes cheerily through life, giving "royal dainties" of kind words of cheer to others, often in reality experiences heavier trials than the one who sighs and cries on account of the roughness of the way; and to them He says, "As thy days, so shall t h y strength be."

It is a glorious thing to dip the foot in oil! Oil is a symbol of the Holy Spirit; the one whose feet even, are anointed with the Spirit of God, will pass over the rough places in life with a heart full of praise and thanksgiving. Under the feet of such a one will be iron and brass — a firm foundation. He will not sink amid the pitfalls of life, for God assures him, "As thy days, so shall thy strength be."

The feet of the one who dips his feet in oil will be shod with iron and brass. When the beloved disciple saw in vision the Saviour officiating as our High Priest in the heavenly sanctuary, His feet appeared "like unto fine brass, as if they burned in a furnace." [1] Brass is formed only in the furnace; and the Saviour's feet appearing like " fine brass, as if they burned in a furnace," would remind John of the fiery furnace of affliction through which the Saviour had passed.

There are some of the human family who are so imbued with the Spirit of God, and follow so closely in the Saviour's blood-stained footsteps, [2] that their feet seem clad with brass, resembling the feet of their Master. Others have their feet covered with iron ; they, too, have special strength given them, but do not come into such intimate relationship with the Master as their brethren.

Twelve thousand of the one hundred and forty-four thousand will be of the tribe of Asher,— those who will dip their feet in oil, and will be so filled with the Spirit of God that they will let the Lord by His Spirit smooth the rough places in their pathway. Like Zerubbabel, the mountains of difficulties will become plains before them. [3] They will yield " royal dainties," words of cheer and comfort, that will encourage others by the way. It is well to learn how to dip the foot in oil, and cultivate the character of Asher.

The Bible gives little more of the history of the tribe of Asher than is given of him as an individual. The tribe is mentioned in connection with the other tribes ; but no independent action is recorded of the tribe in the sacred history.

Asher is the only tribe west of the Jordan, except Simeon, which furnished no hero or judge to the nation. The obscurity which enshrouds the members of the tribe is pierced by only one noted character,— Anna the prophetess, who " served God with fastings and prayers night and day " in the temple. She had the honor of bearing the glad news of the birth of Christ to the faithful ones who were looking for redemption in Israel. [4]

The territory of Asher bordered on the Great Sea, and em-

[1] Rev. 1 : 15.
[2] 1 Peter 2 : 21.
[3] Zech. 4 : 6, 7.
[4] Luke 2 : 36-38, margin.

braced Mount Carmel, the scene of Elijah's great victory, a n d continued northward. The descendants of Asher did not have the fierce, warlike propensities of some of the other tribes, and did not drive out the former inhabitants of the land; "but the Asherites dwelt among the Canaanites, the inhabitants of the land." [1] As the result of mingling with the heathen, they w e r e greatly weakened.

When Israel was numbered at Sinai, Asher was a strong tribe; [2] but in the days of David they had become so reduced that their name is not mentioned in the selection of chief rulers. [3] Although as a tribe they departed from the ways of the Lord, yet among them were honest hearts who feared God.

When Hezekiah held his great

"Anna the prophetess"

Passover and invited all Israel to join in celebrating the feast at Jerusalem, some entire tribes laughed at the messengers and mocked them; "nevertheless divers of Asher . . . humbled themselves, and came to Jerusalem." [4] It takes moral stamina to be true to God when the surging masses on every side are rejecting the light of

[1] Judges 1 : 31, 32.
[3] 1 Chron. 27 : 16-22.
[2] Num. 1 : 40, 41.
[4] 2 Chron. 30 : 10, 11.

God's word. That spirit of faithfulness never left the tribe, and when the Saviour entered His temple for the first time in human form, of the *two* persons in all the city of Jerusalem who were in a spiritual condition to recognize the " Babe as the Redeemer of the world," one was the prophetess Anna of the tribe of Asher. [1]

SUMMARY

Asher had four sons and a daughter, from whom sprang the tribe which bore his name. I Chron. 7 : 30.

The tribe numbered 53,400, when they entered the promised land. Num. 26 : 47.

Asher furnished no hero or judge to the nation.

Anna, the prophetess, is the only noted character of the tribe of Asher, mentioned in the Bible. Luke 2 : 36-38.

[1] Luke 2 : 36.

CHAPTER XLIV

ISSACHAR

ISSACHAR was the ninth son of Jacob and the fifth son of Leah, the first wife. Of Issachar as an individual the Bible is silent after recording his birth. Of his associations with his brethren, we know nothing; but the old father's dying blessing reveals the history of Issachar's life of self-sacrifice and burden-bearing, and his meek and quiet spirit.

Jacob likens him to the patient ass or donkey, bearing two such heavy burdens that he couches down beneath them. The fact that this is not a common animal, but a *"strong"* one, indicates the strength of Issachar's character. " Issachar is a strong ass couching down between two burdens." Then the patriarch reveals the secret of Issachar's self-sacrificing life by giving the motive that actuated him in carrying the double burdens: " He saw that rest was good, and the land that it was pleasant; and

(329)

bowed his shoulder to bear, and became a servant unto tribute." [1]

Many lose the blessing by murmuring and complaining when they are required to carry double burdens. But Issachar was sustained by the thought of the pleasant land in store and the rest by and by. The same hope will sustain burden-bearers at the present day.

In the battle of Megiddo we find Issachar true to the character portrayed in Jacob's dying blessing. " The princes of Issachar were with Deborah; even Issachar, and also Barak." [2] From the words of Deborah, it would seem that Issachar bore the burden of the battle even more than Barak.

The same characteristic is given of Issachar when all the tribes gathered to crown David king of Israel. Issachar had clear discernment. The record states, " The children of Issachar . . . were men that had understanding of the times, to know what Israel ought to do." [3] They represented men that bore heavy responsibilities, pillars in the cause of God. They were not like Zebulun, expert warriors, ready to rush impulsively into the fiercest of the fight on a moment's notice; but they were able to plan the battle, and to carry the burden of the work.

It takes all the different phases of Christian character to represent the perfect character of Christ. The burden-bearer fills as important a place in the work of God as the kingly Judah or the Levitical teacher.

There will be twelve thousand of each class in that wonderful company,— the one hundred and forty-four thousand, " which follow the Lamb whithersoever He goeth."

The children of Issachar were a laborious, hardy, valiant tribe, patient in labor and invincible in war. They " were valiant men of might." [4] They possessed one of the richest portions of Palestine. It was bounded on the east by the river

[1] Gen. 49 : 14, 15.
[3] 1 Chron. 12 : 32.
[2] Judges 5 : 15.
[4] 1 Chron. 7 : 1-5.

" At the gate of the city of Nain . . . the Saviour's words, 'Young man, I say unto thee, Arise,' brought life and health into the dead."

Jordan, on the north by Zebulun, and on the south by the half tribe of Manasseh.

Many places noted in sacred history were within the borders of Issachar. It was there that the great victory of Barak and Deborah was won " in Taanach by the waters of Megiddo." [1]

In Shunem was the residence of the noble woman who, when she found her house was not large enough to entertain Elisha, the " holy man of God," built an additional room and furnished it that she might have the privilege of his association in her home. [2]

By the rich blessings that came into her life, [3] she realized

[1] Judges 5 : 19.   [2] 2 Kings 4 : 8-10.   [3] 2 Kings 4 : 12-37.

the truthfulness of the words, " Inasmuch as ye have done it unto the least of these My brethren, ye have done it unto Me." [1]

It was at the gate of the city of Nain in the borders of Issachar, that the Saviour's words, " Young man, I say unto thee, Arise," brought life and health into the dead body of the man whom his friends were carrying to the tomb. [2]

The same territory that was hallowed by the footsteps of the Saviour and the prophets of God, also witnessed the power of the devil. Endor, in the land of Issachar, was where Saul committed the crowning sin of his life by consulting the witch, and thus took himself entirely out of the hands of God and became a prey of the devil. [3] Saul was slain because he asked counsel " of one that had a familiar spirit, to inquire of it." [4] Those who follow the same course to-day will eventually meet the same fate; they will die spiritually, and be eternally separated from the Lord. [5]

Jezreel, situated in the fertile plain of Esdraelon, was the scene of the wicked murder of Naboth; [6] and in the streets of the same city, dogs ate the flesh of Jezebel. [7]

Tola, under whose rule of twenty-three years Israel had rest, was of the tribe of Issachar. [8]   Baasha, who ruled over the northern kingdom twenty-four years, was an Issacharite. " He did evil in the sight of the Lord." Elah, his son, followed in his footsteps, and was slain by Zimri, and the kingly power passed out of the hands of the tribe of Issachar. [9]

Issachar was the center of Jezebel's power, and the Baal worship introduced by her exerted an influence long after her death.

About five years before Issachar was carried captive into Assyria by Shalmaneser, [10] Hezekiah celebrated his great Passover at Jerusalem. The tribe of Issachar had so far departed from the true worship that they had forgotten to make the necessary

[1] Matt. 25 : 40.   [2] Luke 7 : 11-17.   [3] 1 Sam. 28 : 7-25.   [4] 1 Chron. 10 : 13, 14.
[5] Isa. 8 : 19, 20.   [6] 1 Kings 21 : 1-19.   [7] 2 Kings 9 : 30-37.
[8] Judges 10 : 1, 2.   [9] 1 Kings 15 : 27-34; 16 : 1-10.   [10] 2 Kings 17 : 3-6.

purifications; yet some of them responded to the invitation, and went to the feast, though ceremonially unfit to partake of it. Hezekiah was in close enough touch with the Lord to discern that the desire in the heart to serve God was of more consequence than forms and ceremonies. He allowed them to eat of the Passover, and, as they partook of it, he offered the following prayer: "The good Lord pardon every one that prepareth his heart to seek God, the Lord God of his fathers, though he be not cleansed according to the purification of the sanctuary;" and the Lord, who "seeth not as man seeth; for man looketh on the outward appearance, but the Lord looketh on the heart," "hearkened" to the prayer of the king, and "healed the people."[1]

SUMMARY

Issachar had four sons, from whom sprang the tribe which bore his name. 1 Chron. 7:1.

When the children of Israel entered the promised land, the tribe of Issachar numbered 64,300. Num. 26:23-25.

Issachar possessed one of the richest portions of Palestine.

The valley of Megiddo, or the plain of Esdraeion, was within the borders of Issachar.

Tola, who judged Israel twenty-three years, was an Issacharite. Judges 10:1, 2.

Baasha, king of Israel, was of the tribe of Issachar. 1 Kings 15:27.

---

[1] 2 Chron. 30:17-20; 1 Sam. 16:7.

CHAPTER XLV

ZEBULUN

EAH was the mother of six of the twelve patriarchs. It is worthy of note that, although Jacob accepted polygamy under what might be termed force of circumstances, yet he recognized Leah, the first wife, as his lawful wife. She was buried in the family burying-place. When he came to die, he requested that he might be buried in the cave of Machpelah. "There they buried Abraham and Sarah *his wife;* there they buried Isaac and Rebekah *his wife;* and there *I buried Leah,*" were among the last words of Jacob. It would seem that he wished his descendants to be able to say of the noted cave, "There they buried Jacob and Leah *his wife.*" [1]

During his life, Jacob allowed circumstances and his love for Rachel to influence him; but when he faced death, he acknowledged God's original plan of marriage. [2]

[1] Gen. 49:31.   [2] Gen. 2:24.

Zebulun was the youngest son of Leah; he was older than Joseph, and was born while Jacob was serving Laban. Jacob on his deathbed prophetically located Zebulun's inheritance, saying, "Zebulun shall dwell at the haven of the sea; he shall be for a haven of ships; and his border shall be unto Zidon." [1]

Zebulun's portion in the promised land lay between the territories of Naphtali and Issachar, bordering on the southern part of the west shore of the Sea of Galilee, and is supposed to have extended also to the shore of the Great Sea. Moses, in his parting blessing, spoke of Zebulun as a sea-faring people. [2]

The Bible records nothing of Zebulun as an individual, except his birth. Three sons are ascribed to him, who became the founders of the tribe which bore his name. [3] There is no record of the tribe having taken any part in the events of the wandering or the conquest of Palestine.

Deborah, in her song of triumph after the battle of Megiddo, says that among the tribes of Zebulun were those who handled "the pen of the writer," or as the margin reads, "they that draw with the pen." [4] This would indicate that they were a literary or artistic people.

In the battle which was a type of the great battle of Armageddon, Zebulun "jeopardized their lives unto the death in the high places of the field;" or, according to the marginal reading, they "exposed to reproach their lives." [5] God and His cause were more precious to them than their own lives or reputation.

Twelve thousand of the one hundred and forty-four thousand will enter the city of God under the name of Zebulun,— twelve thousand who, when the enemies of the Lord are numerous and popular, will expose "to reproach their lives unto the death in the high places of the field." There will be men in high places who, like those of Zebulun of old, "handle the pen of the writer,"

[1] Gen. 49:13.   [2] Deut. 33:18, 19.   [3] Num. 26:26, 27.
[4] Judges 5:14.   [5] Judges 5:18.

and wield a wide influence; these men, when the cause of God is in a crisis, will rise up and "jeopardize their lives unto the death in the high places," thus bringing victory to the cause of God.

It was pure love that actuated Zebulun in that ancient battle, for Deborah says, "They took no gain of money."[1] From the record it would appear that Zebulun and Naphtali were exceptions in this respect. Whether they were more prosperous in this world's goods and better able than the other tribes to go to battle as self-supporting warriors, the record does not state.

After Israel returned from captivity and the cause of God was again in a crisis, Nehemiah, a self-supporting worker, came forward and did what others could not do. When the Saviour hung dead upon the cross and ignominy was heaped upon His disciples, Joseph and Nicodemus, two rich men holding high positions, came forward and performed a work for the Saviour which those who loved Him perhaps more sincerely were not able to do.

While Zebulun and Naphtali may not have loved God more than the other tribes, yet from the record given by Deborah, it would seem that they turned the tide of the battle by risking their lives, and they "took no gain of money" for their service.

It seems that Zebulun was an intelligent tribe, blessed with this world's goods; but when there came a crisis in the cause of the Lord, we find them risking all to maintain the honor of God's name.

Over two hundred years later there was another crisis in the cause of God. Saul was dead, and the true hearted in Israel "came to David to Hebron, to turn the kingdom of Saul to him, according to the word of the Lord."[2] Every tribe was represented, but no tribe excelled Zebulun in number and equipage. Fifty thousand expert warriors came, bringing their own instru-

[1] Judges 5 : 19.   [2] 1 Chron. 12 : 23.

" Every prayer of faith was granted by the Great Physician."

ments of war. They were " rangers of battle," able to " set the battle in array;" and what was of more value to the cause of God than numbers or skill, " they were not of double heart," but men the Lord could trust in a crisis. [1]

Who is prepared to perfect such a character in the fear of God, and have the seal of God placed upon his forehead? Who will covet Zebulun's character so earnestly that he will be willing to expose to reproach his life for Christ's sake?

[1] I Chron. 12:33, margin.

22

The land of Zebulun has the high honor of being the child-hood home of Jesus. Nazareth was situated within its borders. The people here had an opportunity of seeing and hearing more of Christ than those in any other place.

Isaiah prophesied that the land of Zebulun would see a great light. [1] Truly this prophecy was fulfilled, for they had within their borders the greatest Light this world has ever seen.

The first miracle performed by Jesus was at Cana in Zebulun. It was also in Cana that the nobleman came to Jesus asking for the life of his son, and the request, like every other prayer of faith, was granted by the Great Physician.

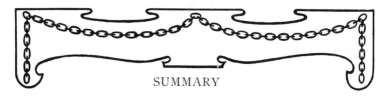

SUMMARY

Zebulun had three sons, whose descendants formed the tribe which bore his name. Gen. 46: 14.

The tribe numbered 60,500, when they entered the promised land. Num. 26: 26, 27.

In the typical battle of Megiddo, they were self-supporting warriors. Judges 5: 19.

Nazareth, the childhood home of Jesus, was within the borders of Zebulun.

Isaiah prophesied that Zebulun would receive great light. Isa. 9: 1, 2.

Isa. 9: 1, 2.

CHAPTER XLVI

JOSEPH

ON THE pages of sacred history, Joseph stands prominent among the few characters of whom Inspiration has recorded no faults.

Joseph received one of the three portions of the birthright. It is interesting to note that each part of that birthright has been immortalized.

Judah, in his home life, perfected such a character that the honor of being the progenitor of Christ was bestowed upon him; and before the throne of God in heaven, holy beings point to Christ and say, " Behold, the *Lion of the tribe of Judah.*" [1]

Levi triumphed in the time of a great crisis in the cause of God, and thus perfected a character which entitled him to the

[1] Rev. 5:5.

priesthood, whose work was a shadow of that of the great High Priest in heaven. [1]

Joseph, separated from his brethren, surrounded by idolaters in a strange land, gained a victory which entitled him to the double portion of the inheritance. Two portions of the promised land were given to the family of Joseph; and throughout eternity, these two divisions of that distinct company,— the one hundred and forty-four thousand,— bearing the names, one of Joseph and the other of Manasseh, the son of Joseph, will be a reminder of his faithfulness. [2] This was prophetically announced in the blessing given by his father:

"The blessings of thy father and of thy mother

Have prevailed *beyond* the blessings of the eternal mountains,

Beyond the glories of the everlasting hills;

They shall rest upon the head of Joseph,

And upon the crown of the head of him

Who was separated from his brethren." [3]

Joseph was the eleventh son of Jacob, and the first-born of Rachel, the beloved wife. [4] The first seventeen years of his life were spent with his father's household. [5]

The principal points recorded in the early life of Joseph were the great love of Jacob for the lad, the coat of many colors, Joseph's dreams, and his being sold into Egypt.

There was evidently a marked significance to that coat of many colors. Joseph was not a child when given the coat, but a young man seventeen years of age, with an exemplary character. The old father knew that Reuben had forfeited his right to officiate as priest of the household; and as the patriarch watched the godly life of Joseph, it would be only natural that he should select him as the one worthy to fill the holy office. It is possible that in vision he may have been permitted to see the great

[1] Heb. 8:1-5.   [2] Rev. 7:6,8.   [3] Gen. 49:26, *Spurrell*.
[4] Gen. 30:22-24.   [5] Gen. 37:2.

heavenly Priest; and that he made the coat as a faint representation of the priestly robe to be worn by his descendants.

But God sees not as man sees; from that group of envious, jealous sons, plotting murder in their hearts, the Lord took one, and purified and refined him until his descendants were fitted to fill the holy office of the priesthood.

The dreams of Joseph, revealing that the family would bow down before him, were more than the jealous hearts of the ten brothers could endure. Benjamin, the twelfth son, was but a child at this time.

When Joseph came to his brothers in the field, at a distance from their father, it would seem that all but Reuben had murderous designs against him. Jewish tradition states that Simeon bound Joseph before they lowered him into the pit, designing that he should perish there; otherwise he might have climbed out and escaped.

When the dreams of Joseph's childhood were fulfilled, and his brothers bowed with their faces to the earth before him, then he remembered his dreams. [1] May we not conclude that Joseph, when he commanded the officers to take Simeon and bind him before their eyes, remembered how Simeon once bound himself, unmindful of his cries for mercy, while these same men looked on without any pity for him? Simeon must also have remembered it, for Reuben had just reminded the brothers of their cruelty to Joseph. [2]

Joseph had no resentment in his heart; he could say to those men, " It was not you that sent me hither, but God." [3] " Ye thought evil against me; but God meant it unto good." [4] Joseph saw only the Lord's hand in it all. When sold as a slave to Potiphar, he realized he was in God's hands. His faith took hold of God; and while serving Potiphar, " the muscles of his

[1] Gen. 42 : 6-9.   [2] Gen. 42 : 21-24.
[3] Gen. 45 : 8.   [4] Gen. 50 : 20.

hands were strengthened through the power of the Mighty One of Jacob." [1]

The psalmist says, " The word of the Lord tried him." [2] He believed the word of God that had been taught him in childhood. It was that word which kept him courageous in prison, and humble when ruling Egypt. His strength, both in adversity and in prosperity, came from the " mighty God of Jacob."

When considering the strict integrity of Joseph in the midst of Egyptian darkness, we must not forget that Rachel, his mother, lived until he was about sixteen years of age. After she had, by her godly instruction, fortified her son for the great life-work before him, God in mercy laid Rachel to rest before Joseph was sold into Egypt, so she was spared that great sorrow. And throughout eternity she will see the fruit of her training; for it was no doubt his mother's godly instruction that enabled Joseph to connect with God so closely that " his bow abode in strength, and the arms of his hands were made strong by the hands of the mighty God of Jacob." [3]

The Septuagint translation of Gen. 49: 26 joins the mother's name with the father's in the blessing: " The blessings of thy father and *thy mother,* it has prevailed above the blessing of the lasting mountains and beyond the blessings of the everlasting hills." The dying patriarch, as he thought of the character of Joseph, remembered the years of faithful instruction which Rachel had given him from his birth until death separated them. The mothers of the other sons are not mentioned in the blessings.

Happy the mother that gives, and thrice happy the child that receives, such instruction. There is a power in godly training in childhood, that moulds the character. It places a " diadem of grace " on the head of the one who receives it. [4]

Joseph saw the hand of God in all the events of his life.

---

[1] Gen. 49:24, *Spurrell.*
[2] Ps. 105:19.
[3] Gen. 49:25.
[4] Prov. 1:7-9.

Job manifested the same spirit; for after God had permitted the devil to take away all his earthly possessions, he left the devil out of the reckoning entirely, and said, "*The Lord gave, and the Lord hath taken away;* blessed be the name of the Lord." [1] This spirit cherished in the heart to-day will make a man great, the same as in the days of Job and Joseph.

The first years of Joseph's life in Egypt were passed in the house of Potiphar, who made him overseer of all his interests. [2] "His master saw that the Lord was with him, and that the Lord made all that he did to prosper in his hand." [3]

Joseph's personal appearance is spoken of as " goodly " and well favored." The wife of his master tried to entrap him; but his reply, " How . . . can I do this great wickedness, and sin against God?" [4] showed his strict integrity; but it cost him his position. From a place of honor he was cast into prison. Again God vindicated Joseph, and he was honored by being placed in charge of all the prisoners. [5] He accepted his position in the prison as from the hand of the Lord.

After several years of prison life, at the age of thirty, [6] he stood before Pharaoh and interpreted the king's dreams, but he was careful to attribute all the honor to God. Then he was exalted to the second place in the kingdom, [7] where he taught the Egyptian senators wisdom. [8]

During the seven years of plenty, Joseph laid up large quantities of grain for use during the seven years of famine. He married an Egyptian wife, and his two sons, Manasseh and Ephraim, were born during these seven years of plenty. [9]

Joseph had been chief ruler in Egypt nine years, [10] when his brothers came to Egypt to buy food. It is interesting to note that when Joseph told his brothers that he would keep Benjamin as an hostage, he had the satisfaction of hearing Judah, the very one

[1] Job 1:21.   [2] Gen. 39:4-6.   [3] Gen. 39:3.   [4] Gen. 39:9.
[5] Gen. 39:20-23.   [6] Gen. 41:46.   [7] Gen. 41:43.
[8] Ps. 105:21, 22.   [9] Gen. 41:45, 50-52.   [10] Gen. 41:46, 47; 45:6.

who, years before, had suggested selling Joseph to the Ishmaelites for twenty pieces of silver, offer to become his bondman for life, in place of Benjamin. [1]

Joseph had the privilege of sustaining his father and his brothers many years, and of seeing the fulfilment of his youthful dreams.

During Joseph's long life of one hundred and ten years, we have no record of his ever proving untrue to God in any way. He died with a firm faith in the promise made to Abraham, Isaac, and Jacob. His last words were, " God will surely visit you, and ye shall carry up my bones from hence." [2] His body was embalmed, and when Moses led the children of Israel out of Egypt, they fulfilled his dying charge. [3]

When the voice of Christ shall call the sleeping saints from their dusty beds, Joseph will spring forth clad in glorious immortality, to greet the " Shepherd, the Stone of Israel," [4] through faith in whom he gained all his victories.

SUMMARY

Two large tribes sprang from the two sons of Joseph. Gen. 46 : 27.

When the children of Israel entered Egypt, the descendants of Joseph numbered 85,200. Num. 26 : 34-37; Gen. 49 : 22.

Joseph received one part of the birthright,— the double portion of the inheritance. I Chron. 5 : 1.

This portion of the birthright is perpetuated throughout eternity by two divisions of the one hundred and forty-four thousand, representing the family of Joseph. Rev. 7 : 6, 8.

[1] Gen. 44 : 33.
[2] Gen. 50 : 25.
[3] Ex. 13 : 19.
[4] Gen. 49 : 24.

CHAPTER XLVII

BENJAMIN

ENJAMIN, the twelfth son of Jacob, was left motherless at the time of his birth. The only recorded request of his mother, Rachel, was that the babe might be called Benoni, "the son of my sorrow;" but Jacob changed the name to Benjamin, "the son of the right hand." [1]

The tender love of the father for his motherless son is shown by his unwillingness to allow him to accompany his brethren into Egypt. [2] Benjamin is often referred to as a lad when he went into Egypt; [3] but the record states that he was the father of ten sons at

[1] Gen. 35 : 16-18, margin.   [2] Gen. 42 : 38.   [3] Gen. 43 : 8.

(345)

that time. [1] The patriarchal form of government no doubt brought him more closely under the direction of his father than are married sons of the present day.

While little is recorded of Benjamin as an individual, the tribe which bore his name acted a prominent part in the history of the children of Israel.

The character of the tribe seems to be portrayed by the prophetic words of Jacob in his parting blessing: " Benjamin shall raven as a wolf: in the morning he shall devour the prey, and at night he shall divide the spoil." [2] These words do not describe an enviable character, but rather that of a child indulged and petted until it is self-willed and petulant, as one might expect the youngest son in a large family would be, with no mother to control him.

This same stubborn spirit was shown by the tribe of Benjamin fighting until they were nearly exterminated, rather than deliver up the wicked men of Gibeah, that they might be punished.[3] Notwithstanding they were at this time reduced in number to six hundred, yet in the time of David they had again become a numerous tribe. [4]

In the days of the judges, the Benjamites could furnish seven hundred men that could " sling stones at a hair breadth, and not miss." [5]

About three hundred and fifty years later, we read that the mighty men of Benjamin " could use both the right hand and the left in hurling stones and shooting arrows out of a bow." [6] The Benjamites were the only tribe which seemed to have pursued archery to any purpose, and their skill in the use of the bow and the sling was celebrated. [7]

Benjamin's territory lay north of Judah's, the boundary line between the two tribes running through the city of Jerusalem.

[1] Gen. 46:21.   [2] Gen. 49:27.   [3] Judges 20:12-48.   [4] 1 Chron. 7:6-12.
[5] Judges 20:16.   [6] 1 Chron. 12:1, 2.   [7] 1 Chron. 8:40; 2 Chron. 17:17; 2 Sam. 1:22.

After the great crisis which resulted from the unfortunate transaction at Gibeah,[1] there were many things that would have a tendency to change the stubborn, self-willed nature of the tribe.

For twenty years the sacred ark of the Lord remained within their borders, in Kirjath-jearim, with a priest to take charge of it.[2]

Ramah, a city of Benjamin, was the home of Samuel the prophet, who had an altar built unto the Lord in this place, and offered sacrifices. Samuel "went from year to year in circuit to Bethel, and Gilgal, and Mizpeh, and judged Israel in all those places. And his return was to Ramah."[3]

Mizpeh, the place where the great assemblies of all Israel were held,[4] was within the borders of Benjamin. Here the Lord wrought a mighty deliverance for His terrified people. "The Lord thundered with a great thunder on that day upon the Philistines, and discomfited them; and they were smitten before Israel."[5]

The prophetic words of Moses in his parting blessing on the tribes, indicate that there would be a decided change from the character portrayed by Jacob: "Of Benjamin he said, The beloved of the Lord shall dwell in safety by him; and the Lord shall cover him all the day long, and he shall dwell between His shoulders."[6]

The same fearless character that Jacob compared to a wolf, destroying everything before it, is changed by the converting power of the Spirit of God; and the strength once used to destroy, is now used to protect the people and interests of the Lord. "The beloved of the Lord shall dwell in safety by him."

It is interesting to notice the similarity between the character of the ancient tribe and that of the leading apostle to the Gentiles,

[1] Judges 19 : 14-39. [2] 1 Sam. 7 : 1, 2. [3] 1 Sam. 7 : 15-17.
[4] Judges 20 : 1; 2 Kings 25 : 23. [5] 1 Sam. 7 : 5-11. [6] Deut. 33 : 12.

who said of himself, " I also am an Israelite . . . of the tribe of Benjamin." [1]

Saul, afterward called Paul, is first introduced to us as witnessing the stoning of Stephen; and " consenting unto his death." [2] Next we hear of him as a ravening wolf, making

The Lord shall cover him all the day long and he shall dwell between his shoulders

Deut. 35:12

" havoc of the church, entering into every house, and h a l i n g men and women," and committing them to prison. [3] Like a savage wolf, thirsty for the blood of his prey, he was " breathing out threatenings and slaughter against the disciples of the Lord." [4] There was no safety for any of the beloved of the Lord near such a character. But the same strength of character that will cause one to " raven as a wolf," and to hurt and destroy the people of God, will, when converted, shield and protect the honor of God and His cause.

From that time, that Saul, the Benjamite, had had one view of Jesus, [5] his wolf-like nature departed, and the beloved of the Lord could dwell in safety by him. The saints at Damascus were in no danger: he who had designed to destroy

[1] Rom. 11:1. [2] Acts 7:58; 8:1. [3] Acts 8:3.
[4] Acts 9:1. [5] Acts 9:3-9.

"The sting of the poisonous serpent was powerless."

them was now their friend, ready to protect them at any time. [1]

God never forgets to return an act of kindness. [2] When Saul shielded and protected the " beloved of the Lord," the Lord covered him all the day long; nothing could harm him. The sting of the poisonous serpent was powerless. [3] There was not enough water in the sea to drown him. [4] God covered him all the day long.

The blessing given by Moses says, " The Lord shall cover him all the day long, and *he shall dwell between His shoulders."* Some commentators think that this refers to the temple being built on Mount Moriah, within the borders of Benjamin; but to the one who has childhood recollections of being carried between the strong shoulders of his father over the rough, uneven places in the road, the words have another meaning.

" The Lord shall cover him all the day long," protect from all harm and danger. And when we come to impossibilities in our pathway, things which our strength could never master,

[1] Acts 9: 10-19.
[2] 1 Sam. 2: 30.
[3] Acts 28 :1-6.
[4] Acts 27: 23-25.

our heavenly Father lifts us in His mighty arms, and carries us safely over that which without His help it would be utterly impossible for us to accomplish. Like the child resting securely between the shoulders of its father, with its arms clasped firmly around his neck, we accomplish that which is beyond all human power. Blessed place to be! but it is for the one by whom the beloved of the Lord can dwell in safety. The voice of criticism and slander must be forever hushed by the one who hopes to fill that place. [1]

Ehud, under whom the land had rest fourscore years, was a Benjamite. [2] He was left-handed, and it seems that by using his left hand, he was able more adroitly to slay Eglon, king of Moab, who was oppressing Israel. [3]

Saul, the first king of Israel, was of the tribe of Benjamin. [4] God not only anointed Saul king over Israel, but He " gave him another heart." [5]   He had associated with him men " whose hearts God had touched;" [6] and as long as he remained humble, the Lord was with him. [7]   When he became exalted in his own mind, he was rejected of the Lord. Then the wolf-like propensities in his character were clearly seen; for he like a ravening wolf, for years chased David as " a partridge in the mountains." [8]   His one desire was to slay " the beloved of the Lord." [9]

In direct contrast with Saul, who spent the strength of his manhood in plotting to destroy the " man after God's own heart," is Mordecai, " the son of Kish, a Benjamite." Their fathers bore the same name and they may have been related more closely than the tribal connection. The whole history of Mordecai is a series of deliverances of people from trouble. He saved the life of the Persian king. [10]   Afterward Satan and Haman planned to destroy every believer in the true God; [11] and while Mordecai was earnestly seeking the Lord for deliverance, [12] God used the kind-

[1] James 1 : 26.
[2] Judges 3 : 15, 30.
[3] Judges 3 : 21-26.
[4] 1 Sam. 9 : 21.
[5] 1 Sam. 10 : 9.
[6] 1 Sam. 10 : 26.
[7] 1 Sam. 15 : 17-23.
[8] 1 Sam. 26 : 19, 20.
[9] 1 Sam. 18 : 11 ; 15 : 28.
[10] Esther 2 : 21-23.
[11] Esther 3 : 8-15.
[12] Esther 4 : 1-3.

ness he had shown to the king as a means of escape. [1] Mordecai was raised to an exalted position in the kingdom, and was used by the Lord to shield and protect His people. [2]

The true, lasting victory that extends throughout all eternity does not depend upon tribal connections or hereditary tendencies, but upon a humble trust in God. "The eyes of the Lord run to and fro throughout the whole earth, to show Himself strong in the behalf of them whose heart is perfect toward Him." [3] God can humble kings when they disregard His word; [4] and He can take captives and give them kingly power. [5]

The natural character of Benjamin is the character of the unconverted heart in every age of the world. [6] Happy the one at the present day who, like Mordecai, will stand true to principle, [7] and will risk all to protect the "beloved of the Lord;" he can claim the promise given to Benjamin of old: "The Lord shall cover him all the day long and he shall dwell between His shoulders."

Twelve thousand having this character, bearing the name of Benjamin, will serve the Lord day and night in His temple throughout eternity. [8]

SUMMARY

Benjamin had ten sons from whom sprang the tribe of Benjamin. Gen. 46: 21.

When they entered the promised land the tribe of Benjamin numbered 45,600. Num. 26: 41.

---

[1] Esther 6: 1-11. [2] Esther 8: 7-17. [3] 2 Chron. 16: 9.
[4] 2 Chron. 36: 1-4, 9, 10. [5] Dan. 6: 1-3; Esther 8: 15; 10: 3.
[6] Jer. 17: 9. [7] Esther 3: 2. [8] Rev. 7: 15.

The Benjamites were noted for archery, and for being left-handed. I Chron. 8 : 40; 2 Chron. 17 : 17.

Ramah, the home of Samuel, was within the borders of Benjamin.

Mizpeh, where Israel held great assemblies, was in the land of Benjamin.

Noted Characters

Ehud, who judged Israel eighty years. Judges 3 : 21-26.

Saul, the first king of Israel. 1 Sam. 9 : 21.

Mordecai, whom the Lord used to save Israel in the days of Esther. Esther 2 : 5.

Paul, the leading apostle to the Gentiles. Rom. 11 : 1.

CHAPTER XLVIII

MANASSEH

 DYING patriarch's blessing meant much in ancient times; and when Joseph heard that his father was sick, he took his two sons, Manasseh and Ephraim, and visited him.

After repeating to Joseph the promise of the land of Canaan which had been given to Abraham and renewed to Isaac and Jacob, the old patriarch said, " Thy two sons, Ephraim and Manasseh, . . . are mine; as Reuben and Simeon, they shall be mine." When Jacob saw the boys, he said: " Bring them, I pray thee, unto me, and I will bless them." [1]

Joseph placed the first-born at Jacob's right hand and the youngest at his left; but the aged patriarch laid his right hand on the head of the younger, and his left hand upon the head of

[1] Gen. 48 : 1-9.

the eldest as he blessed them. When Joseph saw it, he attempted to place Jacob's right hand on the head of Manasseh, the eldest, saying, " Not so, my father: for this is the first-born." But his father refused, saying, " I know it, my son, I know it: . . . he also shall be great: but truly his younger brother shall be greater than he." [1]

Like his great Uncle Esau, Manasseh, although the first-born, received the second place in the blessing; but the circumstances were entirely different. Manasseh did nothing to forfeit his privileges in the family blessing. While he did not have the warlike propensities of Ephraim, which enabled him to build up the kingdom of Israel, yet Manasseh's name will outlive that of Ephraim.

"The Angel which redeemed me from all evil, bless the lads."

There was one portion of the patriarch's blessing which seemed to be shared more largely by Manasseh than by his more prosperous brother. " The Angel which redeemed me from all evil, bless the lads." [2]

The blessing of the Lord was prized by Manasseh and his descendants. Although they lived at a distance from the center of the nation, and from the temple, and though they had become a part of the northern kingdom, yet they took an interest in all the reforms instituted by the good kings of Judah. When

[1] Gen. 48: 15-20.   [2] Gen. 48: 16.

King Asa broke down the idols and renewed the worship of the Lord, they came to him " in abundance " from Manasseh, " when they saw that the Lord his God was with him." [1]

When Hezekiah held his great Passover feast, representatives from Manasseh humbled their hearts and came and partook of the Passover. [2]   They also joined in the work of breaking down the images in their own territory. [3]

The work of reform in the days of Josiah was also carried to the land of Manasseh. [4]   They did not lose their interest in the temple at Jerusalem, but gave of their means to restore it after its defilement during the reigns of Manasseh and Amon. [5] It is supposed that the eightieth Psalm was written by some inspired penman of the house of Joseph during one of these seasons of reform.

Little is recorded of the tribe of Manasseh after the settlement in Canaan, but it is gratifying, that faint and scattered as the passages are that refer to that tribe, they all indicate a desire on the part of many to serve the Lord.

The blessing of the Angel rested upon Manasseh, and while Ephraim and Manasseh were the names of the two portions given to Joseph in the earthly possession, the names given to the two divisions of the one hundred and forty-four thousand in the kingdom of God will be Manasseh (Greek, Manases) and Joseph. [6]   The name of Manasseh is thus immortalized, while that of Ephraim sinks into oblivion.

Gideon, the greatest of the judges, was of the tribe of Manasseh.   He seems to have been the only great warrior in the western half of the tribe; the eastern portion were more warlike.

When David went out with the Philistines to battle against Saul, warriors from Manasseh joined themselves to David; but when the lords of the Philistines would not allow David to go

[1] 2 Chron. 15 : 8, 9.   [2] 2 Chron. 30 : 1, 10, 11, 18.   [3] 2 Chron. 31 : 1.
[4] 2 Chron. 34 : 1-6.   [5] 2 Chron. 34 : 9.   [6] Rev. 7 : 6, 8.

with them to the battle, seven mighty warriors, "captains of the thousands of Manasseh," joined David at Ziklag. "They helped David against the band of the rovers" who had carried captive David's family; "for they were all mighty men of valor." [1]

After the death of Saul, eighteen thousand of the half tribe of Manasseh "were expressed by name, to come and make David king" at Hebron. [2]

The five daughters of Zelophehad, of the tribe of Manasseh, are the first women mentioned in the Bible as holding an inheritance in their own name and right. [3]

If Reuben had never lost his birthright through sin, or if Dan had not formed a character so near akin to Satan that his name was omitted from the list of the twelve tribes, Manasseh's name might never have been given to one of the divisions of the one hundred and forty-four thousand. In all this experience are lessons for every child of God.

When God says, "Behold, I come quickly: hold that fast which thou hast, *that no man take thy crown,*" [4] it is well that we heed the admonition. If we do not, we may find, when too late, that we have allowed the world to rob us of our love for the Master; and that our judgment has become so darkened by sin and unbelief that, like Reuben, we fall far short of doing the work the Lord designed we should accomplish. Some one who, like Joseph, has been separated from those of the same faith, without the opportunities we have enjoyed, will by simple faith and trust in God, do the work we have failed to do, and receive the reward we might have obtained.

The pathway of time is strewn with the wrecks of character,— men who were once true and faithful members of the Israel of God, [5] and who were "written to life in Jerusalem;" [6] but who allowed Satan to fill their hearts with envy, jealousy,

[1] 1 Chron. 12 : 19-22. [2] 1 Chron. 12 : 31. [3] Num. 27 : 1-8.
[4] Rev. 3 : 11.   [5] Rom. 2 : 28, 29.   [6] Isa. 4 : 3, margin.

and criticism, until, like Dan, they have lost their hold on heavenly things, and are no longer numbered with the Israel of God.

"Hold that fast which thou hast, that no man take *thy crown.*"

SUMMARY

The only son of Manasseh mentioned is Machir, whose mother was a concubine; from him sprang the tribe of Manasseh. I Chron. 7 : 14.

When Israel entered Canaan the tribe of Manasseh numbered 52,700. Num. 26 : 34.

Gideon, the greatest of the judges, was of the tribe of Manasseh.

The first women mentioned as holding property in their own names, were of the tribe of Manasseh. Num. 27 : 1-8.

CHAPTER XLIX

THE ONE HUNDRED AND FORTY-FOUR THOUSAND

ENESIS is the book of beginnings, Revelation the book of endings. The most important lines of truth given by all the Old Testament writers meet in the Revelation. Genesis introduces us to the twelve tribes of Israel; Revelation shows us the last representatives of those tribes standing upon Mount Zion in the eternal kingdom of God. [1]

The redeemed of the Lord are an innumerable company, which no man can number; but among that multitude is one separate company, who are numbered and are designated by their number,— one hundred and forty-four thousand. This company is composed of twelve different divisions, each containing twelve thousand redeemed souls; and each division bears the name of one of the twelve tribes of Israel. [2] The list given in Reve-

[1] Rev. 14:1.   [2] Rev. 7:4-8.

lation varies somewhat from the list of the twelve sons of Jacob, [1] as Dan is omitted, and the extra division is given the name of Manasseh, Joseph's eldest son.

This company have special privileges. They stand upon Mount Zion with Christ, [2] and "follow the Lamb whithersoever He goeth." [3] They have the exalted privilege of serving Christ in the heavenly temple; [4] and like all the redeemed host, they are faultless before God, and in their mouths is no guile. [5]

The great reaper death has laid one generation after another of the saints of God in the silent tomb; and lest some might fear that the grave would be the final end of the faithful, God gave the following pledge through His prophet: "I will *ransom* them from the power of the grave; I will *redeem* them from death." [6]

The one hundred and forty-four thousand are redeemed from the earth — from among men. [7] They are alive upon the earth when the Saviour comes, and will be translated, together with the innumerable host who will come from their dusty beds, clad in glorious immortality, when Christ comes in the clouds of heaven. [8]

The one hundred and forty-four thousand are distinguished from all others by their having the seal of the living God in their foreheads. All who have this seal are included in this company. [9] This distinguishing mark is called the "Father's name." [10] Ezekiel was evidently shown the same work, and speaks of it as a "mark" upon the forehead. [11]

We are familiar with the term "seal" in connection with legal documents. A seal contains the name of the person issuing the document, his office or authority, and the extent of his jurisdiction. The seal placed upon the foreheads of the one hundred and forty-four thousand, is the seal of the living God. Seals are attached to laws and legal documents; therefore we should look for God's seal to be attached to His law. The prophet Isaiah,

---

[1] 1 Chron. 2:1, 2. [2] Rev. 14:1. [3] Rev. 14:4.
[4] Rev. 7:15. [5] Rev. 14:5. [6] Hosea 13:14.
[7] Rev. 14:3, 4. [8] 1 Thess. 4:16, 17. [9] Rev. 7:2-4.
[10] Rev. 14:1. [11] Eze. 9:4.

looking down through the ages, saw a people who were expecting Christ to come from the heavenly sanctuary to the earth, and the message of God to them was, " Seal the law among My disciples." [1]

The Bible was given through prophets, — holy men whom God used as mouthpieces, to make His will known to His people; [2] but the law of God— the ten commandments—was not given through any human agent. God the Father, Christ the Son, and myriads of heavenly beings came down upon Mount Sinai, [3] when the ten commandments were proclaimed to the vast multitude of Israel — over a million people. [4] Then, lest there might be some mistake in writing out the law which He had given, God called Moses up into the mountain, and gave him two

" The law of God . . . was not given through any human agent."

tables of stone, upon which He had engraved with His own finger the same ten commandments that He had spoken in the hearing of the multitude. [5] This law will be the standard by which every son and daughter of Adam will be judged. [6] Has God attached His seal to this law, whereby all may know its bind-

[1] Isa. 8 : 16.   [2] 2 Peter 1 : 20, 21.
[3] Ps. 68 : 17.   [4] Deut. 4 : 10, 13, 32, 33.
[5] Deut. 10 : 1-5; Ex. 31 : 18; 32 : 15, 19. [6] James 2 : 10-12; Rom. 2 : 12, 13; Eccl. 12 : 13, 14.

ing claims? Remembering that the seal must contain, *first,* the name of the one issuing the law; *second,* the office or authority vested in the lawgiver; and *third,* the territory over which he rules, let us look for the seal in the law of God.

The first three commandments, and also the fifth, mention the name of God, [1] but do not distinguish Him from other gods. [2] The last five commandments show our duty to our fellow men, but do not contain the name of God. [3]

The fourth commandment contains, *first,* the name, " the Lord thy God;" *second,* the statement that the Lord thy God is the Creator of all things, and therefore has power to issue this law; *third,* a record of His territory, which consists of " heaven and earth," which He created. [4]

The fourth commandment requires all who dwell in the territory of the Lord God the Creator, to keep holy the seventh day of the week, which He has sanctified and blessed, [5] as a memorial of His creative work.

The Sabbath commandment contains the seal of the law. The word sign is sometimes used as a synonym for " seal." [6] Of the Sabbath God says: " It is a *sign* between Me and the children of Israel forever." [7] " Moreover also I gave them My Sabbaths, to be a *sign* between Me and them, that they might know that I am the Lord that sanctify them." [8]

God blessed and sanctified the Sabbath; [9] and to the one who will keep it holy, it is a sign, or seal, of God's power to sanctify him. [10] There is a knowledge of God in the proper observance of the Sabbath. " Hallow My Sabbaths; and they shall be a *sign* between Me and you, that ye may know that I am the Lord your God." [11]

During the Dark Ages, when the word of God was hidden from the people, the seal was taken from God's law. Sunday, the

[1] Ex. 20:3-7, 12.   [2] 1 Cor. 8:5.   [3] Ex. 20:13-17.   [4] Ex. 20:8-11.
[5] Gen. 2:2, 3.   [6] Rom. 4:11.   [7] Ex. 31:13, 16, 17.   [8] Eze. 20:12.
[9] Gen. 2:2, 3.   [10] Isa. 58:13, 14.   [11] Eze. 20:20.

first day of the week, a day upon which God worked, [1] was sub-stituted for the seventh-day Sabbath, upon which He rested. [2] The Lord revealed through Daniel the prophet that a power would arise which should "think to change" the law of God, [3] and that the law would be given into his hands during twelve hun-dred and sixty years, a period of time mentioned by both Daniel [4] and John. [5] After that period had passed and the Bible was

" A faint light, steadily increasing until it lightens the whole earth."

again in the hands of the people, the true Sabbath of the fourth commandment was to be restored and observed. The breach in the law would be repaired, [6] and the law sealed among the dis-ciples of the Lord, who would be eagerly looking for His return. [7]

In Rev. 7:2, this sealing message is represented as coming from the east, or sun-rising. We should understand from this that it would begin like the sun-rising, first a faint light, steadily increasing until it lightens the whole earth.

Four angels were commissioned to hold the four winds until the work was accomplished. Winds are a symbol of war. [8] In

[1] Gen. 1:1-5; Eze. 46:1.   [2] Gen. 2:2, 3.   [3] Dan. 7:25.   [4] Dan. 7:25; 12:7.
[5] Rev. 11:2; 12:6; 13:5.   [6] Isa. 58:12.   [7] Isa. 8:16, 17.   [8] Dan. 11:40.

fulfilment of this we should expect to find that during some period of the world's history the winds of war were miraculously held, while the work of restoring the seal to the law of God was going forward in the earth.

There have always been upon the earth some adherents of the seventh-day Sabbath; but the work of restoring the breach which had been made in the law was begun about 1845, by those who were then watching for the second coming of the Lord. After the time set for Him to come had passed, in the autumn of 1844, the attention of those who had expected Christ to return to the earth at that time was directed to the heavenly sanctuary, where by faith they saw Christ officiating as their High Priest. As they followed the Saviour in His work, " the temple of God was opened in heaven, and there was seen in His temple the ark of His testament." [1] Their attention was attracted to the law contained in that ark, [2] and some of them recognized the binding claim of the Sabbath of the Lord, and accepted it as the seal of the law. About 1847-48 the Sabbath began to be preached as the seal of the law of the living God.

In 1848 occurred one of the greatest upheavals in the national affairs of Europe that had been for many centuries. Decided changes were made in some of the leading nations. In a brief period of time, many of the crowned heads of Europe submitted themselves to the people. It looked as if universal war was inevitable. In the midst of the turmoil and strife, came a sudden calm. No man could assign any reason for it, but the student of prophecy knew that the angels were holding the winds until the servants of God could be sealed in their foreheads.

The forehead is the seat of the intellect; and when the honest in heart see and acknowledge the binding claims of God's law, they will keep holy the Sabbath. The seal placed in the forehead

[1] Rev. 11 : 19.   [2] Ex. 25 : 16.

by the angel can not be read by man, for God alone can read the heart. Simply resting upon the seventh day from all physical work will not place the seal upon the forehead of any one. The resting is necessary, but with the rest must be also the holy and sanctified life that is in harmony with the holy and sanctified day. [1]

Ezekiel saw an angel placing a " mark " upon the foreheads of those who were distressed because of the abominations practised by the professed people of God. [2] Those who are at ease in Zion drifting with the current, their hearts' affections centered on the world, will never receive the seal of the living God.

The Sabbath reform — the sealing work of Rev. 7: 1-4 — arose as the sun. For some years there were only a few that kept the Sabbath of the fourth commandment; but as individuals here and there, in all parts of the world, found that the entire Bible from Genesis to Revelation teaches that the seventh day is the Sabbath, and that Christ [3] and the apostles [4] kept it, they accepted it; [5] and to-day in every division of the earth there are those who honor God as the Creator, by keeping holy the day which He sanctified and blessed as a memorial of His creative work.

In the Christian church there is neither Jew nor Gentile; all are one in Christ Jesus. [6] We are all grafted into the family of Abraham. [7] The one hundred and forty-four thousand are not necessarily literal descendants of the Jews, [8] but they are those who have received the seal of the living God in their foreheads, whose lives are in harmony with the holy precepts of Jehovah.

In Rev. 14: 9-14 we are told of a power that is opposed to God's law, and that has a mark which it will try to enforce upon the people by means of the civil power. [9] Since the Sabbath of

[1] Isa. 58: 13.   [2] Eze. 9: 1-4.   [3] Luke 4: 16; Matt. 5: 17, 18.
[4] Luke 23: 54-56; Acts 17: 2; 16: 13; 18: 4, 11.   [5] Rom. 3: 19.   [6] Gal. 3: 28.
[7] Rom. 11: 17-21; Gal. 3: 29.   [8] Rom. 11: 21-23.   [9] Rev. 13: 13-18.

the Lord is given by Jehovah as a sign of His power and His right to rule, the counterfeit sabbath, or Sunday, the first day of the week, will be the mark of the opposing power. God's law commands all to keep holy the seventh day of the week, God's memorial of creation; but the laws of the land will command all to rest upon Sunday, the first day of the week. [1]

When this test comes, each person will have to de-

"**We ought to obey God rather than men.**"

cide for himself. Many, like Peter and John, when they faced the magistrates and imprisonment, will say, "We ought to obey God rather than men." [2]

This conflict will continue, says John, until the dragon, Satan, will become so angry with the church that he will "make war with the remnant of her seed, which keep the commandments of God, and have the testimony of Jesus Christ." [3]

Out of this conflict the one hundred and forty-four thousand

[1] Rev. 13 : 16, 17.   [2] Acts 5 : 29.   [3] Rev. 12 : 17.

will be gathered. Their experience will be similar to that of the children of Israel coming out of Egypt. Pharaoh would not allow them to rest on the Sabbath. He called the instruction of Moses and Aaron " vain words;" [1] or as Dr. Adam Clarke expresses it, Pharaoh said, " Let religion alone, and mind your work." On " the same day " [2] that Pharaoh complained because Moses and Aaron were instructing the people to rest, the king gave the command, " Ye shall no more give the people straw to make brick," and the burdens of the children of Israel were greatly increased. [3] Satan was determined that the Israelites should not honor the Sabbath of the Lord; but God delivered His people and destroyed Pharaoh and all his host. [4]

On earth the distinguishing mark of the one hundred and forty-four thousand is the seal of God in their foreheads; in heaven it will be the wonderful song which they will sing: " They sung as it were a new song before the throne: . . . and no man could learn that song but the one hundred and forty and four thousand, which were redeemed from the earth." [5] " They sing the song of Moses, the servant of God, and the song of the lamb." [6] It is a song of experience — wonderful melody! Not even the angel choir can join in those marvelous strains as they echo through the arches of heaven. Even Abraham, the friend of God, with all his faith, cannot join in that song. What a chorus that will be! one hundred and forty-four thousand voices all in perfect accord, singing the " song of Moses, the servant of God, and the song of the Lamb."

As the twelve tribes, after crossing the Red Sea, all united in the song of triumph, so the last representatives of the twelve tribes of Israel on earth, as they stand a mighty phalanx on the sea of glass before the throne of God in heaven, will sing the song of Moses and the Lamb.

[1] Ex. 5:9.
[4] Ex. 14:10-31.
[2] Ex. 5:5, 6.
[5] Rev. 14:3.
[3] Ex. 5:7, 8.
[6] Rev. 15:3.

SUMMARY

The one hundred and forty-four thousand receive the seal of the living God in their foreheads. Rev. 7 : 2-4.

They obtain the victory over the beast and his image. Rev. 15 : 2.

Are redeemed from among men. Rev. 14 : 3, 4.

Stand upon Mount Zion. Rev. 14 : 1.

"Follow the Lamb whithersoever He goeth." Rev. 14 : 4.

Sing a song that no one else can sing. Rev. 14 : 3.

Serve Christ in the heavenly temple. Rev. 7 : 15.

A seal attached to a legal document must give the name, office, or authority, of the one issuing the document, and the territory over which he rules.

God has a seal; this seal is connected with His law. Rev. 7 . 3, 4; Isa. 8 : 16.

The fourth commandment contains the seal of the law of God. It gives His name,— Lord God; His authority,— the Creator; and His territory,— the heaven and earth which He has made. Ex. 20 : 8-11.

Sign and seal are synonymous terms. Rom. 4 : 11.

The Sabbath is the sign, or seal, of the law of God. Eze. 20 : 12, 20.

A blessing is pronounced upon the one who will keep the Sabbath. Isa. 56 : 1, 2.

CHAPTER L

THE LOST TRIBES

UCH has been said and written about the lost tribes of Israel, and many fanciful theories have been invented in regard to them. We will not attempt to follow any of these lines of argument, but will speak of those tribes which are truly lost.

In the previous chapters we have seen that Reuben, Simeon, Levi, Judah, Naphtali, Gad, Asher, Issachar, Zebulun, Joseph, Benjamin, and Manasseh, not only had a part in the land of Palestine, but that their names are immortalized, and will be represented in the kingdom of God throughout eternity, while the names of Ephraim and Dan sink into oblivion. They are the lost tribes of Israel.

(368)

Why was proud Ephraim, who was the strength of the kingdom of Israel, and Dan, who was surpassed only by Judah in the number of its warriors when they entered the promised land, left out of the final great gathering of Israel as tribes?

Ephraim was the son of an Egyptian princess who was an idolater, as far as we have any record. It is very probable that most of Ephraim's life was spent among the Egyptians, for we can hardly suppose that with his proud connections he associated much with the Israelites in Goshen, until a king arose that knew not Joseph. [1] Manasseh lived in the same surroundings; but the fact that Ephraim had received first place in the blessing of the patriarch, may have filled his heart with pride and given a different mould to his life. Ephraim was about twenty-one years of age when he received Jacob's blessing. He had the godly example of his father before him for many years; for Joseph lived to see Ephraim's children of the third generation. [2]

Only one glimpse of the individual life of Ephraim is given. The record states that his sons, in a marauding expedition, stole the cattle belonging to the men of Gath, and the men of Gath slew them. "Ephraim their father mourned many days, and his brethren came to comfort him." [3]

While Ephraim was still mourning the loss of his children, another son was born to him, and he named him Beriah, or "evil," "because it went evil with his house." [4] Strange as it may seem, from Beriah came the most illustrious of all his descendants,— Joshua, the great leader of Israel. [5] "Oshea, the son of Nun," [6] was chosen as one of the ten spies, and after his faithfulness had been tested on that occasion, his name was changed from Oshea, "help," to Joshua, "the help of Jehovah." This change of names was common in ancient times, for names then indicated the character of the bearer. Abram became Abra-

[1] Ex. 1:8.   [2] Gen. 50:23.   [3] I Chron. 7:21, 22.
[4] I Chron. 7:23.   [5] I Chron. 7:27.   [6] Num. 13:8, 16.

24

ham when he received the promise; and a f t e r the night of wrestling, Jacob, the supplanter, became Israel, the prince of God. [1]

Another illustrious descendant of Beriah was his daughter, Sherah, who built two cities. [2]

"Hannah gave Samuel to Eli, the priest."

Samuel, the last judge of Israel, was of the tribe of Ephraim. It was in Shiloh that Hannah gave Samuel to Eli, the priest. [3] Samuel is one of the strong characters of the Bible. Few men have filled so many offices during a long and useful life as did Samuel. He officiated as priest, but he was not a priest. [4] He judged Israel all the days of his life. [5] He was also a great educator, and established the schools of the prophets. When but a child Samuel was entrusted with the Spirit of prophecy, [6] and it is usually supposed that a portion of the Bible was written by him.

Ephraim as a tribe had many advantages; but they failed to profit by them. They were envious and jealous, always sensitive over supposed slights. [7]

---

[1] Gen. 17:5; 32:28, margin. [2] 1 Chron. 7:24. [3] 1 Sam. 2:24-28. [4] 1 Sam. 7:9.
[5] 1 Sam. 7:15. [6] 1 Sam. 3:1-21. [7] Judges 8:1; 2 Sam. 19:41-43.

After the death of Solomon, the kingdom was divided, and from that time the history of Ephraim is the history of the kingdom of Israel.

Jeroboam, their first king, was an Ephrathite. It was God that rent the kingdom out of the hands of Rehoboam, and gave ten tribes to Jeroboam;[1] and if he had walked humbly with God, an entirely different history would have been written of Ephraim. It was the same spirit of jealousy and sus-

" The Lord sent a message of warning . . . but Jeroboam returned not from his evil ways."

picion that had marred the history of his tribe, that influenced Jeroboam to make the golden calves, and set them up in Bethel and Dan, thus establishing a system of idolatrous worship.[2] The Lord sent a message of warning, and even performed a miracle

[1] 1 Kings 11 : 29-31.   [2] 1 Kings 12 : 26-33.

upon the person of the king;[1] but " Jeroboam returned not from his evil way."[2]

There are few things more mournful than the steady descent of the haughty, jealous tribe of Ephraim from the pinnacle of success, — their leader the leader of the entire nation, and the center of the worship at Shiloh within their borders, — to the sudden captivity and total oblivion which closed its career.

Some most pathetic messages were sent by the Lord to the tribe of Ephraim. Almost the whole of Hosea's testimonies were entreaties for Ephraim to repent. " I taught Ephraim also to go, taking them by their arms; but they knew not that I healed them. I drew them with the cords of a man, with bands of love; . . . but the Assyrian shall be his king, because they refused to return."[3]

Hosea gives the reason for the downfall of Ephraim: " Ephraim, he hath mixed himself among the people; Ephraim is a cake not turned."[4] God's kingdom and the kingdoms of the world are entirely distinct. No one can serve God and mammon. Ephraim was " a cake not turned;" he did not have a thorough experience in the things of God. One cannot mix himself among the people of the world, spending his strength in the pursuit of wealth and fame, and at the same time be a member of the true Israel of God.

The Lord pleaded with Ephraim, saying, " How shall I give thee up, Ephraim? how shall I deliver thee, Israel?"[5] Again, He said, " I have written to him the great things of My law, but they were counted as a strange thing."[6]

Idolatry was the great sin of Ephraim; he failed to appreciate the sacred things of God. After the pleadings of the Lord were rejected, then the word went forth, " Ephraim is joined to idols: let him alone."[7] " My God will cast them away, be-

[1] I Kings 13: 1-6.   [2] I Kings 13: 33.   [3] Hosea 11: 3-5.
[4] Hosea 7: 8.   [5] Hosea 11: 8.   [6] Hosea 8: 12.   [7] Hosea 4: 17.

cause they did not hearken unto Him," [1] nor accept His love.

There are many idolaters in the world to-day, traveling the same road over which Ephraim passed. They are not worshiping idols made of metal, wood, or stone, for the popular gods of the

Solomon's Temple

present day are not of that form; they are money, wealth, pleasure, and high position. God is calling after them, but they, like Ephraim, are joined to their idols. Like Ephraim of old, they are reckoned as a part of the church of God, but the theater and pleasure resorts have more attraction for them than the house of prayer, and worldly society is more enjoyable than the com-

[1] Hosea 9:17.

panionship of saints. They will one day be taken captive by a King greater than the kings of Assyria and Babylon. The great King of all kings will arise and shake terribly the earth. " In that day a man shall cast his idols of silver, and his idols of gold, which they have made each one for himself to worship, to the moles, and to the bats, . . . for fear of the Lord, and for the glory of His majesty, when He ariseth to shake terribly the earth." [1]

Dan was the fifth son of Jacob, and his descendants composed one of the strong tribes of Israel. Sixty-four thousand four hundred warriors were marshaled under the standard of Dan as they entered the promised land. [2] For some reason the large tribe of Dan was given one of the smallest portions of the inheritance, and in time they pushed northward and fought against " Leshem, and took it, and smote it with the edge of the sword, and possessed it, and dwelt therein, and called Leshem, Dan, after the name of Dan their father." [3] Jeroboam set up his golden calves, one in Bethel in the territory of Ephraim, the other in the city of Dan; and the Danites were given over to idolatry. Even before the days of Jeroboam, we find the Danites worshiping graven images. [4]

When the tabernacle was built in the wilderness, God especially endowed Aholiab, of the tribe of Dan, with wisdom to " devise cunning works, to work in gold, and in silver, and in brass," [5] and also gave him ability to teach others the same art. [6] These gifts remained with the tribe of Dan, and were doubtless the reason why they were attracted toward the wealthy city of Tyre, and intermarried with its inhabitants. [7]

Years afterward, when Solomon built the temple, Hiram, king of Tyre, sent a descendant of Dan, one still possessing the gifts given his forefathers by the Lord, to make the cunning

---

[1] Isa. 2 : 20, 21. [2] Num. 26 : 42, 43. [3] Joshua 19 : 40-48.
[4] Judges 18 : 30. [5] Ex. 31 : 3-6. [6] Ex. 35 : 34. [7] 1 Kings 7 : 13, 14.

work in gold, silver, and brass, for the temple,[1] in Jerusalem.

The tribe of Dan still kept its place among the Israelites in the time of David;[2] but after that the name as applied to the tribe vanishes, and it is seldom mentioned, except when referring to the northern city by that name.

Samson is the only ruler furnished Israel by the tribe of Dan. He judged Israel for twenty years.[3]

The blessing pronounced upon Dan by Jacob, portrays his character: " Dan shall judge his people, as one of the tribes of Israel. Dan shall be a serpent by the way, an adder in the path, that biteth the h o r s e heels, so that his rider shall fall backward."[4] Like t h e blessing pronounced upon Reuben, the first part portrays the character he might have possessed, if he had embraced the opportunities God placed in his pathway.

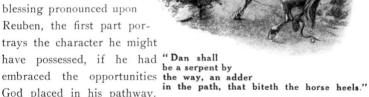

"**Dan shall be a serpent by the way, an adder in the path, that biteth the horse heels.**"

What a contrast between a judge, respected and honored by all, and a serpent by the roadside, ready to fasten its deadly fangs into the flesh of every passer-by!

Dan was the first son born of the concubines, but the old patriarch gave him an honored place among the tribes of Israel. Naturally he was endowed with the quick, keen discernment that makes a good judge; but he did not exercise the gift as God designed; he used it in detecting the evil in others, instead of the good.

[1] 2 Chron. 2 : 13, 14.   [2] 1 Chron. 27 : 22.
[3] Judges 13 : 2 ; 15 : 20.   [4] Gen. 49 : 16, 17.

"An adder in the path, that biteth the horse heels, so that his rider shall fall backward!" What words could better describe the evil tongue that "is set on fire of hell" and is "full of deadly poison"?[1] Dan represents the backbiter, for the adder strikes the *heels* of the horse. Such characters are hated by both God and man. The word of the Lord says, "Whoso privily slandereth his neighbor, *him will I cut off.*"[2] The prophetic words of Jacob reveal why the tribe of Dan has no part in the eternal inheritance; God had decreed, long before they sealed their destiny by their wicked course, that no backbiter should ever stand on Mount Zion.

The psalmist asks the question, "Lord, who shall abide in Thy tabernacle? who shall dwell in Thy holy hill?" In other words, Who will serve Thee day and night in Thy temple, and stand with Thee upon Mount Zion? "*He that backbiteth not with his tongue,* nor doeth evil to his neighbor, *nor taketh up reproach against his neighbor,*" is the answer of Jehovah.[3]

Reuben, by "great searching of heart," overcame his natural character, which was "unstable as water," until it could be said of him, "Let Reuben live, and not die;" and Levi, by the grace of God, changed his father's dying curse into a blessing. Judah, by the help of the Lord in his daily life, "prevailed above his brethren" to such an extent that the dying father could say, "The scepter shall not depart from Judah, nor a lawgiver from between his feet, until Shiloh come, and unto him shall the gathering of the people be." Gad, although overcome by a troop of temptations, gained the victory, and "overcame at last." Benjamin, from ravening "as a wolf," learned to trust in God so fully that of him it could be said, "The Lord shall cover him all the day long, and he shall dwell between His shoulders." Asher learned to "dip his foot in oil," and pass smoothly over the trials that,

[1] James 3 : 6-8. [2] Ps. 101 : 5. [3] Ps. 15 : 1, 3.

without the spirit of God, could never have been mastered.

Ephraim and Dan, with the same opportunities that their brethren had of overcoming evil traits in their characters, failed to gain the victory, and are not reckoned with the one hundred and forty-four thousand who will stand on God's holy hill and abide in His tabernacle.

In families all over the land to-day the same story is being repeated. Brothers, reared by the same parents, surrounded by the same en-vironments, are passing over the same ex-periences as are recorded of the sons of Jacob. Of them, like the wheat and the tares, the command-ment is given, "Let both grow together until the harvest."

"Let both grow together until the harvest."

The same sunshine and storm that ripen the golden heads of wheat for the garner, ripen the tares for the final destruction; so the same daily blessings from the Father of lights ripen one individual for the kingdom of God, and the other for final destruction.

Each one is the architect of his own character. To all the call is given, " Look unto Me, and be ye saved." The one who will keep his mind stayed on God, by beholding will be changed. Day by day a transformation will take place in the soul, which will cause angels to marvel at the work wrought in humanity.

The same Christ who once walked the earth, clothed in human form, will by His divine Spirit, dwell in every human being who will open wide the door of his heart and bid Him enter. He who will meditate upon Christ, and study His sinless life, by beholding the glory of the Lord will be " changed into the same image from glory to glory."

" Christ is sitting for His portrait in every disciple." It is possible for poor fallen humanity through the power of God to reflect the divine character. Christ covers the marred life with the spotless robe of His own righteousness. God and angels beholding the individual thus clothed, see only the perfect character of the divine Son of God; and throughout the ceaseless ages of eternity, the redeemed will witness to the transforming power of the blood of Christ.

INDEX OF TEXTS